TRUE

SEA

STORIES

TRUE *SEA* STORIES

PAUL ASTON

STERLING PUBLISHING CO., INC.
New York

Library of Congress
Cataloging-in-Publication Data Available

10 9 8 7 6 5 4 3 2 1

Published in 1997 by Sterling Publishing Company, Inc
386 Park Avenue South, New York, N.Y. 10016

Originally published in Great Britain in 1997
by Robinson Publishing Ltd

Text copyright © Paul Aston 1997
Illustrations by Chris McLoughlin

Distributed in Canada by Sterling Publishing
c/o Canadian Manda Group, One Atlantic Avenue, Suite 105
Toronto, Ontario, Canada M6K 3E7

Printed and bound in Great Britain

Sterling ISBN 0-8069-9661-7

Contents

Acknowledgments

The author gratefully acknowledges the help of the following in preparing this book:
Leon & Gillian Carberry, the National Maritime Museum Greenwich, residents of Ballycotton, Cork Library, the RNLI Poole, Von Whiteman, Kinsale Museum, Joan Davis of Padstow Shipwreck Museum.

and the following published sources of factual information:

Manning Clark, *The History of Australia* (Pimlico); Alexander McKee, *The Golden Wreck* (Souvenir Press); the *National Geographic Magazine*; Christopher Ralling, *The Kon-Tiki Man* (BBC Books); Nigel Tangye, *Cornwall and the Tumbling Sea* (Wm Kimber); *Lifeboat*, the RNLI Journal; Basil Lubbock, *The China Clippers* (Brown, Son); the *Whitby Gazette*; *Whitby Archives, Local History Series No. 5*, by Paul Pearson (Whitby Pictorial Archives Trust); *Nursing Times*; Ken Wilson, *The Wreck of the Rohilla* (Carrprint); Walter Lord, *A Night to Remember* (Longman); Leslie Reade, *The Ship That Stood Still* (Patrick Stephens); the *Cork Examiner*; the *Daily Mail*; *The Times*; Robin Lidster, *Robin Hood's Bay as It Was* (Hendon Publishing Company); Hoehling & Hoehling, *The Last Voyage of the Lusitania* (Longman); Bailey & Ryan, *The Lusitania Disaster* (Free Press); *Chronicle of the Second World War* (Longman); Cdr Edward Young, *One of Our Submarines* (Hart-Davis); Alexander McKee, *Against the Odds* (Souvenir Press); Charles Dagget with Kris Shaffer, *Diving for the Griffin* (Weidenfeld & Nicolson); A R Martin, *Whales & Dolphins* (Salamander); John Keegan, *Battle at Sea* (Pimlico); *Collier's Magazine*; Lawrence Blair, *Ring of Fire* (Bantam Press); James Hepburn, *The Black Flag* (Headline).

For Anselm & Eloise

CHAPTER 1
MARY BRYANT

"Mr Boswell? We have kept a seat for you." The lawyer slipped quietly into the seat indicated by the court official, nodding to numerous acquaintances.

"A dreadful squeeze here today," sighed his neighbour, another lawyer, "all to gawp at five escaped convicts."

He took a pinch of snuff.

"Not so surprising, Mr Turner," said Boswell drily. "These are after all no ordinary convicts. They are from Botany Bay, and sailed many thousands of miles across the seas in an open boat in order to escape the rigours of our justice."

He smiled sardonically.

"That, I presume, is your present concern, is it not? To see justice done rather than gaze on such miracles of fortitude?"

Boswell affected not to notice Turner's embarrassment.

"You or I would not have been capable of it, I think, Mr Turner," he continued airily. "Indeed, I am more inclined to regard them as unlucky heroes than as criminals."

Turner looked put out. Thinking kindly of convicts was not a habit of his. Boswell allowed his neighbour no time to protest.

"I believe the public is quite right to be here in great number. The fate of these unfortunates is a matter of public interest."

The court was indeed packed. The news that ten mutineers from the *Bounty* had been brought back from Tahiti in the frigate *HMS Gorgon* had been the first sensation to excite the crowds. When it further came out that escaped convicts from Botany Bay were on the same ship, public curiosity knew no bounds.

———

Boswell had first heard about the convicts at his club.

"Interesting case today," said Sir Sampson Wright. Wright was a magistrate at Bow Street. "Those people from Botany Bay, y' know. Quite extraordinary."

Outside the majesty of court, Wright was not given to talking in full sentences.

"Ten weeks in an open boat! Three thousand miles, y'know!

Personally, I find one mile at sea more than enough." He shook his head with the landsman's mixture of contempt and wonder. "The broadsheets are full of it – a miracle, they say."

Boswell mused as Wright rambled on. To him, a miracle would hardly justify a day in the public gallery in court. Misfits and underdogs were his line, lost causes where he could put his modest efforts and means at the service of justice, as he saw it. He was suddenly startled to attention.

"The girl, y' see – that's the real wonder," said Wright. "She survived, while many of the men ..." He waved a hand dismissively. "Just a slip of a girl, too." He paused. "Pretty as a picture, not your type of course, Boswell, you like 'em fleshy, but... Had to wring every word from her, y' know. Felt quite sorry for her in the end, when I heard all they'd gone through."

Wright rarely felt sorry for anyone except himself, when he was deprived of his dinner.

"Alone on the far side of the world, long voyage, lost her husband, lost her children, remarkable. Very cool, very quiet, had to ask everything twice. Wouldn't speak, y' see."

Boswell had not realized that one of the five convicts was female. His attention was caught. He waited, but Wright seemed to have run dry.

"What now?" he asked.

"Old Bailey, seventh July. You attending?"

Boswell felt stirred. He was a man who could resist neither a pretty face nor a fellow human in trouble. The combination was irresistible.

"Ye'll see me there, na doot," he said, at his most Scots. He knew it irritated Sir Sampson.

A hush fell on the court as the prisoners were brought in. The pallor of prison was visibly ousting the weatherbeaten look on their faces from long exposure to wind and waves.

The charge was read out:

"... whereas on 28th March 1791 William Allen, John Butcher, Mary Bryant, Nathaniel Lilly, James Martin and six other persons since deceased did unlawfully steal a fishing vessel belong to the Crown while prisoners in the Colony of Rose Hill, New South Wales, and make their way across the Southern Sea to Timor in the Dutch East Indies."

The clerk stumbled several times during the long sentence.

"Poor drafting, that," grumbled Boswell's neighbour, a legal stickler. "How could a three-year-old and a babe-in-arms be accused of stealing?"

Boswell was silent. He knew nothing about the "six other persons" mentioned in the charge.

The clerk coughed, and continued briskly.

"Whereas the aforesaid living or now deceased persons were arrested on the island of Timor in the Dutch East Indies and given into the care of Captain Edwards, formerly of His Majesty's frigate Pandora. Which said captain brought them to London and delivered them to the justices for consideration of their case. Pray silence for the court."

Gazing on the convicts at the bar, the inquisitor was uneasy. After their dreadful voyage, public sympathy with them was strong. Further punishment, it was thought, would be unfair. But the law was the law, and prisoners could not be allowed to escape from a prison colony with impunity. And they had stolen Crown property!

He played for time and asked questions.

Like most of the world, the court knew very little about the transportation of convicts. The five people in the bar in front of him were among the first shipment of 750 convicts sent from England to New South Wales.

Transportation to Australia was a new system, a way of solving the problem of overcrowded prisons. The prison colony it established was new, a settlement in the wilderness. The convicts were in fact the first European residents of Australia.

As far as London was concerned, the 750 had sailed off the edge of the world.

William Allen was brought up.

"You are an escaped prisoner from Botany Bay?"

No answer. The beadle standing beside Allen poked him in the ribs.

"Answer when you are addressed," he said.

"Yes."

"When did you land there?"

"Twentieth January, four year ago."

There was a pause while the clerk wrote this down.

"Who had command of the colony?" asked the court.

No answer. The beadle nudged Allen again.

"Answer the question," he said roughly.

"Governor Phillip," said Allen, in his surliest voice. "Captain Phillip as was."

Allen expected nothing, and would therefore give nothing. He would not answer helpfully. He had risked his all to escape, and had lost.

"And you lived at Botany Bay?"

"No. We was kep' at Rose Hill, in Sydney Cove. The finest harbour in the world, they said. A place for savages it war."

The clerk intervened.

"The place is now called Parramatta, so I am informed, my lord."

The justice ignored the interruption.

"Were you locked up at night?"

"No."

Eventually the court gave up on Allen, and Butcher was called. More forthcoming, Butcher described the wilderness they'd seen when they arrived, and how the colony tried to make a living.

"Where did you live?"

"In tents and huts."

"How did you spend your days?"

"Workin'. They was always pushin' us to work."

Being mostly thieves, the convicts disliked work.

"Farm work?"

"Yes. Clearin' the ground. Diggin'. Most of'un hated it."

"You grew things?"

"So to speak. The seed rotted or got ate by weevils. We was allus short of food. Lots of people died. Specially at first."

"Didn't the governor get more food from London?"

"'E tried. 'E sent the *Sirius* to the Cape for food and more tools, but the ship got wrecked on Norfolk Island. We was dreadful hungry that winter. I misremember what year it were, but April tide, anyways. Las' year we lost another store ship, the *Guardian*. Hit an iceberg rounding the Cape, so we 'eerd."

"What happened when people were hungry?"

"They stole food from the public stores. All the food was in the public stores, no one was allowed private food. There was thievin' all the time."

"What happened if they were caught?"

"They was flogged – 300 lashes, they got. Then they was chained together and had their rations cut for six months."

There was a murmur round the room at this. The court hastily moved to safer topics.

"What happened at night?"

"We was supposed to be guarded. Them danged Abos was always ready to attack us. We'd stole their land, they reckoned. The guards, sojers they was, they was supposed to shoot at 'em, frighten 'em orf. They was meant to shoot at us, too, if anyone went out a-nights, but they never did. Too idle, most on 'em. Or jus' fed up, thinkin' about home. You could hear 'em snorin' if ye wanted to go out."

"What happened when someone completed his sentence?"

"Most of 'em, they jes' wanted to go 'ome. Everyone wanted to go 'ome. That's all we could think about."

Another murmur of sympathy. The court moved on.

"Who organized your escape?"

"Bryant."

"Mary Bryant?"

"No, 'er 'usband, William."

"Why was he transported?"

"Dunno. Cornish, he was, like 'er. Thievin', I expect."

The clerk intervened.

"William Bryant was a smuggler, sir. He was convicted of resisting the revenue officers who came to seize the goods he had smuggled ashore."

"What was his sentence?"

"Seven years, sir."

"And why is he not here? Did he escape?"

"The sickness took 'im, milud, after Cap'n Edwards got 'un in his care, on board the *Gorgon*."

The court returned to the main issue.

"Why did the escape take place?"

Silly question, thought Butcher. Why does anyone want to escape from prison? Couldn't say that out loud, though.

"Well, sir, Bryant and his wife – they was married out there, being both Cornish, y' see, and they was mad to get back to Cornwall. They 'ad two young children, a boy Manny, and little Charlie, the bebby girl. They didn't want their chillun to grow up in no savage swamp, among bad people like their parents."

The clerk intervened again.

"The children were called Emmanuel and Charlotte, sir, three and one years old. They died on the ship, like their father."

Boswell leaned forward. The plight of the luckless Mary Bryant was growing more dreadful by the minute. And she was so pretty!

"How did he organize it?"

"Well, Bryant, he was a fisherman, and out theer anyone that could help get food was made a trusty, y' see. Bryant had charge of all the boats used for fishing. Good for 'im and Mary it was, they was allowed to keep for themselves all the fish they could eat. Jus' to encourage 'em, like."

Butcher waved his hand, to emphasize what he meant. Boswell foresaw what was coming.

" 'Course, he couldn't resist temptation. Who could, in them danged miserable parts? It was them or us, God rot 'em! The sojers was just as 'ungry as the rest on us, tho'."

He stopped.

"Go on. What did Bryant do?"

"He used to keep back a lot of the fish, cause he was a good fisherman and catched a lot. What'd'e do? 'e'd swap it or sell it for un's own use, that's what 'e done. After a time, Lieutenant King guessed what was goin' on."

"So they took him off the fishing boats?"

"No, they couldn't. He were a good fisherman, the on'y one they 'ad, they needed the food. Instead, they give 'im a hun'ed lashes, and kep' watch on 'un after that."

"And?"

Butcher thought back.

"When they give 'im the lashes, 'e changed, Bryant did. 'E was always reckless, like, but after the whippin' 'e was so mad to get away, 'e could think of nothin' else. Mary, now, she was frightened an' begged 'un to stop, but 'e went on mekkin' preparations."

"How did you come into it?"

"Well, Bryant 'ad talked around, and there was quite of lot of us that 'e convinced, yes, we could do it, we could escape, with Bryant's help. We reckoned 'e knew enough about boats to do it. Had a way wi' people, he did. Talked us into it."

The court was puzzled. Sailing round the Cornish coasts is one thing. Sailing halfway round the world in a twenty-foot open fishing boat is quite another. The question was on everyone's mind.

"But ... did it not occur to you how far you would have to go?"

"We was desp'rate to get away."

A simple answer! marvelled Boswell. We cannot imagine such desperation.

It appeared Bryant had drawn seven or eight convicts into his plans. There'd been hitches. One day, after dark, someone heard them talking about getting away, and reported to Phillip, who ordered a close watch on them.

A day later, Bryant was out fishing in the boat that he'd chosen for the escape. A wind blew up, and the cleat anchoring the foresail snapped.

Bryant swore with fury. Used to having snugly fitted fishing boats in Cornwall, he was enraged by the constant shortages of proper equipment.

"Danged fool thing!" he shouted, flailing after the flapping foresail.

He could not save the mast. The boat got out of control and filled with water as the stern swung round and was buffeted by driving seas. Soon, the vessel was wallowing.

"Git out 'n swim, Mary! I can't hold 'un," he shouted over the wind.

Panic-stricken for her children, who were with them in the boat, Mary seized the baby and jumped overboard. Another convict aboard took little Manny. The sea was not cold, and by some miracle, all of them reached the shore alive.

Luckily, friendly Aborigines saw the incident from the shore. They rushed to their canoes and brought the foundering vessel safely back to land, with Bryant fuming in its wake.

The court thought it had heard enough. The distressing story was making the public perilously restive. Time to adjourn.

When the hearing resumed, the clerk read out the circumstances of the escape.

"On 29th March, Governor Phillip received a report from the guards. Bryant and his family, along with seven other convicts, had escaped the night before in a fishing vessel belonging to the colony."

"So it took a month to put the boat right," thought Boswell. "No materials, I suppose." Butcher had reported that supplies of every kind were in short supply.

By now, the convicts had become human beings in Boswell's eyes. In particular, he had convinced himself that Mary was in dire need of his help.

A letter received from Governor Phillip was then read out. Soon after the escape, Phillip had resigned his post and returned to England. Sir Sampson Wright had sought his help.

The news of the escape had been met with disbelief:

> We were sure they would not get far. [wrote Phillip.] My officers were adamant that they had no hope of surviving. The nearest point of civilisation was Batavia, three thousand miles away. Our knowledge was that they had no instruments to guide them, no charts, nor any knowledge of the sea routes. They could have had little in the way of water or food for such a lengthy journey.

The packed room was agog to hear how they had overcome such insuperable obstacles.

"Call the prisoner Mary Bryant!" called the clerk.

Like Wright, the justice found it difficult to get a single word from her. Clearly, the experiences of the past year had eaten into her soul. She would not speak – nor even think – of them. He called on Lilly instead, who proved quite informative.

Bryant had had a terrific piece of luck. Shortly before the escape, a Dutch ship, the *Waaksamheyd,* had arrived to take the crew of the wrecked *Sirius* back to England.

Phillip was outraged at what happened.

> I regret to say that the captain of the Waaksamheyd, much to his discredit, sold a compass and a quadrant to William Bryant. Thus equipped, Bryant was able to escape twelve hours after the Dutch vessel put to sea.

Why Bryant needed a quadrant was a mystery to the former governor. Quadrants are for expert navigators, requiring knowledge of the night sky. A fisherman could not have such knowledge.

Nonetheless, Bryant had somehow managed. Clearly highly intelligent, he had gleaned enough information from the Dutch captain to make use of it. He would not give good money for something he could not use.

After the escape, the Bryants' hut was searched, said Phillip, and various hidey holes were found. Obviously the man had been storing things for a long time.

As to why the prisoners escaped, one of them, James Cox, left a letter to a female convict, Sarah Young, [continued Phillip's letter.] Cox's sentence was for life. He said that he had no hope that it would be reduced. Though the others had shorter sentences, no doubt their minds were warped by desperation and evil companionship.

Phillip regarded the convicts as hopeless cases beyond redemption by kindness. This was why he had resigned.

Cox's letter also revealed that Bryant hoped to reach the Dutch East Indies, and there find a Dutch vessel to carry them home. For Phillip, the final outrage was that Bryant was no longer available to run the fishing boats.

Such were his skills, we were hard put to do without them in our colony, [he wrote in summary]. Their escape was, I was convinced, utter folly. Even if they reached Timor or Batavia, they would scarce convince the Dutch authorities that they were indeed what they must claim to be, to wit, survivors from a wrecked vessel.

Events proved otherwise.

"Exceptional fellow, Bryant," said Wright, who had joined Boswell. "Shame he was depraved. He'd completed his sentence, y'know. She was the problem. She was sentenced for life."

Boswell contemplated the woman before them. He understood why Bryant would not go alone. Such a woman was not to be given up.

Boswell did not attend the rest of the hearing. He learnt afterwards that the five convicts had been ordered to serve out their sentences in Newgate prison. Life meant life.

"Got off lightly," was the verdict of the broadsheets. By law, those who escaped from Botany Bay merited hanging.

The government did not intend to enforce this. Under Secretary of State Evan Nanpean said to Boswell:

> "We shall not deal with them harshly, nor shall we be kind and encourage others to escape."

According to one rather fanciful newspaper report, the convicts thought Newgate "paradise compared with the sufferings they had endured on the voyage."

The words raised a wintry smile in Boswell. He had been to Newgate.

He now renewed his acquaintance with it, to visit Mary Bryant.

He asked questions about the voyage, trying to bring her to talk. At first, she said nothing, or answered with monosyllables.

"Are you all right here?"

No answer. Looking round at the dirty cell full of women, girls and children, Boswell could understand. He signalled to the guard and slipped a shilling into the outstretched palm. Mary was brought to a separate room. The guard watched at a distance.

"Have you money for your needs?"

No answer.

"How old are you?"

No answer.

"Give the ginnleman an answer!" came a rasping voice from behind.

"Leave her alone," said Boswell.

Eventually he got Mary to tell him about herself.

"Where were you born?

"Fowey."

"What is your father?"

"A seaman."

"Do you want to see him again?"

Silence. She hung her head.

"Perhaps she is ashamed," thought Boswell.

"Why were you transported?" he asked.

"Stealin'."

"What did you steal?"

"A cloak."

"Was it just you?"

"No, there was two other girls."

"How long was your sentence?"

"I doan' know. They didn't say."

It seems no limit was set on her sentence.

"How many of you were in the boat when you escaped?"

"Nine."

"Including your children?"

"No. Eleven, including them."

"Did you have food?"

"Bryant collected food before we escaped, and hid it under the floor in our hut."

Talking about her husband brought colour to her pale cheeks. "Aha, she seems pleased to talk about him," thought Boswell.

"He prepared everythin', everythin'!" she continued emphatically. "He kep' askin' me, now, think, girl, think: what else could we need? An' we caught fish when we could. Bryant always knew where to find fish."

She paused.

"When he first talked about escapin', I didn't believe him. I thought, you silly fellow, you'll kill us all, we'll niver escape. I was frightened for the children. I told him once, you go, you done your sentence, you go and get yoursen a mort of land and start a farm, instead of dreamin' dreams about crossin' the ocean in yon fishin' boat. But he stuck with it, and I believed him."

Boswell waited for her to continue. When she remained silent, lost in her thoughts, he asked:

"Did you stop anywhere to get water and food?"

"We jes' followed the coast, northwards from Sydney Cove. Sometimes we went ashore, and got on land, where there was a harbour, but the others reckoned it was dangerous. They was always sayin', no, we can't, it's too risky, but Bryant knew we had to – we'd starve if we didn't. Once we got ashore, they'd stop arguing – they had to. There was Abos about, we 'ad to be careful. They'd attack if we give 'em the chance."

She blinked, and held her hand to her mouth.

"Once we did hit a reef ..."

"Tell me about it."

For what seemed an age, she said nothing. The screams and quarrels of the prison in the background seemed to become very loud. Then she started talking again.

"Twere 'bout ten days or so after we started. In the end, Bryant got the boat off all right, but 'e reckoned it was damaged an' we'd better put in to shore to repair it, soon as we could. We did find a nice little harbour before she took too much water aboard."

"How did you repair the boat?"

"The men dragged her ashore, and started payin' her seams, jes to make 'er watertight agin. Bryant had brought the tallow along, he'd thought of ev'rythin', that man.

"But then we 'ad to stop, the Abos kep' comin' at us wi' their bows and arrows, there was nothin' we could do to stop 'em, so we hauled her back in the water pretty quick an' made for an island not far off, where we finished the job."

"Did you catch things? Animals?"

"Sometimes. Animals. Dingoes. Big birds. One of the men could throw a powerful sling. We was often hungry for days, though. There wasn't always anything to catch."

"What about water?"

"It rained all the time. We wrung the water from our clothes. Our clothes was wet nearly all the time, from the sea or the rain."

"What about your children? Did you have enough to feed them?"

She shook her head fiercely. Tears welled up in her eyes. She would not speak about them. After some minutes of silence, Boswell tried another subject.

"Did the others handle the boat, or just Bryant?"

"They did what Bryant said. He'd showed them things before we left. Sometimes they didn't like it, being told, they'd start saying, no, we won't do it, who d'you think you are, Governor Phillip or something? Then he'd say, you do as I tell yous or we's all dead."

"So you just went further up the coast of New Holland?"

"We followed the coast, along New 'olland, where we could. Once, we couldn't hold the shore. A powerful current drove us off-shore thirty leagues or more, an' we got messed up among a lot of islands. One good thing, there was plenty of turtles there, we 'ad plenty to eat then. Manny was tryin' to ride on the turtles, so funny 'e looked!"

"Did you lose sight of the mainland for good?"

"No, we found it again, but better nor we 'adn't."

She lapsed into a brooding silence.

"What happened?"

"We hit a reef... I thought I was goin' to die. Two of em did. Drowned, they did, before we was driven on shore."

It was clearly an unpleasant recollection.

"Well, it was the start of summat worse, because when we got to the straits north of New 'olland, it was nothin' but reefs and shoals, and we had such 'ard work to keep off. On top of that, the men was arguing wi' Bryant, tellin' 'im we should go north and Bryant saying, no, we 'ad to go east across the Gulf of Carpentaria, that was the way he remembered it from the chart, that was the way the Dutchy cap'n said."

She swallowed a sob, recalling Bryant.

"In the Gulf, the natives there had all these bigger canoes that could hold thirty men each, and they had sails and platforms for fightin'. We was forever gettin' away from 'em. I was sure they'd come to eat the children. The only way we could stop 'em was to row to windward. That was a terrible time. The children were so brave ..."

She stopped, and looked at him with stricken eyes. Boswell felt uncomfortable.

"Did you use the quadrant?"

"Bryant did, mostly. I helped him sometimes. I don't know if he got it right. He'd told me what the Dutchy cap'n had said, about how to use it. We went over and over it, the first day. Once we started, I got used to looking at the stars, and got to reco'nize them. We had plenty of time to look, specially when it was cold and bright. We used the Dutchy's chart, too. It warn't much good, but it give us an idea which way to go."

"Didn't the chart get wet?"

"Fell in the sea, once, one of the men rescued it. Then another time a wind took it, and that's how we lost it. But it were fallin' to bits anyway. Bryant knew it by 'eart."

"How many of you reached Timor?"

"Eight. Nine, mebbe. I don't remember."

"What happened to the others?"

"They died, like I said."

"When did you get there?"

"Beginnin' of June. Took us about ten weeks."

The more he listened and watched, Boswell was struck by Mary's courage. She did not complain, and she did not let herself go. Though her cheeks were pale and her brown hair long and unruly, she evidently tried to keep herself as clean and tidy as prison allowed.

"What happened in Timor?"

Mary looked at him, then looked away, as if the memory was too much. Then a sudden smile broke the tense lines of her set expression. It was like the sun coming out.

"I didn't believe it. It didn't seem possible we'd ever get there. But we did."

She was almost triumphant. She smiled again.

"I looked at Bryant, standing wi' one foot on the shore in Timor, an' I thought, there's a man, that's my man, I was so proud. But he was thin, thin as a besom. He give all our food to the children and me."

She paused, then added defiantly, looking Boswell full in the face. "They called him bad, but to me he was a good man, always. A bit wild, mebbe. He was more a man than all the others put together."

"What did you tell the Dutch authorities in Timor?"

"They was very good to us, gave us food an' everythin'. Bryant told 'em we'd been wrecked on the way to India; he made it all up. Described the storm we'd had, how we'd 'it the reef, and we were the only ones that escaped. Course, we knew all about that sort of thing, for real. They b'lieved it. I b'lieved it, too, listenin' to 'un."

She showed no remorse at the lies.

Why should she? thought Boswell. Most of his circle would have condemned her as wicked and vicious, just for the lies.

"How was the truth discovered?"

"Them fools with us, the other men, they couldn't hold their liquor and started blabbin'. The Dutch was suspicjus anyway, because the men didn't behave nor like wrecked passengers nor seamen – they started behavin' like convicts agin, lookin' around for what they could steal. So they rounded us all up and put us back in prison."

She laughed mirthlessly.

"All that way, and back to a different prison. What fools men are!" she added with contempt.

———

As he left her, Boswell gave Mary Bryant some money to buy things to make life easier.

He had already learnt from the broadsheets about events after they reached Timor. Soon after their arrival, the brutal Captain Edwards had landed with the mutineers from the *Bounty*. The

Dutch passed the escapees into Edwards's charge, thankful to be rid of them, and the whole party set sail for England. With Edwards was marine officer Captain Watkin Tench, who had sailed out to Australia with the first convicts on the *Charlotte*. Tench knew the Bryants and had great admiration for their exploits.

> I confess that I never looked at these people without pity and astonishment. They had miscarried in a heroic struggle for liberty, after having combated every hardship and conquered every difficulty. They had both of them been always distinguished for good behaviour. [he wrote.]

At Batavia, Mary's little boy Manny died of a fever. A month later, William Bryant himself succumbed to the same sickness, weakened by long exposure. Then, five months later, while still on the way home, the baby Charlotte died. Mary was the sole surviving Bryant.

Boswell sat long in his rooms, gazing at the fire. He pictured Mary's hopes gradually fade to despair as the journey progressed. They had left New South Wales, on the other side of the world, on 28th March as a family. A year and a week later, she arrived in England, in chains and alone. She had spent most of that time

at sea, in extremes of hardship.

Boswell thought of the girl he had seen in Newgate prison and then of his own life. Had he done anything half as great as she had? He resolved to do something about her plight.

For all his resolve and contacts, things did not move quickly after that. The law never moves quickly. Mary grew paler than ever in the foul gloom of Newgate prison, in the company of hundreds of others. She remained composed, and kept herself to herself as much as was possible.

Boswell endeavoured to talk to those who were in a position to take action, such as politicians and high-ranking lawyers. He knew many such people. A pardon was what he wanted.

Some months later, he began to feel he was making progress. He had got as close to the top as possible, to Secretary of State Dundas, the man who could advise the king to grant Mary a pardon – if he so minded.

Unfortunately, Boswell and Dundas were chalk and cheese. Boswell disliked Dundas's manner, Dundas disliked being pushed. They quarrelled.

Boswell left Dundas's office in dismay, fearing that his work on Mary's behalf had been wholly undone. He only half-told Mary the bad tidings, saying he was hopeful of better news shortly.

Mary listened calmly. She had no longer entertained any hopes.

While in Newgate, Boswell also visited the four other convicts from Botany Bay. He told them of his efforts on their behalf as well.

More weeks passed without any further developments.

Then, nearly a year after she had returned to England in chains, the gaoler came to the grim cell.

"Mary Bryant! Where's Mary Bryant?" came the call into the gloom.

Mary hardly dared stir. People were called from the cell for terrible reasons as well as good ones. What the law might do to her, she did not know. She trembled, and stayed rooted to the spot. In the end, the guard came in and half-dragged her out.

"Git out of 'ere when you's told!"

Kindness was not a feature of Newgate.

Half an hour later, the dazed prisoner found herself out in the street, in the bright sunlight she had not seen for many months. She was free to go.

Dundas had changed his mind.

In her fourth month of freedom, Boswell went to see Mary, taking with him a man called Castel. Like Mary, Castel came from Fowey, but he worked in London as a glazier. He said he knew Mary's family. It was a brief visit, but Boswell promised to return soon, with more news.

That evening, there was a knock at the door. Mary opened it cautiously, fearing the unknown.

A slim figure stood outside, dressed in the simple clothing of a servant.

"Dolly!"

It was her younger sister Dolly, who was working as a cook for a family in London.

The sisters hugged each other in silence, and wept.

At last, Mary had found someone she could talk to freely. The two of them stayed up as late as Dolly dared, talking. Dolly could scarcely believe some of things her sister told her, even though Mary let slip little about her worst experiences.

Mary had many ghosts of the past to lay to rest before she could agree to Dolly's suggestion that she return to Fowey and see her family.

"You must go hoam, Mary. Our fayther wants to see you agin," she said earnestly. "I do know he does."

In the end, Mary agreed. It was easier to agree than argue with Dolly. With Boswell's help, it was arranged.

And so, one evening in October, Boswell took a hackney coach to Little Titchfield Street, near Oxford Circus, where Mary lived. He motioned to the coachman to knock at the door. It opened, the coachman went inside, re-appearing a moment later carrying a small box with Mary's few possessions. Mary herself followed, shivering slightly in the cold. She got into the carriage, the first time she had been in one.

The carriage clattered away noisily down the street towards the river. After a bumpy journey full of stops and starts and interrupted by numerous cries and oaths from other users of the street, it came to a stand at Beale's Wharf in Southwark. Boswell looked out of the window and was satisfied. The ketch *Ann and Elizabeth* lay alongside the quay, being loaded with goods for Fowey.

Boswell and Mary got out of the coach and entered the inn beside the wharf. Here, at Boswell's instruction, Mary was served with food – Boswell had already dined. Much to his concern, she hardly touched the food.

"What troubles you, Mary?" he asked, as they sat in the kitchen. "Are you not pleased to be returning to your family?"

She shook her head, looking woeful.

"They will not want me, sir, I know. They will not treat me kindly."

"Nonsense, Mary! They are your family," riposted Boswell sharply. He would not let her slide into depression. "It is quite ordinary to feel distressed before setting off on a journey. I myself have felt wretched many times before departing on a journey. Believe me, it happens often. I will not have you feeling distressed."

He added, "If it is money that worries you, do not concern yourself. I have arranged for enough money to be sent to you every six months that you can leave your relations if you so wish and live an independent life.

"Now. Let us go into the bar. I believe Captain Moyse will take a glass of punch with us before you go aboard."

Moyse remembered the story of the escape. He was rather proud to have such a noted survivor on board his vessel, even if she was female.

Half an hour later, Boswell took his leave. He briskly wished them a safe voyage and returned to the carriage. Departures upset him, and he did not wish to prolong this one. He knew it was the last time he would see Mary Bryant.

At first light, the little vessel nosed out into the stream and headed down river.

Mary went on deck and watched the dawn. She had watched many watery dawns in her life, mostly in unpleasant circumstances. This one was different.

She suddenly felt a change inside her. The feeling of being hunted fell from her, like an old garment. She shook her hair loose, as if to shake off the weight of it.

Passing her on deck, Job Moyse nodded to her and went into the wheelhouse. Boswell had given him special instructions that his passenger was to be treated with all due respect. As he glanced through the opening at her, Moyse thought her pale face looked unusually flushed.

"She've seen more rough water than ever you or I done," he said to his mate.

Boswell slept soundly, untroubled by the dawn. He had no fears for Mary. He knew from Castel that Mary's family had recently inherited a large sum of money and would be both able and pleased to keep her. The poor family had made good. Castel had assured him she would be well received.

By the time Boswell's man pulled back the curtains to let in daylight, the *Ann and Elizabeth* was already past Gravesend.

CHAPTER 2
A LONG WEEKEND AT BALLYCOTTON

Listen!" said Joe, sitting up in bed. "There's that howling noise again."

"It's the wind in the eaves," said Andrew, three-parts asleep.

"No, it isn't," said David, without looking up from his book. "It's Mother McCarthy's yowling again."

Mother McCarthy was their name for a local singer who had told them off for swapping jokes loudly during supper.

"You're right, it's the wind," said Joe.

" 'Course I'm right," said his younger brother Andrew sleepily. "It's from the south-east."

Joe made a show of expert listening.

"No, it's easterly," he said authoritatively.

"It's north-easterly," said David. "Don't argue. I'm the eldest, I know."

"Well," said Joe, stretching luxuriously, "we're agreed at least that it's coming from the sea. Where three wise men agree, it must be true."

None of them stirred to check who was right.

Guessing the direction of the wind was a game they'd invented en route to Ireland, on board ship. Their father, a keen amateur sailor, had remarked as they strolled on deck, "Stiff westerly, veering two points north." Or something like that, Andrew thought. They'd been very impressed.

Voices were heard outside in the corridor. David quickly turned out his reading light and buried himself under the clothes.

"Wind's picking up," said a deep voice. "Probably reach gale force over the weekend."

It was their father.

"That'll be trouble for the Slineys, then," said another voice, which they recognized as Mr Mahony from the lifeboat.

"I'll just check that the boys are all right, Robert," said the deep voice, "then I'll stroll down to the harbour with you."

There was a knock at the door. It opened, and a bearded head appeared, framed in the light.

"Everything OK?"

"Aye-aye, cap'n," came the muffled voice of Andrew out of the darkness.

"Why will there be trouble for the Slineys, Pa?" asked David, propping himself on his elbow. "Who are they?"

"Four Slineys are members of the lifeboat crew. Patrick Sliney is the coxswain, Tom Sliney is the motor mechanic. There's at least two others. Then there are three Walshes in the crew, I think."

"A family business," said Andrew darkly, from under the bed-clothes. He had the makings of a wit.

"Why will there be trouble?" persisted David.

"There's a gale on the way, and that's work for the lifeboat," said their father briefly. "Now, you've had a long day getting here, and we have to be up early. Early it'll be, I promise you. Goodnight! Sleep well, God bless!"

The door closed behind him.

No sooner had the footsteps retreated down the passage than Joe and David leapt to the window.

They looked out over the harbour. Clouds were racing past from over the headland. David opened the window a crack and stuck his finger out, to test the wind. Joe tried to do the same, but David trapped his hand. A terrific draught whistled through the crack.

"I'm right!" they both exclaimed at once, and laughed immoderately.

"Ow!" said Joe, trying to get his hand out.

The boats in the harbour creaked and rocked impatiently, as the choppy waves slapped at their sides. Beyond, the light from the lighthouse flashed steadily.

On...off... pause. On... off... pause. It was mesmerizing.

"Shut that window," murmured Andrew. "It's beastly cold."

They were staying in Fawcett's Hotel, overlooking Ballycotton Harbour. Cork-born John McCabe came over from England frequently on business – this time he had brought his three sons with him for a family celebration later in the week.

" 'Tis time ye knew some of your family," he said, sounding more Irish than usual.

The traditional fishing village of Ballycotton nestles in the southern corner of a bay not far from Cork. It is protected from the prevailing south-easterlies by the headland behind it, which rises to over 200 feet.

The McCabes returned there on Sunday afternoon, in a howling gale. As they drove up the headland, the full force of it hit them. Rain cascaded down the windscreen and trickled through at the sides.

"Can you see ahead, Dad?" asked Andrew. "I can't."

"The floor's soaking," grumbled Joe.

Despite the foul weather, the harbour was busy when they arrived.

The harbour is formed by a pier at the seaward end of the headland, while the inner area is protected by a jetty. Several men dressed in oilskins stood on the slipway, holding ropes. Another was out in a dinghy, which pitched to and fro. He was trying to reach a larger boat that strained at its moorings.

"Isn't that larger one the lifeboat, Pa?" asked Andrew.

The lifeboat, the *Mary Stanford*, was quite distinctive. Over fifty feet long, its low, graceful shape with a funnel and cabin midships distinguished it from the shorter, chunkier shapes of the deepsea fishing boats.

It was moored at the end of the slipway, some 30 yards out, but in the gusty conditions it kept swinging round violently. It seemed anxious to cast itself to pieces on the jetty.

They sat in the car and watched the drama.

"The man in the dinghy's got aboard, Pa," cried David. "They're trying to throw him a rope."

As the lifeboat lurched suddenly, the rope fell off and slithered into the water.

"That's Patrick Sliney and his brother Tom on the slipway," said John McCabe. "The others I don't know."

"What's the rope for?" demanded Andrew.

"To moor the lifeboat more securely," said David tersely. "The wind's driving it on to the jetty."

"Why not keep it in the boathouse?" asked Joe, watching intently. "They wouldn't have all this trouble then."

"You can't imagine what it's like, launching in really bad weather," said their father. "It's pretty rough even now."

A cloud of spray broke over the jetty.

"Launching a lifeboat into rough water is no joke. The crew need all their strength at sea. No point in wasting it at the land end."

"Why ...?" began Andrew, then saw Joe's face. "I've forgotten what I was going to ask. It's your fault, Joe, you made a face."

"Why, why, why," said John McCabe. "Come on, it's time to have something to eat." He knew his sons.

"Just my thoughts," said Joe. Joe was always hungry.

With difficulty, their father dragged David and Andrew away and they all went up to the hotel.

"There's no potatoes," said Joe dramatically, sticking his head through the restaurant door. "We'll starve."

"No," said his father with a smile, "we won't."

___

On Monday night, it was not just potatoes that kept Joe awake. Incredibly, the gale had got worse. Joe tossed and turned, unable to sleep for the noise. At around three, a violent gust loosened a tile, which began to rattle.

He slipped out of bed quietly and went to the window.

In front of the hotel, grey figures were moving urgently to and fro. Beyond, the boats were just restless white patches gleaming in the darkness.

"Must be high tide," thought Joe. Most of the pier and jetty was invisible as the sea washed over them.

Joe lifted the sash window slightly. A cold draught whirled round the room, lifting the curtains.

Snatches of conversation blew up from below.

"… your boat's drifting … broken her moorings, Pat."

"What's up?" yawned a voice behind him. It was Andrew, who had been woken by the noise.

"The Slineys' fishing boat has broken loose in the harbour."

Andrew came over and peered out at the shadowy shapes moving around below them.

"What's that cracking and grinding noise?" he asked.

Joe listened. Andrew was right. Against the howling wind an occasional sharp crack or horrible grinding noise could be heard.

"Sounds like a huge torture chamber," whispered Joe.

"Look down there, at the quay!" Andrew whispered back. In the pounding storm, rocks were being thrown about and ground together. "It's weird. I've never seen anything like that."

"They must weigh tons each!" marvelled Joe. "You'd need to be a giant to pick them up."

Huge clouds of spray leapt up from behind the pier and washed over into the harbour. A heavy thump heralded each cloud, as hundreds of tons of seawater on the far side collided with the rigid stone wall.

"Brr! I'm cold. Shut the window," said Andrew after a while. "I'm going back to bed."

They were wakened on Tuesday morning by David.

"Come and look!" he said in excitement. "They've just rescued a boat which was drifting out to sea. It was ever so daring – one of them had to jump from one rocking boat to the other to lash a rope to her. It must be the lifeboat crew."

"We know," said Joe without stirring. "We saw it last night. They've been at it all night."

"Beasts! Why didn't you wake me?"

Half an hour later, Robert Mahony, secretary of the lifeboat station, bustled past the hotel, big with news. He encountered the Slineys trudging wearily up from the harbour.

"Pat! A messenger has just come from Queenstown. The *Daunt* lightship is adrift. She's broken her moorings, the Guard told me, and is drifting this way. She'll be the devil to find in these seas."

Patrick Sliney nodded but said nothing.

"Mind, I'm not saying ye should go out for her in this weather, Pat," called Mahony over the wind, "No reasonable man could say that." It was the secretary's job to order the lifeboat out.

The two of them looked down towards the harbour. Towering seas piled high behind the lifeboat house and then collapsed forward over it with an intense roar. The pier was virtually invisible in the continuous wash of spray and water. The storm was at its height.

"Now listen, Pat, there's nothing to be done," said Mahony intently. "Ye've put the boarding boat away in the lifeboat house. I don't think ye can even get out to the lifeboat. And if ye did, ye would not get beyond the harbour bar."

Pat Sliney nodded, but said nothing.

"No sane man would do it, believe me," Mahony added earnestly. "It would be p'intless. I'm going back to the phone. Maybe the Civic Guard has had word that the *Daunt* is back at its moorings."

Mahony hardly believed himself what he was saying, but he could not bring himself to order the boat out. He thought that the lifeboat itself could hardly survive those horrendous seas, let alone find the lightship. It was a storm such as no-one in Ballycotton had ever experienced before.

A knot of villagers had gathered to watch and offer advice. Patrick Sliney listened and nodded again. As soon as Mahony had gone, he turned and retraced his steps towards the harbour. His colleagues went to call the rest of the crew.

The Civic Guard had of course no further news for Robert Mahony. The phone lines were down outside the village, trees lay across the lanes and trying to get through had been hard enough for the first messenger.

The lifeboat secretary returned to the harbour, pulling his sou'wester over his head more tightly as protection against the rain.

He was dumbfounded to reach the water's edge and see the lifeboat already approaching the harbour bar.

"The ould divil!" he breathed, as footsteps came up behind him. It was John McCabe.

"Morning, Robert."

"Pat Sliney's gone off without a word. Isn't that just like him now! He didn't even fire the maroons in case we should take fright. The ould divil!"

A mixture of respect and affection shone through his tone.

"Will they get beyond the harbour bar?" asked David, who had just come out, wrapped in his father's greatcoat.

Indeed, the formidable seas visible beyond the bar did seem from the shore an insuperable obstacle.

"If it's like that in the lee of the islands, you can imagine what it's like past on the open sea," said Mahony, pursuing his worries. "They must turn back. It's p'intless."

On the seaward side of the pier there are two islands. The nearer, Sheep Island, can be reached on foot at low neap tides. The further, larger island is separated from the shore by a stretch of deeper water called the Big Sound. The lighthouse, at the far end of the outer island, marks the point where the water reaches a depth of five fathoms.

Deepsea ships do not venture into Ballycotton Bay, but even smaller fishing vessels generally set a course round the outside of the lighthouse. It's safer that way.

"Aaahh!" David thought someone had spoken aloud, but it was his own sudden release of breath.

The lifeboat had at last reached the pounding seas at the bar. It hit a tremendous breaker, and was immediately swallowed up in the wash. An interminable pause, then it reappeared.

"He must come back," repeated Mahony hopefully, half to himself. "He must come back, there's no sense in it. He won't find them."

The watching villagers knew each member of the crew out there. The anxiety was writ large on some faces as the lifeboat rose up to meet each succeeding wave.

"Why is the boat standing up in the air like that?" asked a child, holding his mother's hand. In truth, the stern of the boat did seem sometimes to be walking on the waves.

"Why, 'tis the Slineys and the Walshes showing the sea a few tricks, my pet," came the reply. "Come, now, we'll be late for school."

———————

"She's turning round," said David. "She must be coming back."

"Oh, that's grand," said Mahony, with evident relief. "I knew they must."

They had repaired to higher ground where they could see across the islands to the lighthouse.

The lifeboat was about a mile out, and had apparently reached the lighthouse. The waves were so monstrous here that the spray from them drenched its lantern, 196 feet up. It seemed impossible that any small vessel could make headway in such seas.

"They've stopped," said Joe. "Do you think something's gone wrong with the engine, Mr Mahony?"

"I can't make out what they're doing, Joe, I reelly cannot. I think they must be coming back," was the hopeful reply. It was difficult to see them clearly in the rain.

"They're taking her t'rough the Big Sound, Mr Mahony," came a voice behind him. "That's what they're doing. Saves them a mile or so."

"Oh they can't do that," said Mahony, horror-struck. "They can't do that – they'll be forced back on the rocks. What is he thinking of?"

Truly, the driving seas in the Big Sound did seem to be sweeping the boat backwards, but it was difficult to make out which way.

Then, after about three or four minutes, it became clear that the *Mary Stanford* was indeed heading through the Big Sound.

Robert Mahony covered his eyes, as if he could hardly bear to watch.

John McCabe watched the motion of the boat. Even from the shore, the lurch from the top of the wave to the bottom of each trough seemed extremely violent. He feared the structure of the boat might not be strong enough to withstand the strain.

"I wonder that the engine has not gone through the floor of the boat," he muttered to Mahony.

" 'Tis just what I fear, John," said Mahony. "In my mind, I can just hear the thud as she hits each trough. Particul'y if they're all sitting in the after cockpit, as I've no doubt Pat has told them."

Watching was an agony for him. He was suffering with the crew out at sea.

"If I know Pat Sliney, he'll be counting heads after each wave," he added. "What goes into a wave doesn't always come out."

The thought of brave men being swept overboard reduced them all to silence.

John McCabe decided it was time to move.

"I think I can be more helpful if we take the car and go over to Power Head, Robert," he said. "With the telephone lines down, you won't be able to get messages through to Queenstown from here. I have my field glasses upstairs, I should be able to keep watch on their progress along the coast."

"Indeed that would be grand," said Mahony, adding inconsequentially, "though I believe they will not find the lightship."

"If they don't, what then?" asked McCabe.

"They will have to put into port, either here or in Queenstown. I shall drive up to Cloyne or Midleton, to see if the phone is working. Sure to God there must be a phone working somewhere so I can ask the Cork pilots where the lightship is! Pat must return here, I b'lieve."

John McCabe took only David with him. He was afraid that the car he had hired would not make it along the rough roads with a full load.

The protests of the two younger boys at being left with a relative subsided when it was revealed that there was a billiards table in the house.

"We shan't be long," their father promised, recklessly.

———————————————————

It took them more time, and the *Mary Stanford* less time, than he expected to reach Power Head, which is about eight miles along the coast in the direction of Cork Harbour.

By the time they had bumped down the farm lane and found a sheltered spot where they could observe the sea, the lifeboat was only about a mile short of them, driven by a following sea. The boat yawed wildly as it hit each wave.

"It looks very dangerous, Pa," said David. "They must be shipping tons of water. Could it capsize?"

"A normal boat might, but the lifeboat shouldn't. I'd say it's just very uncomfortable." He sounded worried nonetheless.

About ten minutes later, they observed a flurry of activity in the after cockpit of the lifeboat. John McCabe took a look through his field glasses.

"They're putting out a sea-anchor now. That slows the boat down and makes it more stable."

"What kind of sea-anchor?" asked David.

"Probably a drogue. That's a sort of bucket on the end of ropes... Oh!" He broke off sharply.

"What is it, Pa? Can I have a look?" David was alarmed.

"I think they've been swept overboard." His voice cracked in the effort of saying the shocking words. "A wave washed over them." He looked away, so as not to show his dismay.

David put his hand to his mouth, stricken.

John McCabe stared out to sea, rigid, not seeing. Then, hoping against hope that he had made a mistake, he handed the glasses to his son. "Here, you have a look, David. Your eyes are sharper than mine. Can you see anyone moving on board?"

David took the glasses and gazed at length, then handed them back, shaking his head. He looked dumbly at the ground, obviously near to tears.

John McCabe was moved. That his son could be so upset by the fate of comparative strangers revealed a new side to his character. He put a comforting arm round the boy's shoulder.

The boat ploughed on in the rain and sleet, clearly with the engine still running.

"Let's go."

John McCabe was profoundly depressed by what had just happened. He raised the glasses to take a last look at the lifeboat, noting with detachment the direction of its drift.

He took so long that David, standing behind him, thought he'd forgotten what he had just said. David shivered with cold.

It came as a shock when his father turned, animation shining from his face. He handed the glasses to David, and nodded at the sea without a word. The rain had slackened, and the boat was now in a brighter patch of sea.

David took the glasses. The vision was blurred. He adjusted the distance, and all at once the lifeboat came into sharp focus.

"They're moving, Pa! They didn't fall overboard," said David, as excited now as he had been cast down a few minutes earlier.

"How many people can you see?"

"Can't make out... They're doing something with the sea-anchor. I think they've changed direction, and are heading out to sea! Why on earth...?"

"The *Daunt* lightship is out to sea."

"But it's adrift!" exclaimed David.

"Yes, but they'll try to keep it near the normal position if they can, otherwise there won't be any warning to ships at all. I think it's time we went. Let's go to Queenstown and report what we've seen."

Though only seven miles as the crow flies, to get to Queenstown by road meant a long detour via Midleton and Fota. It was gone half past ten when they reached the quay at Queenstown.

⎯⎯⎯⎯⎯⎯⎯⎯⎯⎯

Queenstown, now called Cobh, is a pretty little seaside town on the north side of Cork Harbour.

Its quayside is a historic spot, full of ghosts. From here, thousands of Irish emigrants left Ireland for ever, to start a new life over the ocean in the New World. The long brick departure building still echoes with their endless sad farewells.

As the McCabes stopped in front of the pilots' building, the lifeboat was already visible in the deep-water channel behind Spike Island. A crowd was gathering on the shore. News of the rescue attempt had spread, and people were anxious to see in the flesh the heroes of the rescue. Newsmen were out in force.

When the lifeboat hove to alongside, the crowd were not disappointed in their heroes. Though almost devoid of individual features under their thick oilskin jackets, hats and leggings, and numb with cold and wet, the men looked the very image of selfless courage. Only the moustaches of motor mechanic Tom Sliney and Second Coxswain John Walsh were visible distinguishing marks.

"How ya been?" called a waiting newsman.

"Ahh, twas a picnic," said one of the crew, "though we did have a spot of trouble trying to get into your Harbour. Did you not want to see us, now?"

This sally caused some mirth, but concealed a less jolly reality. The breaking seas at the estuary bar undoubtedly gave them many terrifying moments. They had lost the sea-anchor while fruitlessly scouring the sea for the lightship. Its ropes were just not up to the strains imposed by the mountainous waves. On entering the estuary, they had had to spray oil on the breakers to provide an easier path through them.

Only Patrick Sliney and Second Coxswain Walsh came ashore.

Tired and cold though they were, they were bent on putting to sea again immediately. They had time for neither food nor a change of clothes.

John McCabe went into the pilots' building to see if there was anything further he could do, perhaps take a message to Ballycotton. He overheard the pilots telling Pat Sliney where the last position of the lightship had been reported.

Apparently she had managed to get an anchor down, not far from the *Daunt* Rock, and had hoisted red lights fore and aft to show she was off position. The British destroyer *HMS Tenedos* and an Irish ship, the *SS Innisfallen*, were standing by.

Pat Sliney then went into the office to try to get through to Ballycotton and report that he was putting to sea again.

"Where is the normal position of the lightship, then?" asked David quietly. He did not want to reveal his ignorance but he had assumed that the *Daunt* lightship would always be near the *Daunt* Rock.

"It's about a mile or two out to sea," said his father equally quietly. "It would be dangerous to be too close to the Rock. In any case, there are other rocks and reefs along that coast. Ships know that if they keep seaward of *Daunt* lightship, they'll avoid them all."

Pat Sliney emerged from the office, having failed to get through. The lines were still down.

And then he was out of the building as unobtrusively as he'd come. They cast off and were away, heading east, then south past the mooring roads and Roche Point, and out to the roaring ocean.

All the McCabes returned to Queenstown in the evening, and found no news of the lifeboat. It finally slid alongside at 9 30 pm, while they were out having a bite to eat.

The sight of that utterly weary crew coming ashore made a deep impression on bystanders. The men were soaked through and numb with cold. They had not eaten for twenty-four hours, and had spent the weekend rescuing their boats.

And yet it was not failure brought them back now. They needed equipment to finish the job.

Quite by chance, John McCabe met an old school chum, a newsman, who had ferreted out the day's drama.

The lifeboat had eventually found the lightship around midday, anchored about half a mile from the shore. *HMS Tenedos* and the *SS Innisfallen* were indeed in attendance, but the merchantman left once the lifeboat arrived.

The lifeboatmen hailed the lightship. However, the crew were adamant – they would not abandon the ship.

"Duty first, ye haveta admire then," said the newsman. "A lightship out of position is a danger to navigation."

"Why the lifeboat, then?"

"They only had an emergency anchor down, which might not hold. So I guess they wanted the lifeboat to stand by."

Which she did. For some reason, she could not anchor, said the newsman.

"Foul weather," said John McCabe. "In seas like that, the anchor would be a threat. It could cause her to capsize."

So they had to keep driving forward past the lightship and drifting back.

The reporter consulted his notes.

"Around 3.30 pm, the weather improved a bit – the wind dropped, or something – and the warship people said, let's get a cable to the lightship and tow her to safety. So they went upwind of her and floated something ... can't read this ... a glass line?"

"Grass line," said John McCabe. "A thin line with a thicker wire cable attached. Floats out on a buoy, someone at the other end pulls it in."

"You've got it," said the reporter. "Well, the lightship tried hooking it aboard several times, but the sides of the lightship are very high. See?"

He made a quick sketch of the scene as he imagined it.

"What with the lightship bucking like a bronco, and these huge

waves washing over them all the time, leaning over the side to fish a rope from the water ten feet below was probably no picnic.

"So the lifeboat had a go, it sits lower in the water. Well, they got the grass line and passed it to the lightship."

"Whereupon it broke," said David facetiously.

"No joke, young man," said the newsman, "but you're right. So the destroyer had a go, it came real close, like that."

He gestured with his hands, to show how close.

"Not so close as to smash into each other, of course, but near enough to get the line aboard."

He paused impressively, watching David with amusement.

"Did it work" asked David with bated breath.

"No sich luck. This time the wire cable snapped. The sea was imposing some pretty severe strains as it pitched them up and down and this way and that."

He stopped, registering David's dejection.

"I'm landlocked myself, so I can't say I've done justice to the situation, but it sounded very nasty to me. To my shame, I'm glad I wasn't there.

"And all this took hours and hours, by which time it was dark, and they had to give up for the night. Pat Sliney thought, well then, let's go and get some more ropes. And maybe a bite to eat. The destroyer would stand by."

Before he sat down to his first meal in 36 hours, Pat Sliney slipped into the pilots' office, and tried to ring Ballycotton.

He had no luck. The lines were still down. He went back and found his crew well into their food. Some were nodding off at their seats.

He went into a huddle with the pilots, and agreed that three of the crew should remain on duty in the boat, turn and turn about. The rest would try to catch up on some sleep.

At around 11 pm, the pilots' office door opened.

"Where's Pat Sliney? Robert Mahony's on the line from Cloyne."

The energetic lifeboat secretary had spent the day driving about the storm-wracked countryside trying to find a telephone that worked. He'd been to Midleton, tried and failed to reach Roche's Point lighthouse by the estuary, returned to Midleton, waited, returned to Cloyne, and finally found a line that worked.

Pat Sliney was as unassuming as ever.

Various lines and ropes were what he wanted, another sea-anchor, things like that.

The line was bad, and Mahony's voice sounded faint. Nevertheless, the message got through.

"I'm returning to Ballycotton right away, Pat," came the reassuring voice from Cloyne. "I'll bring everything over."

Sliney knew he could rely on Mahony, and went back to his boat.

Somewhat later than planned, the McCabes set off for Ballycotton. Within ten minutes, David nodded off. The "long weekend" in Ballycotton was proving almost as exhausting for him as for the lifeboatmen!

Robert Mahony reached Queenstown at three on Wednesday morning, after a long, circuitous journey of twenty-three miles, avoiding fallen trees, collapsed earth banks, stones dislodged from walls and the like. He brought everything the lifeboatmen wanted, plus a change of underclothing.

"Oh, that's grand," said one of the crewmen as he changed. Exchanging soaked garments for dry clothes was an unbelievable luxury.

The McCabes heard the rest of the story as it was retold in Ballycotton later. David had been very taken with the newsman in Queenstown, and compiled his own report. All ears during the narration, he subsequently made copious notes from memory, in a brand new notebook.

"First-hand information, that's the key to good reporting, me bhoy," the newsman had stressed.

The lifeboat set off again at first light on Wednesday. Some of the crew had managed to snatch some sleep. Crossing the breakers, their clothes got drenched again.

Thankfully, the *Daunt*'s emergency anchor had held, but the destroyer left once the lifeboat arrived. News had come through that the *Isolda*, the Irish lightship authority's vessel, was on its way from Dublin.

"'Twas strange, now," said the lifeboatman. "The wind eased, the fog came down, but the heavy swell didn't let up like you'd expect. The *Daunt* was rolling like she was drunk, and we were pretty tipsy ourselves, shipping water all over the place. The *Daunt* was getting pretty nasty weather reports on the radio, so they hailed us and asked us to stand by."

The *Mary Stanford* was still there in the morning, surging and drifting to remain in position. It was tiring and so uncomfortable that two of them were seasick – probably due to the long periods without food, followed by a hasty meal two nights before. They were soaked through, and mostly ravenously hungry.

"And we were getting low on petrol."

They had to go back. The *Mary Stanford* had a sail, but this was useless for standby duty.

By nine on Thursday morning, they were back in Queenstown, after twenty-six hours at sea.

"Of course, our petrol was at Ballycotton, and we had no lorry," said Robert Mahony. "So I asked Cork, could they provide some? They promised 80 gallons. Grand, I said, thinking that was all organized."

Then came a call: the Cork driver was injured and there would be a delay.

The crew hung around till 4 pm, fretting. Waiting was neither resting nor working. When fuel came, they scudded off at top speed.

They reached the stricken vessel not a moment too soon. The *Isolda* had arrived, but the wind had veered round, driving the lightship towards the Daunt Rock.

"The *Daunt*'s emergency anchor started to drag. To make matters worse, a huge sea washed right over the lightship, dislodging one of the red warning lights. Things were getting very bad on the lightship. We took a turn round the stern and fetched out the searchlight to find the crew."

The lifeboatman paused, recalling the scene.

"John here played the light on the stern, and there they were, all eight of them, looking mighty miserable. In mortal fear of their lives probably. The *Daunt* was rolling forty degrees or so. She had these deep bilge-keels, stabilizers, sticking out two or three feet each side."

He demonstrated with his hands.

"As it rolled, the bow plunged into the sea on the starboard side, throwing the stern high in the air. Then down she'd come again, thrashing and churning the water with these bilge-keels. Frightening it must have been, standing on the stern. They were holding on like grim death, expecting to be washed overboard with each sea. And they were pretty tremendous seas, too, pushing her towards the Rock. Like I said, the anchor was dragging.

By then she were, oh, maybe under a hundred yards from the Rock. If the wind veered round again, she'd be on it."

Absent-mindedly, he smacked an emphatic fist into his left palm, startling Joe.

"I thought, there's no time for ifs and buts. We shifted up to the *Isolda* and told thim, we'd take the crew off now. Carry on, carry on, they said. They knew they'd not get a line to her themselves in those conditions.

"It was no joyride, for sure. We couldn't go alongside to windward on account o' the cable. The bilge-pieces were churning it up to leeward, but we had to go that side, we had no choice."

David and Joe hardly dared move, lest the speaker lose his thread. Andrew fidgeted and yawned, a sign that he too was listening keenly.

"We drew as near the stern as we could and got out the hailer again, and told 'em what we had in mind. We were going turn the motor up to full speed and bring her alongside, I said, then cut it suddenly, so as not to go past her. The risk was, we'd foul her cable and be dragged under.

"And in that instant, I told 'em," he tapped the table with his finger, "in that instant when it stopped going forward, they'd have to jump. Niver look down, I said, don't even think about it. One look down and they'd be lost."

He half-smiled.

"Couldn't have done it myself, mind, throw myself overboard in the pitch dark like that, not even in terror of my life."

John McCabe smiled. The phlegmatic lifeboatman in terror of his life indeed!

"So we made ready to go. We pumped our bit of oil on the waves, which did no good at all, and made our first run alongside. Maybe I hadn't plied the Blarney hard enough, but on'y one of them jumped. We got him safely sat down, and then tried again. John trained the light on the deck, to show them where to jump. Come on, come on now, I said to myself as the motor drove us forward. Jump, now! I willed them to do it, but not one of them did. They were all for holding on.

"Back we drifted, and then had another go. This time five of them risked their necks. Brave bhoys, that's it, I thought, that's how it's done, let's show 'em! That left two."

"The next time was not so good. We came up to her just as a big sea caught her and tipped her over towards us. This is it, I thought, we're sunk. Down she came over us, smashing into the rails and the deck. The two men near brushed my nose as they whooshed past. T'ank God, John jumped clear in time without dropping the light. He said some things which I won't repeat before these tender ears.

"I thought, we'll go in again quickly, afore they have time to think about it an' git scared. Pyschology." He paused. "Good idea. Didn't work, mind."

Andrew had clapped his hands to his ears. They were going to drown, he knew.

"The p'int was, I didn't know what to do. The two of them were hanging on like limpets, paralysed, like, couldn't let go.

"So I said to Michael Walsh and Tom – Tom Sliney – some of ye get forward, now. We're going to pull those men in, I b'lieve they can't act for thimselves any more. I shouted all this, thim being upwind. I said, it's no time for bein' polite and saying, 'Please jump now, we're waitin' for you', I said, get hold of them an' pull thim in.

"So Tom revved her up and we went forward."

He paused, as if recollecting an unpleasant moment.

"We had no choice. It was grab them or leave them. So we grabbed them. We got one in all right, but he hit his face, on a stanchion probably. Made quite a deep cut. T'other one, I don't know how it was, no way would he let go. He took a tremendous knock in both legs when we finally got him off."

It was clearly an uncomfortable memory.

"Fortunately, our first-aid box was intact, and Tom patched them up for the while. It was one of the others that we couldn't help. The strain had got to him."

"What happened?"

"He lost control and started shouting and waving his arms about and lashing out. He'd had a hard time – maybe I'd want to hit someone in his place – but anyway we pinned him down, two of us had to hold him. I was skeered he'd really lash into someone and knock him overboard."

He added, "Besides, we were pretty done-up ourselves. We'd been away from home seventy hours by then."

The tale was over, though not all told.

David looked round the audience. There was an impressed silence. Then, gradually, general conversation resumed.

Joe was taken with the facts and statistics, and noted them down, to tell his class back home.

The *Mary Stanford* reached Queenstown just before midnight, where the injured men were taken to hospital. It then returned to Ballycotton, arriving the following midday where it had left 76.5 hours earlier. She'd been away from the shore for 63 of those hours, at sea for 49 hours. On average, the lifeboatmen had slept three hours during that time.

The weather was atrocious throughout, with rain and sleet falling almost non-stop. Temperatures were little above freezing.

Not surprisingly, the crew were in poor shape when they reached home.

The story lost nothing in the telling when the three boys reached home after returning from Ireland. It had featured in newspaper headlines in England as well as Ireland, and all kinds of people were moved to send money to the Lifeboat Institution for the "wonderful work of rescue off the Irish coast".

The most exciting accounts were given in a school near Newbury. One was based on copious jottings from a brand-new notebook.

"Just think! They were awake without a break for longer than we spend at school in a fortnight," marvelled David.

"Most of you lot can't stay awake for one lesson," commented his teacher sarcastically.

"Oh, I expect they did it for money," muttered a cynic at the back. A sharp jab was administered from the next desk, and the cynic was ostracized for at least five minutes.

Indeed, the lifeboatmen were paid for their work, as was quite proper. Each man got nearly £9.50 for his service, plus a £10 bonus for its heroic nature.

In Ballycotton, the other part seemed more important. Coxswain Patrick Sliney was awarded the Gold Medal for outstanding gallantry, Second Coxswain John Walsh and Motor Mechanic Tom Sliney got Silver Medals and the other crew members – Michael Walsh, Tom F. Walsh, John Sliney and William Sliney – got Bronze Medals. Mr Mahony was given an inscribed binocular glass.

The McCabe boys did not see the presentation, but John McCabe told them, "Next time we won't need our own glass – we'll borrow Mr Mahony's."

The old salt tapped the arm of mine host.

"Bring me another pint of yer best, Robert," he said.

"William's the name, Master Carron, William Fyne! Robert's the publican at the Sun, down the street, as well ye'd remember if ye weren't jug-bitten already. Where's thy farthing, then? I won't give it thee for nothin'."

The hoary mariner reluctantly pushed the coin forward.

"Here you are, ye rogue, charging an honest seaman a week's pay for a pint o' beer."

William the Publican picked it up and bit it before signing to a servant to bring a jug of ale.

Richard Carron turned to his neighbour, James the Weaver from Christmas Steps. James sat nearest of a devoted group of listeners. He never stirred from his workshop except to come to the inn to hear Master Richard Carron, seafarer extraordinary, tell tales of foreign parts. Being a Bristol man through and through, James could hardly tell – nor did he care – whether the tales were entirely true. That they were wonderful in the extreme was all that mattered.

"Did I tell ye," began Carron, "of how it were from this very tavern that His Majesty King Henry – him being king of Castile 'bout twenty year ago, as I'm sure you all well know" – Carron winked heavily at his audience, knowing they'd never heard of either Henry or Castile – "it were from this very tavern that His Majesty of Castile did first discover and subsequently acquire a valuable island."

He hrrmphed, and took a sip of mine host's best.

"An' I hope it's not his worst, neither," said Carron. "As I were sayin', this island bein' on the edge of the world, is called Madeera, and lies somewhere in the direction of fabulous Cathay, of which you've all heerd tell, for sure.

"Well, I can hear ye all starin' and see ye all listening and sayin' to yerselves, what's this island called Madeera to do with our Master William Fyne's tavern?

"Well, now. It were 'bout fifty year afore that when a gently born young Brissol lad called Robert Macham come into this very tavern one morning and said to mine host – that were Master William's grandfather William, or his great-grandfather William, mind, not Master William ye sees over there – he said, Master William, tha's allus been a good friend to me and mine, here's ten pence and tha can be a mortal great friend to me tonight.

"And what he told Master William's grandfather were, when Master John d'Arfet the merchant should come to the inn tonight, he were to ply the good Master John with his best and keep the said honest citizen at the inn as long as he could, till at least past midnight.

"Master William looked very distressed at this, and was afeerd that Robert Macham had evil designs on Master d'Arfet's house and property. Young Robert made haste to assure mine host that he had no such designs, but said that he was in love with Master d'Arfet's daughter Anne and wished to speak with her alone that evening. That was all.

"Master William looked severe at this and said, 'What are the young come to these days?' Humsoever but he would accept the young gentleman's word this once, he said, looking at the ten pence."

Richard Carron looked round at his audience. To a man, they were spellbound. He allowed himself a wetting of the whistle, and continued.

"Well, that were the last time Master William ever saw young Robert. That same night Robert carried the young lady of his heart down to Brissol Bridge. There they found waiting for them a ship laden with cloth for Cadiz, and away they went to Spain. When Master John returned 'ome with a sore head in the early morning, he were in no state to enquire whether all his household were at home."

The narrator paused and made a face.

"You could see that the good Lord in Heaven Above were in two minds about the affair, because our Robert and his sweetheart never did reach Spain but was struck by a cruel tempest, on account o' which they sought refuge in Hatchet. That's the name of a bay on the island of Madeera.

"The young lady were very ill by then, what with the storm an' the ship's food, and young Robert were cast down in despair. He said to the master of his vessel, we must go ashore a day or two so that my lady may recover."

"Where's the tragedy, Master Richard?" said James the Weaver, all eager. "I can't bear to hear no further! 'Tis certain it will all end in tears."

"Alas," said the narrator, relishing the tension. "The master of the vessel was no honest man, though Master Robert had paid him honest silver for the boat. He gladly agreed that Robert and his friends should put ashore in the boats; which they did.

"The company found the island very agreeable, and were preparing to pass a pleasant time when the lady turned and said,

'Richard my lord and love, why is our boat hastening away?'

"And indeed it was. No sooner had the company set foot ashore when the false knave of a master found that the wind were set fair and he hurried forth with the ship and the valuable cargo."

There was a deep sigh from the audience. That a Bristol captain could behave in this fashion was inconceivable.

"That were no Brissol master!" exclaimed James hoarsely. "No Brissol man would treat thus dishonourably."

The narrator held up his hand, to silence their protests.

"To be sure, 'twas no Brissol man but a foreigner from Lunnon. Anyway, Robert were struck all a misery by this double treachery and feared that all he touched would turn to woe. It seemed he were truly in the right of this thinking acos his young lady turned thin and died. She were taken with distress that God had abandoned them and they were cast away and far from our Lord Jesus Christ.

"So there she lay on distant soil, all unshriven. Young Macham loved her dearly and could not bear that she should be placed in unhallowed ground. So he built a hermitage to bury her in, and told the mason to write his name and hers upon the tomb, and the date of their arrival in the island."

The audience gazed at Master Carron, stricken with grief that such terrible things could happen to young lovers. Carron continued.

"The good Lord took this as a sign of true penitence for all their sins, and led young Robert into miraculous paths. All round about the island there were trees of great girth such as ye scarcely see in England. Robert commanded his men to build a boat of one of these trees, and it was so great that they all could sit aboard it.

"And in this boat they were blown steadily across the ocean until they came to the coasts of Africky. When the Moors in Africky saw them coming over the ocean without sail or oar, they said, they said —

"Tis a miracle!" breathed James devoutly.

"Exactly what they said," cried Carron. "And the king of that country was of the same mind, and sent them all straight way to King Henry of Castile."

Carron looked round expectantly.

"And what d'ye think King Henry did?"

"He made the young Englishman a prince and give 'im a castle," said an apprentice hopefully.

"He told his minstrel to compose a virelay," said James, shaking his head mournfully, "sure as I'm a weaver. Such deeds must be recorded in song for ever."

"Why, both of you is completely wrong!" laughed Carron, delighted to have outwitted them. "What does he do but send a ship to find yon island and keep it for hisself! That's what he done!"

There were many shakings of the head at this cleverness.

"My, that were indeed a kingly thing to do," said James. "That's why he were a king."

Another tale of Richard Carron's was over, and splendid it was too. But James the Weaver wanted the last word.

"As I remembers, Master Carron, ye did tell us once that yon island of Madeera were the king of Portugal's."

Carron was only momentarily nonplussed. He scratched his head and said, "Ah, yes, well, that were another story how King Henry stopped being kingly awhiles and came to lose it."

James was satisfied.

CHAPTER 4

THE GREAT TEA RACE

1866

Woo-HO! Woo-HO! Woo-HO!

The six oars swung in unison, pulled by burly Chinamen in white duck uniforms.

The gig rounded the point in the Min River. The sudden sight ahead of him almost took the young man's breath away: sixteen front-rank British clippers at anchor behind Pagoda Island.

Able Seaman Ben Law felt a surge of excitement. In his six years as a seaman, he had never served on a tea clipper. He had never even aimed so high.

Thanks to sheer chance, he was now signed up for one. Misfortune had stranded him in Foochow without a berth. For two weeks, he had kicked his heels. Then came a piece of luck.

Short of a crewman, the legendary Scottish Captain Keay had scoured the wharves of Foochow. Not just any seaman would do. He sought men with a certain resilience of spirit. For some reason – probably his Scots name – Law had caught his fancy. And so he found himself on his way to the *Ariel*.

He shook his head in astonishment. It was no mean feat to crew one of the front-runners for the annual Tea Race.

Foochow was a Treaty Port. It was one of the few ports in China where foreigners could trade with the Celestial Empire. Behind Foochow lay the rich province of Fukien, with its fine black teas. Tea was fast becoming the British national drink.

In the 1860s, fashion intervened. Top people must drink the new teas from China, and the tea merchants rushed to meet the demand. Clippers were built to fetch the tea as fast as technology knew how. *Ariel*, built in 1865, represented all the latest ideas.

One of the Chinese rowers spat over the side. Law felt put out. It did not fit his mood of exaltation.

"Foreign devils," murmured Deason, the petty officer beside him.

"What?" asked Law, looking round.

"Spits when we gets near a British ship, that one. Puttin' us in our place as foreign devils, I reckon. Not got much time for us, have the Celestials."

"But we're not foreign," said Law.

Deason glanced at him in amusement.

As they drew nearer, Law idly watched the men clambering over the clippers. They were painting the sides, holystoning the decks, applying gold paint to the gingerbread work at the stern, varnishing deck fittings and polishing brass – things he'd done himself a thousand times before, with far less splendid results.

"I'll be doing that," he thought, and was pleased. Hanging around Foochow with nothing to do had seemed good at first, but soon became irksome.

They passed behind the *Fiery Cross*, the *Black Prince*, the *Serica*, the *Taeping*. Some of the names he knew from the talk in the ports. Others were new to him.

"We're at the end," said Deason.

The *Taitsing*. The *Falcon*. Other names Law could not read.

At last they swung round under the stern of a low black hull. It was nearly 200 feet long, and seemed longer. *ARIEL, LONDON*, said the ornate lettering. Greenock-built, London-owned.

"Here we are."

Ariel lay beyond the rest of the fleet, not far from Pagoda Rock. To Law, she seemed special, apart. He'd heard she was one of the favourites. He looked up at her as they came alongside.

"God bless all who sail in her!" he thought, pleased with what he saw.

And they were finally aboard.

───────

Masts and spars tinted the colour of flesh. Bulwarks and midshiphouse painted brilliant white, lined out with green, the centre fields picked out in pink. Decks gleaming milkily from repeated holystoning. Brass rails shining like a blaze of fire in the evening sun.

Such a feast to the eye! It would have put the richest Manchester cotton merchant's yacht to shame.

The next day, off Pagoda Island, the breeze was stiffening. Gangs of coolies had been brought aboard the ships, to help with the ballasting.

"Fellers ashore must be moving at last," observed Deason in his peculiar accent. "The Old Man only orders ballasting when the tea's on its way. Probably cheaper that way. Got an eye for the pennies, has Cap'n Keay."

Deason was an old hand at the Tea Race.

Law walked down from the midshiphouse and peered into the hold. Urgent bumping noises were heard from below.

"Check the ballasting, if you please, Law."

Law nearly leapt out of his skin. He had not heard Captain Keay approach.

"Mr Madder will be down to check at the end of the watch," added Keay. Madder was the Second Mate.

"Yes, sir!"

Law clattered down the companionway. The coolies needed no instructions, Deason had said – they knew their job. Someone had to be on hand, guessed Law.

Ballast provided stability. The bottom of the boat was lined with 100 tons of iron kentledge, fixed permanently. Another 20 or so tons of pig-iron was moveable. It was adjusted every trip, to give the best balance or trim.

On top of this came 200 tons of clean, hard shingle. Clean and hard because it must contain no water. The tea chests would sit on it. If the ballast contained wet, porous stone, the tea would soak up the water and be spoiled.

Proper ballasting was essential for a fast voyage.

The following day, Law was one of the crew detailed to go with the captain's gig to the shore.

"Things are hotting up with the cargoes," said Madder. "Cap'n's got to be on the spot. Fix the deal, an' that."

On the foreshore in Foochow, knots of seamen waited outside the Officers' Club. The evening air was punctuated by their guffaws and animated tales of piracy and adventures on the high seas.

Inside the club, high drama was being enacted. To an inexperienced eye, it seemed unlikely that the seamen appreciated that. But every man jack of them was aware of it. They had seen the captains go in. The tension written on their skippers' faces had been all too obvious.

The sailors had got used to the comings and goings over the last week. It was the general view among them that talks with the tea merchants were at a tricky stage. It was make or break time.

"You should ha' seed the Cap'n go in two days ago," said a Somerset seaman from the *Serica*. The *Serica*'s skipper, Captain Innes, was a fiery Edinburgh man, well-known for his excitable temperament. "Face as black as a pirate's beard, 'un waar."

It was a common illusion that pirates had beards. Those who had met them in the flesh in the China seas – and there were many – knew that pirates were young and smooth-faced. It was their hearts that were black.

The babble of conversation suddenly died away. Captain Robinson, followed by Captains Keay, Nutsford, McKinnon, Innes, the tea-men and others, emerged from the Club and hurried down the steps. They looked none too pleased, but were evidently intent on action. Orders were barked.

The deal had been done.

"We're on!" said a *Fiery Cross* man out of the side of his mouth.

He was not sure that Robinson was in the mood for cheerfulness.

There was a general cheer. As they turned to follow their respective captains, the crews of the *Fiery Cross* and *Serica* settled their last piece of business.

"A month's wages we'll beat you home," said a *Serica* man.

"Done!"

"Good luck!" Then an afterthought. "Better luck to us, though."

There was a raucous laugh from the *Fiery Cross* crew.

Up in the clubroom, Captain Inglis of the *Black Prince* puffed comfortably at his cheroot before taking it from his mouth. Gunn of the *Falcon* sat beside him.

"My beaver hat we're in London ahead of you, sir," said Inglis.

"Done, sir."

They both laughed lazily. They would be among the last to arrive. Inglis lost his hat.

Later in the day, huge bets would be placed on the front runners.

Meanwhile, the first cargo junks and sampans loaded with tea chests were already casting off and heading down river.

Law had been detailed to supervise the tea boats as they arrived. Junks and chop boats were being hauled alongside in quick succession. A gang of stevedores chatted and joked as they lifted the tea chests aboard. Two other crew members checked quantities.

The bottom layer of chests, the flooring chop, was already aboard – 391 chests and 22 half chests. The cheapest tea was used as flooring chop, in case it got spoiled.

There was a brief lull in the arrival of tea.

"What's that banging?" called Law to his colleague as he mopped his brow.

"Last flooring chest being forced down. Has to be a tight fit," came the voice, preoccupied.

From time to time, smiling Chinese women brought comfortable sampans alongside. They bore additional supplies or took messages to the shore. Work went on through the nights.

As Sunday dawned, the fourth day of loading, there were still sixteen chopboats alongside. Law was bug-eyed with sleeplessness. Madder noticed him nodding off.

"Half a day an' we're done," he said encouragingly. "Keep awake now. The Old Man doesn't take kindly to slackers."

Over on *Fiery Cross*, they were about twelve hours behind. Captain Robinson stomped up and down the deck, booming impatient orders. His gaze raked the row of clippers. Down at the end of the row, the *Ariel* was loading the last chops. The sight maddened him. Blast Keay!

Taeping and *Serica* were still further in arrears, but McKinnon and Innes were confident of their seamanship. They would catch up any lead Keay or Robinson could start with.

The fifth front-runner, *Taitsing,* had scarcely begun loading. Pagoda Anchorage echoed with a babble of frenzied commands.

By 2 pm, the last chest was stowed on *Ariel,* making a total of 1,230,000 pounds of tea on board. The chow-chow chop had brought innumerable last-minute packages and left. *Ariel's* crew were enjoying their first break for four days.

Captain Keay climbed down into his gig to go ashore. He had only to get clearance at the chop house, sign the bills of lading, and they could be the first away.

At 5 pm he was back on board, having sent the paddle tug, the *Island Queen*, ahead of him. It was already lashed alongside.

He gave the order to unmoor.

Tug and clipper passed safely through the seven-mile gorge of the Mingan Passage and dropped anchor for the night.

The bellow of Robinson's voice echoed across the anchorage as they moved out of sight.

"A tael for every gang if we're finished tonight!"

A tael was worth six shillings and sixpence.

Early the following morning, Captain McKinnon of the *Taeping* went ashore to clear his cargo. As he entered the chop house, he found Captain Innes nearly paralysed with excitement. Purple in the face, he strode up and down the room in a rage.

"The de'il's gone! Bolted! Whusht awa' in the night like the thief he is."

"Who?"

"Robinson. The blackguard! The ould rogue! I canna believe it. Hove up during the night wi'oot coming ashore ta get his papers! The scoundrel's got twelve hours on us. An' he's tekken my tug."

He flung out of the door, only to re-enter equally tempestuously a few minutes later.

"Ah went wi'out ma papers."

He banged out of the room again, still in a fearful dudgeon.

At first light on Tuesday, *Ariel* hove up and ventured down river, to catch the tide. Yoked alongside the clipper, the paddler entered the Middle Ground channel. Keay bit his lip with suppressed anger. The tug was so desperately slow. The others must surely catch up.

At 8.30, they neared Sharp Rock. Keay paid off his Chinese pilot. The *Island Queen* moved ahead to tow.

At this point, the Min River runs between sandbanks and is very fast-flowing. Many fine vessels have met their doom here through bad luck or carelessness.

Unfortunately, the *Island Queen* was pretty feeble as tugs go. As she moved head, she started to swing about in the choppy currents. Disaster was imminent as the current pulled them towards the North Sand Bank. Keay fought to regain control of the helm.

"Drop anchor!" came the sharp command from the wheelhouse. The anchor was run out with a rattle. The forward motion was checked just in time – just clear of the sandbank and doom.

The *Island Queen* drifted back alongside.

Over the sound of the paddles, Keay shouted instructions to the mate, who went to the rail. He gesticulated at the master of the tug, waving him closer.

"Try again, 'longside this time," he bellowed.

The master gestured, and berated his hapless Chinese crew as they muddled the lines. What he said was lost in the noise of the thrashing paddles. Eventually the two vessels were hitched together again.

Slowly, putting on every ounce of steam, they moved forward together. It was highly risky. A powerful cross current buffeted them, forcing them towards the wreck of the *Childers*. This lovely clipper had run aground on the North Sand Bank three years earlier, carrying 1,388,000 pounds of tea.

"He's messing us up," growled Keay to the mate. He strode over to the rail. The current was grinding the two vessels together, ruining *Ariel*'s gleaming black paint.

"Stand off, sir!" he barked. "We'll try again ahead."

Smidt, the Dutch pilot, refused. The tide was ebbing fast, and he would not go forward until the flood. Fuming, Keay had no choice but to anchor.

Matters were made worse by the sight of Robinson in the *Fiery Cross*, coming up behind them. Drawn by a much better tug, she was making good headway. Morover, she had only 854,000 lbs of tea aboard and stood higher out of the water. She could negotiate the shallow waters more safely.

She ploughed steadily past. Mocking cheers echoed over the water from her crew.

As the tide flooded back that evening, Keay prepared to weigh anchor. This time the weather baffled him. It turned misty and wet, and Smidt refused to move. Bad news also came from Madder, returning from the bow.

"Five inches by the head, sir."

The trim was badly out, no doubt due to their adventure with the sandbanks.

"All hands below deck!"

It was back-breaking work. All the heavy moveable things in the bows – chains, twelve casks of salt, stores – were dragged aft. Some of the tea was shoved in the captain's cabin. This was no hardship for Keay, as he would stay on deck until they were safely across the China Sea.

At 9, *Ariel* got underway again, with the *Island Queen* ahead. Keay stared ahead in vexation. *The Fiery Queen* was now fourteen hours ahead, and the *Taeping* and *Serica* were close on his heels.

They crossed the bar to the open sea almost together, and hove to, to drop pilots. This was where the race officially began.

Island Queen had still not done with *Ariel*, however. As she lowered a boat to bring off Smidt, she managed to capsize it, throwing the crew in the water. So long did it take to rescue them that Keay signalled impatiently for another pilot vessel to come for Smidt.

By 11.10, all three ships had set sail in an east south easterly direction, heading down the Formosa Strait. All day, a steady north-easterly wind blew. By noon they had passed the White Dogs, *Ariel* managing to pull ahead of the *Taeping* and *Serica*. During the afternoon, low cloud descended and the three ships lost sight of each other.

On the after deck, Law took a deep breath. It was good to be at sea again.

Apart from the *Taitsing*, about a day behind them, the other eleven ships were still at anchor, awaiting their cargoes. They had no chance of catching the first five.

Winds are generally very light across the China Sea in early June, and very unpredictable. The *Fiery Cross* was still ahead of the *Ariel* as they tacked close to the land, trying to catch the breezes.

Stood in towards shore, in hopes of land wind, Keay wrote in

his log. Then the wind would sometimes come. Sometimes not. *Midnight, fresh breeze came from off SW. Land of Cochin China [Vietnam] 4 miles distant.*
7 pm: tacked off-shore. 9 pm: tacked in-shore.

Keay sat on deck throughout, keeping an anxious eye on the weather. His spare black frame hunched over his charts like the recording angel, observing all, missing nothing.

"The Devil himself could not look more completely in charge," thought Law admiringly.

Much lightning on western horizon, noted Keay.

Sometimes the lookout brought exciting news.

"*Taeping* in sight SE by E," heard Law, as he stowed rope on the anchor deck.

"Small vessel 100 yards ahead," was the call later, after darkness had fallen. They lurched to avoid a collision.

Keay kept the crew busy.

Took three doors off their hinges, to put hawsers and lines etc. in my cabin.

Put nine casks of pork in after store-room, leaving only two of beef in lower forecastle, [he noted in his log.] Ship seems to steer easy and is probably almost in trim.

Painted the rails over the brass work, to save polishing.

"The Old Man keeps us busy," Law complained cheerfully to Deason.

The weather could change alarmingly. Broken masts and torn sails gave the crew plenty of variety in their work. The carpenter was the busiest man on the ship, inventing ever new ways to repair spars. All the seamen helped sew the torn sails.

Strong squalls to SSE. Very confused SW sea. Ship pitching and surging to leeward considerably. In all small sails, rope of main topgallant sail gave way and split the sail.

On 10th June, the *Taeping* was seen about four miles away. It signalled: "Passed *Fiery Cross* two days ago."

There was a cheer on the deck. If that was true, *Ariel* could be in the lead!

We are probably the headmost ship so far, noted Keay with satisfaction.

Alas, it was an illusion. *Fiery Cross* and *Taeping* had merely crossed, tacking in opposite directions. *Fiery Cross* reached Anjer at noon on 18 June, and passed out of the China Sea. She was a day and a quarter ahead of *Ariel* and twenty-one days from Foochow.

"Anjer 6 miles to South East!" called Law, on lookout at 7 am on 20 June. Anjer was on the narrow Sundra Strait, between Sumatra and Java. It was a fabled spot in the mind of seamen, especially on the China run. When ships passed Anjer from the China Sea, they left the mysterious Orient behind. They also passed out of the pirates' reach.

"Pretty little town," thought Law as they passed less than a mile from the shore. He could see individual houses.

"Wonder who lives in them," he mused. "Fellers like me, mebbe."

Eighteen years later, he passed through Sundra Strait again. The memory of that bright morning in 1866 came to him. The little town had been totally destroyed by the floods that followed the eruption of Krakatoa. In 1884 there was nothing to be seen except an incredible sunset.

The *Taeping* passed Anjer six hours behind *Ariel,* two days ahead of the *Serica.* McKinnon and Innes had been less lucky catching the land breezes off Cochin China and Borneo. Nutsford in the *Taitsing* trailed a good four days behind them.

From Anjer, the racing clippers could really show their mettle. Gone were the tricky days of coaxing forward motion out of the South West Monsoon. From Anjer, the steady trade wind of the Indian Ocean hurled them across the Indian Ocean to Africa. Mileages leapt from 70-150 miles a day to 200-350 miles a day.

First landfall was the island of Mauritius, which they passed still in the same order, but more spread out: *Fiery Cross* on June 29, *Ariel* and *Taeping* on July 1, *Serica* on July 4, *Taitsing* on July 9.

From here to the Cape of Good Hope, at the tip of Africa, the weather turned fickle again, shifting abruptly from light airs to storms.

1 am, [wrote Keay as they neared the coast of Africa], ship almost unmanageable in the strong current. She came round against the helm. Till 5 am, strong gusts and confused sea. 5.30 am, it suddenly moderated. Set all sail on wind. PM wind very light, then calm.

Though average runs dropped to well under 200 miles, the tea clippers were still outclassing every other ship.

"Ship ahead, 6 miles north by north east!" called the lookout at noon.

It was the speedy little *City of Bombay*. By 4, *Ariel* had outstripped her. Five days later, chased by a stiff southerly breeze, *Ariel* made as short work of the *Tantallon Castle*, on her way from Calcutta to London.

July 15th, passed the Cape. 44 days from Foochow.

Had Captain Keay known, the *Fiery Cross* was now only a few hours ahead. Robinson had been less lucky with the wind. The *Taeping* was half a day behind.

It was anyone's race.

From the Cape, the race opened up completely. *Taeping* and *Serica* steered a course closer to the African coast and found good winds. Further out, *Fiery Cross* and *Ariel* were checked by light winds.

Calms and baffling airs, [wrote Keay.] Light, baffling NNW wind veering with every cloud.

It was very frustrating. The crew enjoyed the balmy weather, and felt guilty.

The first three ships were now jostling for the lead, though out of sight of each other. *Taeping* gained ground and was first past the lonely island of St Helena, the last home of the dying Napoleon. *Ariel* was now lying fourth, just behind *Serica*, a day behind *Fiery Cross* and two days behind *Taeping*.

Three days later, with a mighty effort, *Ariel* almost caught up with *Fiery Cross*, gaining a day on *Serica*. The new month brought a good day's run.

August 1st. PM. Sighted Ascension Island. Saw three ships during the day, left them all fast. Distance 270 miles.

Hands were still busy, lest they get bored and up to mischief. *Capn. got the hands scrubbing inside of boats. Also finishing off odds and ends about the rigging,* wrote Deason in his diary.

"My, he's stickler for smartness. Does everything twice if we're too slow," said Law admiringly.

At the Equator, it was almost a dead heat, though the captains did not know it. The first three ships crossed the Line on 4 August, with Serica about two days behind. The crews remained blissfully unaware, and went on with their "odds and ends".

On 9 August, the *Taeping* and *Fiery Cross* were near enough each other to signal. From there the leader kept changing. Captain Keay betrayed no excitement as he logged the daily tasks of the crew. No other ships were in view, and speculation was idle. But *Ariel* had moved into the lead. *Taeping* and *Fiery Cross* pursued their parallel courses in hot pursuit, still in sight of each other.

Then *Fiery Cross* struck a dead calm, which held her captive for 24 hours. Robinson watched in impotent fury as *Taeping* picked up the breeze and vanished out of sight. His rage may be imagined as his chances ebbed away.

Finished scrubbing inside and outside, records Keay on the same day.

Ariel held the lead past Cape Verde Islands, a day ahead of the next three. *Taitsing* was doing well and catching up, too.

Commenced to oil the bright work and paint inside ship, notes Keay with majestic calm.

On 29 August, all four leaders passed the Azores within 24 hours of each other, 91-92 days out from Foochow. The *Taitsing* was now only two days behind. All five ships were now blessed with a fresh westerly or south-westerly winds.

On 5 September came the call they had long awaited.

"Bishop Light, 10 miles north-north-east!"

The Scilly Isles! They were in British waters. Now a last dash for victory!

Busy on the watch, Able Seaman Law paused in his work to look over the rail at the speck of light and the invisible shore.

"Home!" said the seaman beside him. "Beautiful, 'n't it."

And what a tremendous last lap it proved, as McKinnon chased Keay up the English Channel. *Taeping* was visible astern of *Ariel*.

5th Sept. 1.30 am. saw Bishop Light. 2.50 am, St Agnes Light about 10 miles away. Set all possible sail. 8.25 am, Lizard Lights 11 miles. Since daylight a ship has been in our company, Taeping probably. 4.15 pm. Portland Lights 6 miles. All flying kites set, wind strong. 12.30 am, Beachy Head Light, north 5 miles.

In the early hours of next morning, at Dungeness, *Ariel* hove to and signalled for a pilot.

The crew leant on the rail and waited, agog. Would they get the first pilot? Or would McKinnon slip ahead and cut them out?

Getting the first pilot was vital. The race would be won by the boat that first picked up a pilot. The length of the race was measured from pilot to pilot: dropping one in China to picking one up in England. Keay describes a tense three hours.

6th Sept. 3 am, Dungeness Light 8 miles. Sent up rockets and burned several blue lights. 4 am, hove to, continued to signal for a pilot.

Keay and his crew had to manoeuvre smartly, to prevent the

Taeping cutting them out.

5 am, saw the Taeping and also signalling. Bore up lest they should run eastward and get pilot first. Seeing us keep away, they hove to and we hove to. 5.30 am saw two cutters coming out of Dungeness. 5.40 am. Kept away so as to get between Taeping and the cutters.

Captain Keay prepared to deal the knockout blow.

5.55 am: rounded close to the pilot cutter and got first pilot. We were saluted as first ship from China this season.

So that was it! *Ariel* was the official winner.

As the pilot clambered aboard and congratulated him, Captain Keay remained unmoved. He waved at the *Taeping* lying astern.

"Yes, and what is that to the westward? We have no room to boast yet," he said testily.

London – and the merchants – lay half a day or more ahead. For the merchants, it was the first ship to dock and unload the tea that mattered.

With their pilots aboard, the captains returned to the fray.

"Hoist all plain sail!" barked Keay.

The two ships set sail again and scurried up the English side of the Channel, the *Taeping* a mile behind throughout.

Off the Downs at Deal, they hove to again. From here, they would have to take tugs.

Now it was McKinnon's turn to crow. The tugs came up from behind, and naturally the first tug threw its line to the nearest ship, the *Taeping*. Outwardly calm, but raging inwardly at being outwitted, Keay watched them steam away.

Taeping's tug proved much better than ours, he wrote bitterly. *It soon towed past us.*

The battle continued all the way up to London. *Taeping* anchored at Gravesend 55 minutes ahead. Steaming up behind, Keay saw a chance to cut his rival's lead.

"Mr Jones, signal me another tug. Do not anchor."

Soon the second tug was alongside. A line was secured, and *Ariel* was ready to follow *Taeping* up river. The water was just deep enough, and rising.

At 9 pm, *Ariel* hove to outside the gates at East India Dock, and waited for the tide. *Taeping*'s tug chugged on. It had further to go, and reached London Docks nearly an hour later.

So that was it. *Ariel* had indeed won. Or had it?

McKinnon saw his chance, taking advantage of the *Taeping*'s shallower draught. He signalled to the dock.

"Leave the outer gates open."

Hawsers were thrown, and willing hands hauled the *Taeping* through the outer gates of the dock. The gates thudded shut, and the dockmaster opened the sluice, allowing water from the inner dock to flood into the lock.

The inner gate opened, and *Taeping* was warped home. She had arrived. It was 10 pm precisely.

Down river Captain Keay watched the tide slowly rising. At 10.16 pm, he judged the moment had come and gave the signal.

"Heave ho!"

The lines tightened, shoulders were bent, and by 10.23 pm *Ariel* was also in dock.

It was a near thing, though Keay did not know it. Close on midnight, the tide was ebbing fast at the West India Dock. The dock master came out of the dockhouse and prepared to close the gates. The sound of a tug caught his ear. In a few minutes, the unmistakable shape of a clipper loomed out of the darkness behind the tug. It was the *Serica*.

Taking advantage of favourable winds, Captain Innes had raced up the French side of the channel. He'd caught the same tide as his rivals.

He signalled furiously that he wanted to come in.

He was in time – just. The *Serica* scraped the bar as she lurched into the dock, but she was in.

By then, dockers were stacking the tea chests from the *Ariel* and *Taiping* on the quayside.

Able Seaman Law was knocking on the door of his family's house, in Wapping.

———

No sooner was he ashore than Innes buttonholed the dock master.

"What news of the *Fiery Cross*, eh? Is she in yet?"

The tempestuous Scot was hardly able to contain himself. The surprised dockmaster told him what little he knew. Robinson had anchored off the Downs because of unfavourable winds. He was probably over a day behind.

"Dished him, have we?"

The dockmaster reeled under the force of the affectionate blow from Innes.

"That'll teach the oul' scoundrel a lesson!"

Innes strode off into the darkness, chuckling and rubbing his hands with satisfaction.

It was marvellous! Unheard of! Ships sailing from the other side of the globe, yet docking within minutes of each other. All day London buzzed with it. The newspapers competed to publish fanciful stories of the voyages, complete with "reports" from the masters.

The owners and agents of the ships had been in a turmoil since the previous day. When the shore stations on the Downs had telegraphed the positions of the ships, innumerable problems sprang up from nowhere.

"What happens if they dock at the same time?"

"Who gets the prize money?"

"McKinnon might still trick us, and dock further down river."

Messengers scurried to and fro between the various offices, bearing veiled threats and more cautious proposals.

In the end, diplomacy won the day over aggression. No one wanted to give the tea merchants a chance to argue. The tea merchants were feeling sour already. The tea when it arrived would be hugely unprofitable, and they knew it.

The owners finally agreed that each ship should make for its home dock and the first one in would claim the money.

And this is what happened. *Taeping* was paid the ten shillings extra per tonne, and Captain McKinnon received the £100 prize money. He shared both with Captain Keay.

"A guid day for Scotland," the noble member for Greenock told a fellow MP at White's Club. He'd betted heavily on McKinnon. His companion smiled sullenly. Robinson had been his man.

Scottish captains had gained the first three positions, and four of the first five ships were designed and built in Scotland.

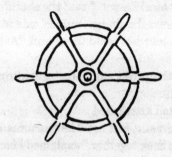

CHAPTER 5

JUSTICE BEFORE LUNCH AND DINNER

There was a hum in the stuffy court. The cub reporter from the Herald looked up from his notepad, hoping the air-conditioning had resumed working. Finally the prosecutor stood up.

"What now, Mr MacPherson?" said the sheriff resignedly.

"We wish to amend the charge, milud," said MacPherson.

"Not attempted murder?" said the sheriff. "Assault and battery, then?"

"No, sir," said the prosecutor. "Just misconduct and breach of the peace."

The sheriff looked astonished.

"That's rather drastic, is it not?" he murmured.

"The couple are back together," explained MacPherson.

"Perhaps you'd better tell us what happened, Mr MacPherson," sighed the sheriff, looking at his watch. It was getting near lunch

time. "I believe the ... er ... incident ... happened aboard a boat
called ..."

He consulted his papers.

"... called *Fat Katz*. Is that right?"

"Yes, m'lud," said the prosecutor. "Strictly speaking, both on and
off it. The argument that led to the incident started on shore and
finished when the accused, Mr Picken, threw his wife off the boat."

"Who owned the boat?"

"They both did."

"Were they arguing about who owned it, then?" enquired the
sheriff, lifting an eyebrow. There was a titter in court. The sheriff
was renowed for his droll wit.

"No, sir."

MacPherson picked up his notes.

"To be wholly accurate, the sequence of events started in the
family house. Mr Picken had been away to visit friends, and
when he returned, Mrs Picken accused him of staying away
longer than he promised. Mr Picken denied the accusation somewhat hotly, I gather. They are, shall we say, a temperamental couple. Mrs Picken asserts that her husband spoke provocatively."

"How provocative?"

"She says he shouted, 'I didn't', in a very provocative way."

"How long did the disagreement last?" asked the sheriff.

"About forty-five minutes, according to Mr Picken, about ten
minutes, according to Mrs Picken, milud."

"Even ten minutes would seem a long time to say, 'You have
been away a long time', would it not?" said the sheriff. "I merely
ask."

"Indeed," said the prosecutor. "I am given to understand that
the argument did, um, recycle just one or two facts."

"Mmm. A circular argument. A feature of marriage. So – what
happened after that?"

"Mr Picken left the house in a rage and went down to his boat,
which was moored in the harbour."

"His and her boat," amended the sheriff, playing idly with his pencil. He drew a yacht with half a moustache and half a skirt.

"Milud," acknowledged the prosecutor, nodding. "Mrs Picken followed but Mr Picken refused to let her aboard, claiming it was his boat. Another set-to ensued, which soon returned to the earlier question of how long the accused had been away. And why he had walked away during the previous wrangle."

"Arguments about arguments," noted the sheriff, doodling As all over his papers. "And during this time he was on the boat and she was on the shore?"

"No, milud. During the argument the church clock struck seven, which was when they always had coffee. Mr Picken let Mrs Picken aboard because she knew how to make it."

"Coffee before dinner?" asked the sheriff, shaking his head at this affront to civilization. "Goodness! Whatever next?"

"I fear so, milud," said the prosecutor. "In fact, they each had a glass of brandy as well, seated at a table by the stern."

"No doubt this stoked the fires on each side," murmured the sheriff, who knew about such things.

"Yes, milud," said the prosecutor. "The quarrel grew heated. In the end, Mr Picken lost his temper and threw the cups and glasses over the side."

"At which ...?" prompted the sheriff, staring at the magnificent ceiling of the courthouse. It had a sort of knife-and-fork design.

"At which Mrs Picken – quite naturally – protested forcefully that they were her presents from her parents and he had no right to treat her property like that."

A pregnant silence followed.

"Yes?"

"Yes, milud. That, I fear, is when the Incident occurred. Mr Picken said to his wife, equally strongly, 'If you want the damned cups, you get them!'"

"And, er, threw her after the cups?"

"Correct, milud. He shouted after her, 'That's just for starters!' He was not thinking of dinner, I fear."

"How deep was the water?"

"About twelve feet, I believe."

"And how far were they from the shore?"

"The boat was moored at a jetty, milud. Mrs Picken was able to swim to it and was helped up by a neighbour."

"What was Mrs Picken wearing? It must have been rather cold in the water."

"She was wearing a fur coat over shorts, milud."

"You are nonetheless of the opinion that he was not trying to murder her?" The sheriff wished to reassure himself on this point.

"No, sir. It was more in the nature of a marital tiff."

Something still seemed not right.

"Why then was a charge of attempted murder preferred?"

"One could say it was a matter of honour, milud. Mrs Picken wished to settle the score. She was very upset that her favourite fur coat had been ruined by the water, and thirsted for revenge. A matter of marital differences, milud."

The sheriff glanced at the clock. Way past lunch time. An amusing incident, indeed, but it must not distract the court from the main matter.

The clerk called the court to order. There had been a lamentable amount of laughter in court during the prosecutor's evidence. The accused stood up and the sheriff fined him £500.

Looking over his glasses, the sheriff declared solemnly, "Let this be a warning to you, Mr Picken, how easily a marital tiff between excitable people may be misconstrued. Had Mrs Picken suffered injury, a very grave interpretation might have been placed on your action. Very grave!"

He added, thinking of the dreadful things he had heard: "If you had had dinner first and coffee afterwards, none of this would have happened!"

The accused looked suitably humble and chastened.

Shaking his head, the sheriff stood up and strode out of the court, intent on his lunch.

Justice was adjourned.

CHAPTER 6

SO NEAR, SO FAR

"Not a night to be out," said Mrs Ellis in Skinner Street, and drew the parlour curtains. The curtains lifted in the draught.

Down the road, another Whitby resident, Dr Francis, stepped out through his front door for his customary evening walk. His little dachshund trotted obediently behind him.

"A gale blowing up, Toby," he commented.

As they reached Captain Cook's monument on the headland, the full blast of the wind hit them. Dr Francis peered out into the soupy blackness of the sea beyond Whitby Harbour, and pulled up his greatcoat collar.

"Hope no poor blighter's out there tonight, Toby," he said in clipped tones.

Five minutes later he had had enough. He saw no point in unnecessary heroism.

"We'll give it a miss this evening," he said to the shivering puppy. They turned back briskly, towards the warmth of home and a blazing fire.

Hundreds of feet below, the sea roared its fury, battering the shore and sending huge clouds of spray in the air.

Alas, all kinds of blighters were out there that night. Among them were the crew of the large hospital ship *Rohilla*. As Dr Francis lifted his knocker in Crescent Terrace, eighty miles to the north a white-painted ship was ploughing into the teeth of a gale, off the rugged coast of Northumberland.

In the stormy darkness, no watcher was on hand to admire the handsome lines of the Belfast-built British India Company steamship, or to note its green line punctuated with red crosses, the symbol of mercy and aid.

On board the *Rohilla*, the 229 souls could expect no mercy from the wind and waves. They had to grit their teeth and put up with whatever the weather threw at them. It was their duty to be at sea. It was 1914, Britain was at war with Germany, and they were on their way to Dunkirk to bring off wounded soldiers.

Among the 100 medical staff were four female nurses. Other passengers included a stewardess, Miss Roberts, who had been aboard the doomed *Titanic* four years earlier, a Catholic priest Canon Gwyder, and the ship's cat.

For most of the medical staff, it was their first voyage.

It did not hit St John's Ambulanceman McPherson until they were about three hours out of Leith. The weather was worsening. Walking along the deck, he glanced at the grey, endlessly surging sea and experienced a moment of overwhelming terror.

"I canna get off!"

He had a horror not to be on firm ground. Now there was nowhere to go. This rolling and heaving beneath his feet would never stop. He could not get off!

A wave of nausea overcame him. He hurried to the gunwales but could not be sick. That was the worst of it.

A clap on his shoulders restored him to saner thoughts.

"Buck up, lad! Think of the boys we're going to rescue."

Ambulanceman McPherson muttered incoherently without turning round and went back to the orderly room. The mental picture of wounded soldiers really did calm the churning in his stomach.

The only patient aboard was a gunner named Nicholson, who had broken his thigh, and was too ill to be taken off at Leith.

The Rohillas were a tribe of fierce, tumultuous Pathans, subdued by the British in 1773. No doubt the ship's name implied that British power could pacify the waves as effectively.

Unfortunately, British power had another enemy to contend with besides the waves. The German enemy could be anywhere. All the aids that captains relied on in peacetime – lighthouses, lightships, warning bells, buoys – were out of service, to make navigation difficult for the enemy.

Still, the lights of the ship shone bright. The *Rohilla* was a hospital ship and did not fear enemy attacks.

And yet what was difficult for the enemy was as difficult for the home fleet. Seamen now relied on dead reckoning – a complicated series of calculations based on time and compass readings, with adjustments for wind and currents. In rough weather, steering by dead reckoning can be a little bit like taking a narrow footpath through a treacherous bog, blindfold, with just your memory to serve you.

The captain called the second officer on duty.

"To the wheel, if you please, Mr Huddy. Hold your course."

In this weather, it was better to have two men by the wheel to control the heavy rudder, despite the steering engine.

Captain Nielson had last taken his position three hours ago, by daylight. As darkness fell, the weather got worse till the wind reached storm force. It was time to take his position again. The captain bent to his task.

A Scot, Captain Nielson had been at sea for forty of his fifty years. He had commanded the *Rohilla* since she was launched, and had often taken her to India carrying troops. Though new to the North Sea, he knew his ship, and his crew trusted him.

In a raging storm, holding course demanded the highest seamanship. It was easy to be a mile or so off course without realising it.

The ship was rolling heavily. Second Officer Huddy anxiously watched anxiously the captain poring over his charts, his pencil twitching and tugging at the scribbled figures. Huddy said nothing. It was not his place to speak first.

"By my reckoning, we are eight miles off the Farne Islands," the captain said finally.

"No sight of Longstones Lighthouse, I suppose, sir."

"No. I don't think we shall see anything until first light."

"Will you go down to dinner, sir?"

"Mr Powell will be bringing it up shortly."

Mr Powell was the chief steward.

Huddy peered ahead into the darkness. All he could see was the wind whipping foaming white crests off the huge waves.

The ship lurched sideways into a deep trough, then the bows

rose again to meet a wall of water.

On deck again, Ambulanceman McPherson watched it with utter dismay. He could not keep away.

———————

Those on the *Rohilla* were not the only ones at sea doing their duty that night. Aboard the ancient brigantine *Laura*, Captain Shuter and his crew of six were sailing north, carrying ore to the Tyne. Conditions were even more atrocious for a small sailing ship.

And all along the coast, though the lighthouses were dark, men were on lookout duty.

At Whitby, sentries of the watch took turns at the end of the piers. As the wind veered round to the east, the temperature dropped sharply. By 3.30 am, two hours in the gusting rain and icy wind was torture.

The sentry on the West Pier cupped his mittened hands together for warmth and huddled against the dark lighthouse. Over on the East Pier, his colleague nursed a flaring match in his great-coat collar, to light a cigarette.

Two hundred feet above them, on East Cliff, Coastguard Jefferies was duty officer. He had the advantage of being indoors. Also, he could see further.

Near 3.40 am, he went to the window and looked out into the stormy night. He could not believe his eyes. He picked up his glass and had a second look.

"By heck!"

Under a mile away, the lights of a large vessel were unmistakable. She was heading straight for the rocky shore below East Cliff. There could be no worse place to head for. He could see no sense in it.

For a moment he was paralysed, unable to think what to do. Then his mind cleared and his training took over. It was his duty to warn the ship of the danger.

"She's off course!"

He picked up his acetylene lamp and rushed out on to the little balcony. He began to operate the shutter on the lamp, slowly, deliberately, lest the message be misunderstood. It was 3.45 am.

At 3 40, on the bridge of the Rohilla *Captain Nielsen was making routine checks. He was holding a steady course seven or so miles from the coast.*

"Mr Graham. Cast the lead."

Casting the lead checked the depth of water beneath the ship. Fourth Officer Graham hurried off towards the poop deck to organise this.

On the way, he got distracted: bolts securing a lifeboat had worked loose. He summoned two seamen to fix it, and another ten minutes passed before the sounding was taken.

The depth was just 144 feet.

"It can't be!"

Alarm bells rang in his brain. If the reading was correct, they were much further inshore than the captain supposed. There was no time to lose. Graham hurried back towards the bridge in something of a panic. It was after 4 am.

"Heck!" said Coastguard Jefferies again.

He was almost in tears from frustration. For fifteen minutes he had been signalling, but the mystery ship showed no signs of slowing down or changing course. They were ignoring him!

He continued signalling desperately. No other way of averting the impending disaster occurred to him. They must see him!

Shortly after, the sentry on the harbour pier caught sight of lights to seaward, apparently bearing straight at him.

"Hey! Hey!"

He signalled wildly to his colleague opposite, in warning. The other pier was empty, silent. He started to run back towards the guardroom.

Jefferies' signal had been noticed. On the *Rohilla*, Second

Officer Winstanley came on duty at 4 am. As he staggered up the heaving deck towards the bridge, a flashing light to starboard caught his gaze.

"What the devil?"

Unfortunately, Winstanley was not a practised signaller, and could not decipher it.

He quickened his pace, lurched up the steps and entered the bridge in haste.

"Light to starboard, sir. Too fast for me, I'm afraid," he gasped.

Captain Nielson had been worrying over his calculations. There was always an element of guesswork in dead reckoning. He called Second Office Gwynn over and spoke to him urgently. Gwynn listened, then nodded and went to warn the engine room to slacken speed.

Nielson thought he might not have made enough allowance for drift. The sideways movement of currents is very difficult to calculate.

"What was that, Winstanley? A light, you said."

"A signal to starboard, sir. 'Fraid I can't read it."

The captain peered to starboard but could see nothing. He opened the door and went out on the gallery. A swirl of icy air swept through the warm bridgehouse.

Neilson returned, frowning.

"Where's Graham?"

"Sir?"

"I sent him to cast the lead twenty minutes ago."

"Shall I go and get him, sir?"

"No. You'd better find Paddock, see what he makes of it."

"Yes, sir."

Thomas Paddock was the signalman. Winstanley never got the message to him.

No one knows why it happened.

A violent shock coursed through the ship. The men on the bridge were thrown to the floor. About to mount the bridgehouse steps, Fourth Officer Graham suddenly found himself sprawling on deck. On the engine room companionway, Second Officer Gwynn was flung backwards by the impact, but kept hold of the rail. Down below the waterline, in the dusty boiler room, the firemen were hurled against hot surfaces. Metal implements clattered about them. In the coal bunkers, piles of coal cascaded rearwards, throwing extra weight on the stern.

No one was prepared – or trained – for the situation. In the darkness of the sleeping quarters, everything seemed worse.

" 'Ere, Ted, what's happened?"

The deck boy nudged his brother anxiously.

"Dunno. Terrible bump, war'n'tit. You OK?"

"I'm 'avin' a look." He clambered down. 'Ere. Bill! The floor's awash! Cmon, we gotta get out of here."

There were feverish rustling noises.

"Bill! I can't find my shirt. What's happened to the light?"

"Never mind that, Ted. Let's git out!"

Half-clad, they rushed out of the cabin.

"Up, Ted, jes' go up!"

Most people had been in bed, though the ship's heavy lurching motion had kept them awake all night. The boys bumped into others just as scantily dressed, many wandering around in a daze.

Eventually, they opened a door and found themselves on the Boat Deck. Luckily they were on the lee side, and huddled for a while out of wind and rain under a lifeboat, before cold forced them to seek shelter in an empty duty room.

As he picked himself up off the floor, Captain Nielson's mind was racing. Suddenly the tiredness was gone. What had happened? They were at war. An immediate explanation offered.

"By God, we've struck a German mine!"

Urgent action was called for. Probably the ship was holed below the waterline, and water could be rushing in.

"Full astern, Mr Winstanley!"

It was essential to slow the ship down, to reduce any intake of water. Winstanley leapt to obey.

It was no-win situation. For what seemed an age but was in fact only a few seconds, Captain Nielson considered his options: to keep the ship where she was, where she might – probably would – sink, or chance his luck further inshore, on the inhospitable Yorkshire coast.

He brooded. The first option was hardly worth considering. In these towering seas, launching the boats was wellnigh impossible. Even if the boats got away, they would hardly survive to the shore. They were eight miles out to sea.

Let them try for a safer shore in the ship.

"Helm hard to starboard. Engines full ahead!"

The light to starboard had passed clean from his mind, and Graham had not returned with the depth reading. Nielson could not know they were not eight miles out to sea. They were in fact under a mile offshore.

Up on East Cliff, flashing his message like a demoniac, Coastguard Jefferies thought he was losing his wits. Contrary to rational explanation, the ship was now heading straight for the Scaur!

Between Whitby Harbour and the headland of Saltwick Nab, sheer cliff runs for about a mile. The coastguard building is up there; so is the ancient church of St Mary. The churchyard runs to the edge of the cliff. The view in summer, on a clear day, is terrific. You look straight down nearly 200 feet, if you have the nerve.

In a howling October gale, the foot of that cliff is no place for man or ship. A ledge of hard rock called the Scaur runs the full length of it. It projects about 600 yards out to sea, then drops away sharply into deeper water. Most often, it is submerged.

At 4.30 am. water covered the ledge, but was not deep enough to float the Rohilla, *which drew 24 feet. With engines turning at full power, the mighty ship drove up on the shelf with a searing, rending noise that was audible on deck, even over the gale.*

She was stuck fast, like a fly at the mercy of a spider. The forward half was lodged tight on the Scaur, while the stern hung unsupported over the underwater escarpment. From the east, a driving sea pounded its prey ceaselessly, chasing clouds of spray right over the ship. It could only be a matter of time before the waves devoured the ship entirely.

Coastguard Jefferies threw up his hands and stopped signalling. Catastrophe had struck. It was time to call for help. Before long, maroons were soaring over the town.

Bang!

500 yards offshore, the first distress signals also rose from the ship's signal gun. Rocket after rocket followed as the extent of the disaster was realised.

Senior Whitby lifeboat coxswain Thomas Langlands was awake at once. He dressed with care but in haste and hurried down to the lifeboat station. A fellow lifeboatman just beat him to it.

"Tha sleeps wi' both ees open, Richard!" said Langlands sardonically.

His gaze swept the turbulent water thrashing the launch ramp. Risky for a launch.

"Let's check the outer harbour," he said. Second Coxswain Richard Eglon went with him.

A small town astride a narrow valley, Whitby rises on steep terraces to headlands at Khyber Pass in the west and St Mary's church in the east. The echoing rockets woke numerous others.

The rescue services – the lifeboatmen, the coastguards and the Rocket Brigade – soon turned out in force. They were later joined by members of the new St John's Ambulance Brigade, on call for the first time. No single person was in charge, and numerous hurried consultations took place.

Whitby is an ancient fishing port with a long maritime tradition. From here, Captain Cook sailed for Australia, in Whitby-built ships. From here, the whaling fleet used to set out for deep, distant waters.

A wreck concerned the whole town, and called out the best in the community. Many acts of heroism marked that night of disaster and the following days, by people who hardly realized they had it in them.

It was heartbreaking. On land, there was such a desire to help a stricken vessel so close at hand. On the ship, the shore seemed tantalizingly close; would the sea overwhelm them before they could reach it? Yet in the dark, what could be done?

"We must act" was the universal cry.

After the first terrible realization of disaster, Captain Nielson had followed procedures. He ordered the crew to lifeboat stations.

Sleepridden, confused, they staggered on deck, unprepared for the nightmarish conditions outside. Before the captain's eyes, two men were swept away by waves washing over the deck. Several others met the same fate elsewhere. Haste was folly. They would have to wait for dawn.

"Lifeboat stations, stand by until further notice!" came the curt command. For a good captain, the safety of those on board outranks even the ship's safety. Now both were in mortal peril. Captain Nielson hid his distress in Scots terseness. He flushed, suddenly conscious that, as captain, sole blame for the disaster might rest with him.

Had he done all he could, even now? At the earliest opportunity, he left the bridge and hurried aft. He wanted to see for himself how bad things were, knowing that the ship could soon break up.

The sight of the poop deck shocked him. A fracture ran right across the ship. Huge waves washed over the stern section beyond it, where a group of men sheltered. They watched petrified as the gap widened.

"Jump, men, jump!" shouted Nielson over the wind.

But they would not. Fear enveloped them.

Midships, one man had refused to await first light.

"I must see to poor Nicholson. He cannot help himself!" exclaimed Canon Gwyder after disaster struck. Nicholson lay with a broken leg in the stern. Brushing aside advice to seek safety on the Boat Deck, the canon hurried below.

He was never seen again alive.

Up at the coastguard station, optimism reigned at first. The wrecked ship seemed so close.

"Fire a line and get a bosun's chair out to them," ordered the coastguard commander, Charles Davy. "Should be feasible."

The rocket would take a line to the ship, which could then carry a rescue cradle. Easier said than done, however.

Normally transported by horse-drawn cart, on East Cliff the equipment had to be moved manually. Willing hands struggled and heaved the heavy cradle along the cliff-top, suffering numerous bruises. Mud and rain made faces almost invisible in the darkness.

Optimism soon waned. When rockets were finally fired, they plunged into the sea, far short of their target.

"Mebbe we can try from the Nab, sir," said the signaller.

It was a sensible suggestion, but not practical yet. Not only would they have to take everything down the cliff-face and across the slippery rocks in the dark, but the tide was still running.

"We'll wait till first light," said Davy reluctantly.

The Nab would bring them 100 yards nearer, but it was a wet, dangerous place for firing rockets.

At the lifeboat station, the mood was more sober. Langlands had decided that the water was too rough to launch No. 1 lifeboat

– even within the harbour. The second, smaller vessel, the *John Fielden*, was normally moored afloat by the quay. The twelve oars would have to traverse the pounding waves at the harbour bar. A roaring flood tide made this impossible – they would be driven back on the West Beach.

Both boats were rowing vessels, like the third Whitby lifeboat at Upgang, two miles up the coast.

First light soon after six brought a dispiriting sight. The bows of the *Rohilla* had broken away, and the rest was clearly undergoing a severe battering. At the fractured stern, the water was creeping up to the Boat Deck.

Ashore, the rocket brigade started to lower their equipment down the cliff, to reach the Nab. It was slimy, dirty work. Though pessimistic, Davy kept his doubts to himself. Something had to be attempted.

"Keep the lines coiled neatly," he called down. "For God's sake don't get them tangled."

"They weigh a ton," grumbled a voice below.

"Sodden through, like," muttered the signalman. "Nobbut the rockets should carry the line even so," he added doubtfully.

They reached the rocks and, sweating despite the cold, dragged their loads on to the slippery promontory. Wet fingers fumbled in the rain and spray to ready the first rocket.

Up it went in a low arc.

"Too low! It won't reach it," said a coastguard. It didn't.

They tried again.

"Still too low! Aim higher!"

"It's not the angle," said the signalman impatiently. "The weight of the line's dragging it down."

They tried again. And again. The result was the same.

"It won't do," said Davy. "Fred, go back to the station and get some dry lines. We'll never manage with these. Keep 'em well-covered, mind!"

No sooner had Fred and his mate gone out of earshot than the signalman croaked in triumph, "Got it!"

The line was certainly holding, but it was not clear where.

"Tha's struck forrard, Jack. They can't reach it."

Indeed the crew could not. The bows were now well clear, resting on the underwater ledge. On shore and ship alike, hearts sank.

"Coom on, lads, keep at it," urged Davy. "We've got the distance."

He knew as he said it that only dry lines would do it, but lives were in peril. Every minute the danger was increasing. The ship was breaking up.

Daylight waxed general. Thomas Langlands could see only one possibility: carry the boat by hand along the shore to the Scaur, directly opposite the wreck. There, they could try to launch it into the shallower surf.

"We can do it," he said to Eglon.

"Tek time, though," said Eglon sombrely, nodding agreement. "Can we do it wi'out holing her? It's nigh on a mile."

He feared the numerous jagged edges they would meet.

"Have to," said Langlands tersely.

Manpower there was aplenty – half the town seemed to be on hand by now – but the task was daunting. It involved raising the heavy boat out of the water, heaving it over a rough stone breakwater six feet high, and dragging it 1,300 yards over sand and rock.

They were not dissuaded.

"Round to the Spa Ladder, lads!" rose the cry among the townspeople waiting anxiously to assist. A surge of muffled figures hurried off towards the harbour bridge. It was a fair walk, across the River Esk and back along the opposite bank to the Ladder. This was a narrow walkway joining the East Pier to the mainland above the breakwater.

They arrived just as the crew of the *John Fielden* shipped their oars alongside the breakwater. Ropes were secured to the boat, and skids were placed underneath.

"Heave! Heave!"

Somehow they got it out of the water and atop the breakwater, where it balanced dripping while they regained their breath. Letting it down on the other side was a beast. Their feet slipped on the damp, seaweed-covered rock, and the ropes burnt and cut even the horniest hands.

"Whoah, there! Gently, lads! Hould it now, ye'll smash it!" shouted Eglon, as the prow tipped forward suddenly. The boat was deceptively heavy, and the ropemen nearly let go.

Having got it safely down on the other side, the helpers – men and women – spread out along lengthy tow ropes.

"Heave! Together, now. That's it. 'Ware that spar-stone, mind it, I said!"

Eglon and Langlands shouted themselves almost hoarse over the next hour or two. By the time they reached the Nab, despite their best efforts, the *John Fielden* had been holed in two places.

The two senior coxswains inspected the holes despondently.

"What d'ye think?" said Langlands.

Eglon shook his head and looked at his brother John, also a member of the crew.

"Good for one trip out. Mebbe two. Not more, I'd say," said John.

Langlands looked round.

"How about it, boys? Are ye willin'?"

To a man, the twelve men were. Of course they were. No lifeboatman would hold back in such circumstances. The cork filling of the boat would keep it afloat, but they could do nothing now to plug the holes, which would get worse.

"Let's go, then."

Eager hands dragged the boat down to the sea. Langlands winced as he heard the bottom scraping on the shale, but with many hands pushing from behind, they were soon afloat.

It was agony, watching their progress from the *Rohilla*. At times, Captain Nielson found himself clenching his jaw, so slow did it seem, but at least something was happening.

145 survivors had gathered on or near the bridge. Many were in their nightclothes. All spare garments had been lent round. The effect was often absurd, prompting the occasional joking remark. A stoker wore the captain's spare uniform.

At first light, Nielson had found to his dismay that the sea had carried away all but one lifeboat. If any use were made of the last boat, it must be soon. He called Second Officer Gwynn.

"Mr Gwynn, call a volunteer crew and lower the boat. We'll try to get a line ashore."

"Aye aye, sir."

Relieved at a chance to do something, numerous volunteers came forward but when the boat was lowered, the sea flipped it over. When it was righted, many oars were found missing, so Gwynn opted for a light crew.

"Mr Wootten, we'll make do with six," he said curtly to the bosun.

Wootten chose well. The six seamen were tough, and got the lifeboat away without getting dashed against the side. The line trailed after them.

To Gwynn, those 400 yards were agonizing. Without adequate oars to control the boat, eddies swept them this way and that, and the line kept catching on submerged rocks until it was a tangled mess. Eventually, the boat found itself held fast by the line and in danger of overturning.

Efforts to free the line proved futile. Gwynn realised he had little choice.

"Cut the line, Mr Wootten," he said.

The bosun had never seen an order given so reluctantly. Far from rescuing their comrades, the eight would be lucky to save their own skins. Their mission had failed.

Freed of the line, they crept towards the shore, where townspeople risked their lives to wade out and pull the boat in.

As he stepped ashore sick at heart, Gwynn turned and looked

back. The funnel of the *Rohilla* was no longer to be seen. Time was running out.

It was nearly 10 am before Coxswain Langlands and his crew were alongside the wreck. The miracle was that they made it at all.

A rope ladder snaked down the side of the *Rohilla*, while the lifeboatmen used their oars to protect their boat from being smashed. Spray drenched them.

"Women first, then the senior medical staff," came the order from the bridge. Doctors could save lives elsewhere.

Calmly, Sister Bennett gazed over the rail at the swinging ladder and seesawing motion of the lifeboat, took a deep breath, and swung awkwardly over the side. Her clothing did not make for an easy or elegant descent, but strong, rough hands grasped her arms. The three other nurses followed.

Stewardess Roberts, escaping shipwreck a second time, found the swaying movement overwhelming. For a moment she clung to the rail as the recollection of that horrible night on the *Titanic* hit her.

The surgeons made ready to descend, but before they could step out, three seamen pushed in front and quickly dropped into the boat. The officers had no time to expostulate. Captain Nielson made a mental note of their names, and vowed to expose the "white-livered objects" publicly if opportunity arose.

The other seamen showed greater discipline, and held back to let the medical staff down. One noted water slopping around in the heavily laden lifeboat.

"Last boat to earth!" he murmured facetiously.

That first trip brought off seventeen people. Langlands and his brave crew immediately pushed off again with the increasingly waterlogged boat.

They brought back another eighteen souls. By then, water slopped over their ankles. The wallowing vessel frequently scraped underwater rocks under its burden. The sea fast sapped their reserves of strength.

Back on shore, Langlands and Eglon examined their
boat and shook their heads.

"It won't make it," said Eglon.

"We need a motor lifeboat," said Langlands.

"Cap'n Milburn's the man for that."

The damaged *John Fielden* was drawn up high in
shore and abandoned. The tide was flooding and their only escape
was up the cliff.

> *Captain Milburn was an influential man – the Lloyd's
> agent and a member of the local Lifeboat Committee.*
>
> *When told of the desperate situation, he pondered for a
> minute or two, then went to his office.*
>
> *"Let's telegraph the other lifeboat stations."*
>
> *The replies were not very encouraging.*
>
> *"South Gare motor lifeboat put out to sea but made no
> headway in heavy seas. Will try again this afternoon."*
>
> *"Tug will tow out Scarborough lifeboat if tide favourable
> at 2 pm."*
>
> *Over the next two days, the seas foiled all attempts to get
> near the wreck. The Upgang lifeboat was dragged across
> country and lowered down the cliff, but could not get off the
> beach.*
>
> *The Scarborough lifeboat was towed to Whitby, but after
> eighteen hours in appalling weather trying to get near,
> retired. The approach was too dangerous.*
>
> *The Teesmouth motor lifeboat no sooner set to sea than
> she sprang a leak.*
>
> *The No. 1 Whitby lifeboat failed to get anywhere near the
> wreck.*

On the stricken ship, all hope left with the *John Fielden*. No
further activity could be seen from the shore. Though the Rocket
Brigade continued firing and one or two lines reached the ship,
lives were lost as brave seamen clambered out to haul them in.

Incredible feats of fortitude were performed by a general servant called Macintosh.

"That man deserves a VC," thought Nielson. He was a great admirer of courage.

Aft, the tragedy was entering its last act. By Friday midday, the tide had almost engulfed the stern section. One by one, the sea picked off the hapless survivors. Desperate, the remaining few tied themselves to rails or made for the poop deck cabin.

Then a huge wave tore the cabin itself from the deck. The stern section rolled sideways and sank, taking the last of the unlucky thirty.

No rescue seemed forthcoming. Depressed, the Captain indicated any that so wished, might take a chance and swim for the shore. The outlook was grim whether they stayed or went.

In early afternoon many jumped over, particularly at low tide. The shore proved deceptively near – the current swept the swimmers obliquely towards the piers, tripling the distance.

Luckily, many townsfolk lined the beach day and night, ready to wade in and assist swimmers. Rescuers formed chains, to counter the violent undertow.

Even so, it was often bodies they fished out. Some swimmers drowned almost within reach of the outstretched hands, sucked under by the sea.

One stalwart rescuer, the bricklayer George Peart, spent hours in the water, carrying the dead and living ashore on his shoulders. Later, his family found deep scratches scoring his back, caused by drowning men clinging to him for dear life.

The exhausted survivors were wrapped in blankets, and taken to local hotels and homes.

Some bodies were carried up the slippery steps to the clifftop. Among them was Canon Gwyder.

Day passed to night, and still the storm raged on, disheartening those still alive aboard the wreck. Some tied themselves to the rails or the rigging, but then died of exposure instead of drowning. Others tried swimming but were swept back to the ship or got tangled in wreckage. The lucky ones caught the lines cast them from the ship, and were hauled back on board, bleeding and exhausted.

In the grey light of Saturday morning, the Upgang lifeboat put off from the shore. For the survivors, it was the first visible hope of rescue for nearly a day. As the boat crept nearer and nearer, spirits rose.

And were dashed again, when, within a short distance of the ship, the oarsmen were swept back towards the shore by the current.

The Saturday morning papers were filled with the story. By evening, crowds of sensation-seekers had swarmed into town. The cafes did roaring business, but the mass of gawping visitors

obstructed the emergency services.

The rescuers ignored them. A local doctor, Dr Mitchell, appealed for stormlamps to help the rescue on shore, should more survivors turn up in the darkness. Captain Nielson had signalled:

"Ship breaking up rapidly. Look out for swimmers."

Some made it, using improvized rafts. One deck boy on a hen coop did not.

Between seven and eight, three more bodies were washed ashore, but one swimmer was still alive. At nine, two more appeared suddenly, white as ghosts but wearing lifebelts, picked out by the bright light of a car lamp trained on the sea. A cheer went up from the shore.

Above all, the lights moving backward and forwards on the shore told the survivors that they were not forgotten. When the tide drove them off the shore, their owners carried the lamps up the cliff, braving heavy rain.

Captain Milburn had had more luck with the Tynemouth Lifeboat, the *Henry Vernon*. When the call came through, its distinguished Captain Burton, of the Royal Engineers, quickly got it ready and it set off at 4pm on Saturday afternoon.

A very heavy swell had developed, and once they passed the harbour bar, the shore vanished from sight. About ten miles out, they hit gale force winds. It took nearly nine hours to cover the 44 miles to Whitby, which they reached at 1 am.

The Royal Engineers also sent a powerful searchlight by special train from North Shields, with a corps of trained operators. They reached Whitby soon after 4 am.

Volunteers bore off with the light to the clifftop, where the operators immediately set it up.

A powerful beam played over the Scaur, then moved seaward.

Rocks. Waves. Foam. Wind. More rocks. Heavy seas.

Finally, it found a few bits of iron, almost unrecognizable as a ship.

It was an appalling sight.

"Poor blighters!" Burton said quietly. "Signal that we're our way at first light."

The signaller did so, but received no answer. The *Rohilla*'s signalman had drowned, trying to reach the shore.

"I hope there is someone left to rescue," said Burton.

Burton kept his word. At first light, the powerful motor-boat nosed out of harbour, carrying cans of oil donated by a local businessman. The oil formed a crucial part of the rescue plan.

To the fifty souls still shivering on the wreck, the *Henry Vernon*'s subsequent manoeuvres were inexplicable and heartless. It went out to sea, steered wide of the wreck, then – for what seemed like an eternity – stood off to windward.

But Tynemouth Coxswain Smith knew what he was about. He had made a wide circle to avoid the submerged stern and bows. And he needed to time his approach precisely.

"Right, lads, pour it out," he barked crisply to the two men holding the oil cans.

They poured, and slowly the current carried the oil in a long narrow slick towards the wreck. The heavy oil dampened the spray and flattened the swell.

"That's the lot!"

With the cans empty, Coxswain Smith put the boat at full speed past the wreck on the landward side, then smartly turned her round to face into the slick, which was just drifting past the wreck. Richard Eglon stood beside him to ensure that he hit no invisible underwater obstacles.

There was a powerful roar from the engine and, despite the fierceness of wind and current, the lifeboat battled its way alongside the bridge. No other part of the *Rohilla* was now visible.

The survivors were calm but numbed after two days and nights aboard the wreck, expecting every moment to be their last. The *Henry Vernon* took off all fifty of them.

In best naval tradition, last to leave was the captain. Unfortunately for him, after two days in cramped conditions, he was less nimble than he thought, and slipped on the way down. He was pulled from the water, still holding the ship's black cat. The cat miaowed in protest.

They reached the shore at 8 am, to cheers from the crowds lining the harbour walls. Church bells pealed. Opportunists gathered bits of wreck as souvenirs.

Most survivors had to be helped ashore. The Captain was made of sterner stuff. Watched by his wife, he stepped confidently ashore, waving aside an outstretched arm. That earlier slip was – forgotten.

> *RNLI Gold Medals went to Coxswains Langlands and Smith, and to Captain Burton. The second coxswains, Richard Eglon (Whitby) and James Brownlee (Tynemouth), received Silver Medals, as did George Peart.* Rohilla *survivor Able Seaman Henry reckoned that Whitby itself deserved a medal.*

What did the *Rohilla* strike, that Friday morning? A German mine, Captain Nielson maintained to the end. A rock is a more likely explanation.

A third possibility was washed ashore some days later – wreckage from the brigantine *Laura*. The small vessel was passing Whitby travelling north that Friday morning. It never reached its destination, and its captain and crew vanished.

What of the survivors? Were they so lucky? Forty of the naval ratings were packed off to Chatham that Saturday afternoon, to rejoin active units.

How many – or few – of them survived the greater disaster of the First World War, now in its second month, is another story.

CHAPTER 7
GOLD IS DIFFERENT

GOLD IS DIFFERENT

Gold was different.

The weather knew it too, and celebrated the day of its first discovery in Australia. It was a find that changed the country for ever.

At Kilmore, near Melbourne, the sun turned bluish red as a fiery north wind filled the sky with dust. Later in the day, balls of fire blew over the housetops from burning grassland. In Gippsland, day turned to night as fires raged.

In Melbourne itself, the temperature soared past 47 degrees. Clouds of smoke drifted over the town, and the sun turned purple red. Reports of terrible destruction in the countryside caused panic among the townsfolk.

In Tasmania, huge black clouds filled the sky. The sun turned a bloody red, and people went down on their knees, thinking that the end of the world was at hand.

One man remained unimpressed by these natural fireworks. Edward Hargraves was a firm believer in the march of human progress – and his own role in it. While others trembled at nature's showy tricks, he was in Lewis Pond Creek looking for gold.

It did not take him long to find it. As he washed away the dirt from his pan of earth and river gravel, a tiny piece of gold gleamed at the bottom.

"There it is!" he said with great satisfaction. "This is a memorable day in history. I shall be a baronet, and my old horse will be stuffed and put into a glass case and sent to the British Museum."

Hargraves named the place Ophir, after the legendary biblical city noted for its fine gold.

It was a momentous find. Madness descended on Australia. The great gold rush had begun.

Though nothing came of the grandeur Hargraves promised himself, the gold rush changed Australia. From a convict colony at the back of beyond, it became the destination of golden dreams.

Those already in Australia had a head start. Within a fortnight, 1,000 men had swarmed to Ophir. Some had tents, others made shelter out of what they could find.

Attitudes changed, too, down by the panning creek. Convicts, gentlemen, shopkeepers and miners jostled for space. There was no superior and inferior – they were all equal, all in it for instant riches.Australia's rulers trembled, but they could do nothing to stop it. Democracy was in the air.

The gold rush also put a final end to transportation – the system whereby British convicts were sent to Australia in lieu of imprisonment. Why should the government provide free transport for "the wrong sort" of person to get rich quick? The very idea!

"Whatever next?" fumed a noble lord in White's Club in London. "They'll steal the cloaks off our backs to get transported."

Then gold was discovered at Clunes, west of Melbourne. Melbourne was stampeded. In September, sensational news hit town: pieces of gold the size of nuggets were being found in the river beds at Ballarat, not far from Clunes. Men, women and children poured out of Melbourne. By November, 1,855 licences to dig had been issued, and Melbourne had become almost a dead town. Teachers, priests and bankers alike abandoned their desks and pulpits, and hastened to join the diggers.

Cottages are deserted, houses to let, business is at a standstill, and even schools are closed, wrote Governor La Trobe in despair.

Once they got down to the creek, men were afraid to wash, cook or eat in case someone else struck rich first; little wonder that beards grew long and unkempt, moustaches waxed bushy.

There were fights, of course, and people were killed in disputes over territory and finds of gold. Quarrels, brawls and murder were the order of the day. Those that found nothing sometimes went mad.

But people who had never dreamt of wealth suddenly found

that hard work or cleverness was no longer the way to success. With a bit of luck, stamina and a thick skin against the hardship and violence of the digger's life, they found wealth such as only aristocrats had enjoyed till then.

They had a way with spending, too. They tricked themselves out in lavish clothes and bought showy jewellery, of course. But spending went to their heads. They made extravagant gestures like washing in champagne, watering plants with good wine and having smashing competitions with valuable china – just to show they could afford *anything*.

News of the gold rush did not hit England until 1852, when a ship called the *Albatross* docked at Liverpool with a substantial cargo of Australian gold. Something clicked in the public mind. Suddenly, the mother country discovered a mighty interest in its distant colony.

"Gold!"

Over all England, indeed, over all Europe, men held their breath for an instant. Then they picked up their hats and headed for the ports.

All at once, thousands of people wanted to get to Australia – *fast*. With a golden gleam in their eyes, men hoarded money they did not have, sold jewellery their wives treasured and betook themselves to Liverpool.

There they besieged shipping offices. They argued with booking clerks or, when that proved vain, accosted ship's officers and begged to work their passage. Failing that, they hung around and waited for the next ship.

Over the next five years, 100,000 Britons left for the other side of the world. At a time when many people hardly ever left their native village, it was a brave thing to do. It was the golden dream that lured them.

Until the 1850s, voyages to Australia took five or six months. Ships could be becalmed for weeks, awaiting a favourable wind. Conditions on board were awful. Dozens of steerage passengers died every trip, like the cattle, pigs and sheep with them on the lower decks.

Came the new-fangled steamship, and all that changed. Ships like Brunel's famous *Great Britain*, launched in Bristol in 1843, combined the best of both worlds. They had sails for speed in a following wind, and a screw for calms. Steamships could cut the trip to ninety days.

For steamship owners, that was good news. They could do two round trips a year instead of one – do more business, make more profits. Glasgow and Liverpool got down to it. The ships began to roll down the slipways.

———————

Gold ... It wanted thinking about. It could take a man from the hard life of a Cumberland tenant farmer and make him rich as a king. Just a little luck, and he could ensure his children never wanted for anything again.

John Armstrong was a Cumbrian through and through. He was deeply attached to his native soil of the Eden Valley, but he did not own his farm. His father had come down in the world in the hungry 1840s. John was only a tenant, a sheep farmer on the upland moors, farming poor land that no one else wanted.

It galled him. It was a hard life, and he saw no prospect of it improving.

Funnily enough, it was Mr Bell, the fire-breathing Methodist preacher at his local church, who showed him the way out.

One Sunday, Mr Bell took as his text a sentence from St Luke: "Be content with your wages." His real theme was the indecent lust for riches in the lower classes. Reports filled the newspapers about ordinary people making fortunes from gold in Australia. It was a bad thing, because it upset the natural order of things. People got rich by hard work, or cleverness; or were rich to start with. Not by luck, fulminated Mr Bell.

The germ of an idea lodged in John Armstrong's brain. The tender shoot grew when, two weeks later, he fell into conversation with a horse dealer at Appleby Fair. The dealer knew – only by report, of course – of someone who had struck gold in Australia.

From that day, John Armstrong began to put money aside. It was eighteen months before he had enough, and only then with money from a valuable tallboy his mother left him. He sold it while his wife Jane was away at Penrith Market. When she came back and noticed it had gone, there was a fearful to-do, and the truth came out.

Jane wept and pleaded with him, but John was adamant. To Australia he would go – for all their sakes. And he went.

"Shall I ever see them again?" he thought dismally, as he hugged his children and his wife. He said goodbye with a smile he did not feel. A leather bag with a change of clothes was all he took with him, plus a few practical bits and pieces. Jane put those in – she was afraid he would not look after himself. John himself had no idea what he would need in Australia.

He arrived in Melbourne with 629 others, on the *Great Britain*. Switched from the New York to the Australia run, Brunel's ship had become the most popular vessel on the route.

It took Armstrong two weeks to find his feet, ask about the goldfields, buy what he needed. People in Melbourne warned him of the terrible dangers he risked on the goldfields: the murders, the thefts, the drunkenness. Respectable Melbourne folk looked down on the diggers.

Then, one morning, he set his face to the west with his meagre belongings. The road was deep in mud.

"Ballarat, here we come!" said his companion jovially, a fellow northerner named Dixon. Dixon had also just arrived.

"Mebbe," said John. "Let's hope it hasn't been washed away."

The rain poured down.

Jane Armstrong heard little from him over the next four years. Just the occasional letter, with news about the heat, troubles with licences, and a lot about the Chinese, who seemed to be pushing honest Englishmen off the goldfields.

Gold-digging had ceased to be an easy road to fortune – there were too many diggers. The gold was there – but only machines could get at it.

"I've gone into partnership with another Englishman," wrote Armstrong. "Let's hope it works out. We've bought some machines – everyone's doing it."

He did not mention that machines cost good money. It might worry her.

The letters did worry Jane. Yet, because of the farm, she had little time to brood. Her brother came to help with the sheep, but she had enough trouble keeping things going.

Then one day – it was summer 1859 – came wonderful news. John was coming home. He expected to leave Melbourne in late August.

Australian gold paid for the *Royal Charter*, owned by the Gibbs, Bright shipping line of Liverpool. There was big money in the Australia run, and the shorter the voyage, the more money there was. The *Royal Charter* had got it down to sixty days, regular as clockwork.

"Steam from Liverpool to Australia. Under 60 Days," cried the posters. "The magnificent steam clipper *Royal Charter*, 2,719 tons register and 200 horse power, is appointed to leave Melbourne for the River Mersey. Fares: After Saloon (First Class) 60, 65 and 75 guineas, Second class 25 and 30 guineas, Third Class 16, 18 and 20 guineas. Children from One to Twelve Years Half Price."

The poster contained an illustration of the ship at full speed. Topsails, jib and spanker billow in a fair wind, but smoke is pouring from the single central funnel as well, as if the engine were working hard too.

Long and narrow, she had the style of a racing clipper but the flush deck of an iron ship. With a strong following wind, she could scud through the water like a greyhound. She easily overtook any other ship she met on the way.

In practice, the engine was just for calm weather: it was not very powerful, and the ship carried only 700 tons of coal – enough to escape the doldrums but no more. Space was precious.

For over three years the *Charter* had plied the Melbourne-Liverpool route, carrying a fortune in goods one way and a fortune in treasure the other way. What was not gold bullion in the hold was gold in passengers' luggage, as coins or jewellery. Gold was the passport to future happiness, and travellers kept it close by, or in safe places.

Every return trip, the *Royal Charter* was a treasure ship like no other. Its passengers had gold in their minds and on their faces. They were – most of them – very happy.

John Armstrong returned from Ballarat to Melbourne in style. Even during his time in Australia, Melbourne had grown fast. A wilderness bought from the Aboriginals in 1835 for a few blankets, knives, tomahawks and trinkets, it now had nearly 90,000 inhabitants.

Despite his homesickness for the Eden Valley, John Armstrong had changed his mind. He wanted to come back to Australia and buy a farm in Victoria. He had even selected the site. He liked Australia. It offered, he thought, a better future for his children. The climate was just like southern England. The difficulty would be to persuade Jane.

In case she did not agree, he took his gold with him. On board, it would be deposited in the hold.

"Looks pretty good, don't she?" said a voice beside him on the quay.

It was Dixon, whom Armstrong had not seen for three years.

"Going home?" asked Dixon. He had changed enormously. He

was tanned, and in his loud check shirt looked more Melbourne than Manchester.

"Yes," said Armstrong. "Maybe I'll be back, though."

"Me too," said Dixon. "Taking the *Charter,* then?"

"Yep," said Armstrong.

They watched a small steamer chugging out to the *Royal Charter*, lying at anchor in the roads.

"Tried to get aboard that," said Dixon. "Couldn't get anywhere near it. Police swarming everywhere."

"Gold, that's why," said Armstrong. "Saw them loading it. Boxes all sealed. Must be a fortune there."

"Where d'they put it, you reckon?"

"Dunno. Must be a strongroom some place on yon ship."

The sealed boxes did indeed contain a fortune, a third of a million pounds, in fact – a lot of money in 1859.

Armstrong thought of his own bag going aboard, and smiled inwardly. He did not covet the sealed boxes.

"We'd better get aboard," said Dixon.

On the way out they chatted, leaning on the rail.

"Captain's name is T. Taylor, it said on the sailing bill," said Dixon. "Don't know him. Fella in Melbourne told me he was called Boyce."

"He retired," said a sailor standing beside them. "Didn't get on with the company."

"Oh, why was that?" asked Dixon. He enjoyed talking to strangers.

"He thought they were mad about speed," said the sailor. 'Faster, faster!' they kep' tellin' 'im. He reckoned it was dangerous. I think he jes' got tired of bein' pushed."

"You with the *Charter,* then?"

"Yep. Five trips now."

"What's this captain like?"

"Taylor? 'E's a proper seaman. Worked his way up from the fo'c'sle. 'E an't one of your gold-braid swells."

"What's he like?"

The sailor pondered a moment.

"He's all right. Drives us like the devil, mind. There's no slacking on board the *Charter*. If we doesn't get 'er home in sixty days, there's all hell to pay."

Armstrong travelled home second-class. Four years ago he had travelled steerage, and had considered returning that way. In the end, he decided he was above that now. You met a different sort of passenger in the second-class dining area.

With 376 passengers aboard, it was very crowded. Except in rough weather, when many passengers stayed below in their cabins, it was hard to elude human company. It was thus better to make friends, because that way the journey passed pleasantly.

Most talk on board was about gold and life in Australia, but it was not usually greedy or boastful. Passengers were travelling home generally because they had done well down under. The atmosphere was good-natured.

One young man called Watson had gold samples in his pocket. They were intended to convince his young lady in England that he could afford to marry her.

Another passenger, a former convict who had worked out his time, had made a fortune from gold. He was saving the boasting till he got home. His neighbours had seen him taken off in chains. Now they would see him return in glory, dispensing gifts to his family and putting the rest of the street to shame.

"They'll see what Gordon Smith is made of!" he said in his booming voice.

"Really, he's very trying," said Emily Thorne to her husband that evening.

"No harm in the fellow," said Mr Thorne. He was a wool merchant and had often met rough diamonds like Smith.

"I wonder what he was transported for," said Emily. "I didn't dare ask."

"Oh, assaulting a policeman, I expect," said her husband cheerfully.

Down in steerage class, the atmosphere was more like the Lone Star Saloon, with colourful cowboy-like characters milling around. Most of the time, snatches of song and fiddle could be heard. In the evenings, conversation became very boisterous.

"Gaar, you never did!" was frequently heard from a farmer, John Steel. He disbelieved every word of the incredible stories the goldminers told.

A painter, Thomas Something or other, sat paper in hand, doing lightning sketches of other passengers.

"Why did you go out to Australia, then?" Steel asked him.

"Didn't know enough lords and ladies who wanted their likenesses painted," said the painter amiably.

"How did it go?"

"Very well. I'm just going back for my wife."

The painter handed them a small sketch he had just done.

"Mr Steel, it's you to the life!" said Mrs Steel. The farmer looked at it over her shoulder and grunted. He did not think the coarse face was a likeness at all.

Much speculation centred on a certain passenger called Garden, who had come on board at the last minute. He shut himself away in his cabin, and was rarely seen in public.

"I reckon he's an explorer," opined a shoemaker-turned-miner. "He has that faraway manner."

"I'm not going near his cabin, then, he might have all sorts of dead things in it," said his wife.

"No, he's on the run," said an elderly woman. Despite her frail looks, she was a veteran of the miners' saloons in Ballarat, and had survived many a brawl by reading character correctly. "He's on the run, you mark my words. I've seen many of his type."

She was right. The mysterious stranger had a bag full of other people's gold. He thought it wise to avoid questions from his fellow travellers.

They sighted the forbidding outline of Fort Charles at Kinsale on 24 October.

"Ireland ahoy!" sighed an Irish voice. "Not long now."

He was thinking of his family, and his ten children.

"Am I ready to be a fayther again?" he sighed, clinking the gold in his pocket.

As they dropped anchor in Cork Harbour, first-class passenger M'Evoy leaned over the rail and watched the luggage being loaded on to the shore-boat.

Many passengers sent messages to England, telling relatives to meet them next day at Liverpool or be prepared for their arrival.

I am looking forward to seeing you and Ruby again, wrote Dixon to his brother, a shopkeeper in Walsall. His brother was his only relative. *Be sure to be at home on Thursday evening. I have something that may surprise you.*

M'Evoy was startled out of his musings at the rail.

" 'Bye, M'Evoy! Thanks for the good conversation," called Daniel McCarthy as he stepped over the side. McCarthy and his wife had been entertaining companions on the voyage. They were returning home to Cork.

M'Evoy went forward to say goodbye, but as he did so, he was overcome by a sudden urge to visit his brother, an Irish MP living in Dublin.

"Wait!" he called to McCarthy. He turned to the steward standing by the gangway. "Stannard, is there time to get my luggage packed and have it transferred ashore?" he asked anxiously.

"Yes, sir," said Stannard. "We'll be here at least two hours."

Stannard went down with him to the cabin. M'Evoy was in haste. It seemed imperative he get off the ship at Queenstown.

Thirty minutes later, he was chugging with fourteen other passengers towards the steep terraces of Cove, recently renamed Queenstown after a visit by Queen Victoria. One of the fourteen was the mysterious Garden.

Another man was just going ashore to see someone he knew in Cork, eleven miles away. By the time he got back, the *Royal Charter* had weighed anchor and was away round Roches Point. That was fortune of a different colour.

Except ... *his wife was still aboard, with his gold.*

As they headed out to sea, Captain Taylor promised they would be in Liverpool within twenty-four hours. Nothing would stop them. The *Royal Charter* always kept to its schedules.

"In twenty-four hours, I'll be drinking tea with Mrs Taylor," he said with a confident smile. If there was one habit that Captain Taylor maintained to the bitter end – at least in front of passengers – it was confidence that all would be well.

He was known as a Sixty-Day Man, and by God he meant to keep it that way! Outstanding seaman though he was, he loved approval from the Quality. When educated passengers listened to him with respect, common sense sometimes vanished. He said what they wanted to hear rather than what was true.

Anyhow, Gibbs, Bright expected him back as soon as possible. If it came to a choice between risking the weather and missing sixty days, he'd risk the weather any time. It was a habit that was to become a fault in exceptional circumstances.

He was not to know that, twenty-four hours later, he would be locked in his last combat with the wind and waves.

The weather knew it, though.

By early afternoon next day, they were abreast of Holyhead, almost in sight of Liverpool. The wind had picked up. This made it most unlikely they could get in to Liverpool within twenty-four hours from Queenstown.

More worrying, they could see the Welsh mountains to starboard. There was a strange, dark haze over them, casting a most unnatural light.

"Filthy weather tonight, Adams," commented a passenger, a sea captain who knew these things. Fortunately, his companion was another seafarer. It did not do to alarm passengers.

They were not to know that the "filthy weather" had already struck the West Country. It had wreaked devastation, leaving hundreds dead in its wake.

And the storm was rapidly proceeding north. In those pre-wireless days, there were no radio signals or telephones to warn ships.

They knew about it that evening. It was not just filthy weather – it was the storm of the century, a Force 12 hurricane that produced huge seas beyond anything that even the most experienced seamen had ever experienced.

"The sea on that beach was such as I never saw in my life before," said Rowland Hughes later. He was coxswain of the Moelfre lifeboat, and knew what rough seas were all about.

Thousands of seamen were out at sea round Britain's coasts that night. If they were lucky enough to survive, they could not even find the words to describe it. They just shook their heads inarticulately.

By six, the ship was rounding the Skerries, north of Holyhead. There, it turned east. A strong wind was blowing from the southeast. It was blowing hard enough to worry some of the passengers. The ship was hardly exceeding a walking pace.

"Signal for a pilot!" said Captain Taylor as they approached Point Lynas. This was the normal place to pick up a pilot for Liverpool Bay.

Soon after, a rocket soared over the ship, the signal for a pilot. Blue lights were displayed.

Seven miles away, Point Lynas Pilot Boat No. 11 saw the signal, but was unable to help. The wind was too strong. An hour or so later, the wind reached gale force: Force Nine. Pilot Boat 11 was itself in difficulty and struggling to survive.

By eight, the *Royal Charter* was headed into Liverpool Bay but hardly making way. Nearly all the sails had been taken in. The mighty ship now relied solely on its engine. The screw threshed the water valiantly but hardly had any effect. Engine technology was still in its infancy.

Before long, the rudder ceased to have any effect at all. They were not moving.

Within minutes, the ship was out of control, entirely at the mercy of the storm – and the wind was still rising!

"Force 10, sir," reported the Second Officer on the bridge.

Captain Taylor stared ahead into the darkness. There was a mountain of spray and white foam. He was a worried man.

"Wind east-north-east, sir."

Taylor could hardly hear what his officer was saying, but he could see it outside. The wind had veered round to north and was rearing straight at the bows. The ship was being blown back towards the shore of Anglesey.

By 10.30 pm, the gale had reached hurricane force: Force 12.

"Prepare to run out the anchor!"

At 11, an anchor was hurriedly run out. Maybe the ship could ride out the storm. The engine churned the water in a desperate effort to reduce the strain on the chain.

Alas, the anchor would not hold. Slowly, it dragged across the sea floor. The crew could do nothing to stop it.

"The ship is no longer under command!"

The first anchor cable snapped at 1.30 am, the second an hour later. Some time after three, the *Royal Charter* went ashore on the beach at Moelfre.

Captain Taylor still radiated confidence to his passengers. What he truly thought can only be guessed.

"We are not ten paces from the shore," he assured terrified passengers. "In ten minutes, you will all be safe," he added. Perhaps he really believed this.

In some respects, it was the truth. In one major respect, however, Taylor was misinformed. He thought it was high tide. In fact it was low tide. Instead of ebbing and gradually leaving them high and dry, the sea was flooding in, to launch a new attack.

They waited until dawn, hardly daring to dwell on what fate awaited them. It is scarcely imaginable, what they were thinking:

men with families, desperate for their wives and children; lovers in panic about each other; nurses comforting sick patients and suppressing wild imaginings of the terrors that faced them.

The gold was forgotten, though many passengers still carried it about their persons. It represented everything they had struggled for. That was a fatal mistake – you cannot swim with a dead weight round your waist or in your pockets.

> *When dawn came, the view was incredible. Land was indeed just paces away, a mere stone's lob of 25 – 35 yards. The ship straddled the shore, facing west. It had turned round completely.*
>
> *On the shore stood a human figure, watching them in amazement.*

Yet what a stone's lob! The sea roared and heaved and sucked and pounded and hissed and churned and threw great clouds of spray in the air.

Hundreds of tons of water rushed up the shore, driven by a mighty wind, and retreated again to renew its efforts, ceaselessly. It would not stop for any human agency.

And what a shore! Jagged rocks jutting out from an unyielding ledge, the harshest environment that a ship could encounter. Local seamen who saw the site afterwards said that the *Royal Charter* had struck land at the worst possible place. There was no hope of refloating her, or of getting ashore.

The story of what happened in the next hours is unbearable even in the telling. The ship found itself broadside on to a merciless sea.

Battered by hundreds of tons of moving water driven by a howling wind, the ship broke up. Most of the crew and passengers were pounded to death by the waves on the rocks when they tried to escape or were swept overboard. It was a dreadful spectacle to those that witnessed it. So near and yet so far!

Thanks to the heroism of twenty-eight men from the poor Welsh village of Moelfre just over the headland, over forty people were saved. They came down to the shore to offer help such as frail humans might provide in the face of overwhelming nature.

An incredibly brave member of the crew, a Maltese seaman called Joe Rodgers, seemed to be the only actor aboard who knew what could best be done, and dared to do it. He looked at the shore and the sea, then swung himself along the jib, to fall clear of the bows. He had a line tied round his waist.

Swim he could not, in those currents. It was the most he could do to stay afloat. After being washed backwards and forwards between the ship and the shore, he was cast up on a rock, bruised and bleeding. The men on shore just managed to get hold of him before the sea reclaimed him.

In Alexander McKee's famous phrase, it was "the swim of the century", and earned Rodgers a special monument, later erected by the *Liverpool Evening Express*.

Thanks to this action, a bosun's chair was set up. By means of this, a number of passengers and crew – all men – successfully got ashore.

Unfortunately, all the women and children had been sent below until the bosun's chair was ready. Before most of them could be brought up, around 7.30 am the ship was washed higher by the incoming tide and thrown violently on the rocks. The ship broke in two, and all aboard were cast into a seething cauldron.

Whether John Armstrong was saved or not, we cannot know. Some survivors did not stay long enough to have their names recorded. However, some months later the Armstrongs' farm was in other hands. If John Armstrong did get ashore, his gold – down in the hold – cannot have gone with him.

Certainly, the story of the *Royal Charter* did not stop there. The human side went on for some time, as it had to. That night, 133 ships were totally wrecked by the hurricane on British shores, another 90 were driven ashore and badly damaged. Altogether over 800 people died in the storm, over half of them on that rocky shore in Anglesey. The *Royal Charter* left a lot of human business to be done.

The nation was shocked, at the height of its industrial prosperity. How could such a calamity happen, at a time when man ruled nature? Was this ship not an example of the latest technology, fitted out with all the comforts and opulence that human brain could devise? Was not the captain the best that mastered the seas, backed by loyal men who would follow him to the ends of the earth?

Somebody, somewhere had to be to blame. The stunned relatives felt this keenly. It was the captain – he had not taken enough care; he should have sought refuge in Holyhead; he was drunk; he had driven the ship too hard.

Poor man! It was not enough that he had died, trying to save his passengers and his ship. His reputation was to be hacked about as well.

Or the shipping company was to blame: they had not built the ship safe enough; it was not properly equipped; they were not doing enough to find the bodies; they cared more about gold than human life.

Or it was the lifeboats' fault: they had not put to sea in time to rescue the stricken ship.

Or ...

The parson at the little church near the wreck received over a thousand letters from desperate relatives of the victims. He answered every one, and then died of exhaustion.

The gold was different. Gold goes on for ever. There are still men scouring the wreck site looking for *Royal Charter* gold.

It interested even those who had no interest in the passengers or the shipping company.

The insurance company worked hard at the wreck. Divers went down soon after. On one day, they found gold worth nearly £100,000. Within two months, nearly all the "official" gold – the bullion – was found.

Ah, but what about the gold that belonged to the passengers?

This was not to be measured and ticketed. How could they identify the gold of John Armstrong, even if they found it on the sea floor? Who could they give it to? Who was he? The passenger list had been lost in the wreck.

If John Armstrong and 450 others lost their lives, how could the sacrifice – and the success – of their lives in the Australian goldfields be measured? Certainly not in gold.

The "unofficial" gold handed in to the Receiver of Wrecks amounted to only £1,200's worth. The passengers on the ship were worth a hundred times as much, or more.

Many of the bodies were washed up by the sea. They were usually quite unrecognizable – only the unchanged gold jewellery in their clothing was distinctive. The body of passenger Captain Withers – the man who had predicted the "filthy weather" – was found nine miles away, identified by a snuff box and £36 in gold. Another victim was identified by some pieces of poetry and £35 in gold.

Gold is different. It reacts neither to sea water, nor to air or oxygen. It is therefore usually found in its free metallic state. For the same reason, it tops the list of precious metals – it resists electrochemical corrosion.

So when the gold digger finds it in the gravel bed, he can take the golden gleam directly to be weighed. Easy for thieves to do the same: the wreck of the *Royal Charter* attracted thieves at once. Not surprisingly, the wreck is still hot news today. SUNKEN MILLIONS: DIVERS FIND FABULOUS GOLD HAUL ran a headline in 1985.

After most of the "official" gold was brought up, the insurance company sold the wreck back to Gibbs, Bright, the owners of the ship, for £1,000. Gibbs, Bright had a go at recovery, then sold the wreck to locals, who found numerous gold coins.

The wreck is now the haunt of treasure hunters. The sea claimed the ship and the people. That leaves the treasure down there somewhere. Doesn't it?

CHAPTER 8

YOU GOTTA BLAME SOMEONE

My great-grandparents never made it to America. That's my big tragedy. That's why I'm not an American millionaire, I'm just an apprentice fitter in a British factory.

My great-granddad went down with the *Titanic*. I'll never forgive him. My great-grandma never did, till the day she died. She used to tell me,

"I didn't want to go. Not ever. He was always the one who said, 'Let's get out of this, Vicky. Let's go to America. We'll never get rich here.'"

He wore her down with it. Eventually she gave in – she had to. And so they sold the furniture, scraped together the money they had, booked tickets for New York.

On the *Titanic*. Stupid idea. I blame him.

The *Titanic*, in case you don't know, was an Atlantic liner. The biggest there was, in fact – all 46,238 tons of it. Its owners, the White Star Line, thought no end of it, the latest in luxury. So did everyone else at the time. All the nobs thought it very swish to travel on it. They paid through the nose to be up there on the Upper Deck. The top price for a First Class suite was nearly $4,350 – and that was 1912 dollars. A fortune in today's money.

My great-granddad was earning five pounds a month at the time. Just shows you, doesn't it?

Still, he got there just as quickly as they did – or didn't. A lot of the nobs finished up at the bottom of the Atlantic with him. That's democracy, in a way.

So there they all were in Southampton, on Wednesday, 10 April 1912. (When you're blaming people, you've got to get the details right.) There were crowds on the quay, come to gawp at all the famous people going on board. At noon, off they went amid great cheering. *Titanic* was off on its maiden voyage.

They got about 40 yards, I'd say. Some careless fella forgot that *Titanic* was rather large. Big engines, you see. Their great propellers thrashed round mightily, as they were supposed to, sucking water like mad. The suction dragged a tiddly little liner called the *New York* from its moorings, right next door. Bad parking, probably. Any minute, there was going to be one great bang as they hit each other.

Was there a commotion up there on the bridge, with these two colossal heaps of metal drifting together at a rate of knots! I'll say! It took some time to connect, but someone soon got the message. Engines were stopped. Tugs rushed in with ropes. Calamity averted. Phew!

Maybe not, on second thoughts. It might have been better to have a little crash then. Avoid the big one later.

Ominous, really. They say the rats got scared and hopped it at that point. How come my great-granddad never got the message? I'd have skipped over the taffrail there and then.

Well, he didn't, of course, and off they went again, with my great Gs at the bottom of the ship, in steerage class. (That was the cheapest sort of ticket. They were crammed in a sort of big dormitory, next to the First-Class baggage.) By the time they left Queenstown, in Ireland, they had 2,200 people on board. They were worth a bit – just the ones White Star knew about knew about had $250 million or so between them.

Funny things, big liners. A bit like small floating towns. At the top (Decks D and E) were the staterooms for the very rich and the well-heeled. Super-de-luxe mansion cabins, you might say. Just round the corner on D and E, convenient but out of sight, were the little terrace cabins, as it were. 900 crewmen packed in these, ready to run errands for Captain Smith or bring Lord X or Sir George Y a clean towel.

Below them (Deck F) were the comfortable burghers – Second Class and respectable Third Class – in decent cabins. Sort of villa class.

Under them were the doss houses, so to speak. The steerage berths, for the likes of my greats. The riffraff class. GG (that's my great-gran) said most of them carried all their worldly goods in their bags with them. Travelling light, as it were.

Only the mole class rated even lower than that – the engineers and stokers. They beavered away night and day to keep the boilers going. Made sure the lights and heating worked. Things like that.

Only trouble was, the town sat on water, not dear old English soil. If it came to sinking, the chances of escaping depended on how high up you were. You couldn't just jump out of the window from the ground floor. I blame my great-granddad for not thinking about that.

So how did my old great-granddad get himself to the bottom of the ocean, thus depriving me of my fortune?

There they were on the high seas, bowling along at a rate of knots, everyone thinking how grand it was to be travelling in style.

On Sunday, the weather turned cold. In the afternoon, the wireless operator – always called Sparks, like electricians now – heard a message. Something about icebergs, from a ship called the *Californian*. On the *Titanic*, Captain Smith was unfazed. Captains always are. He was making a cracking pace, 23 knots or so. Anyway, as all the world knew, the ship was unsinkable.

Clever design, you see. It was divided into watertight compartments. Two, three, even four compartments get holed, no sweat. The rest would keep good old *Titanic* afloat.

Just to show what a smashing ship it was, the toppest brass turned up for the trip: Bruce Ismay (managing director, White Star Line) and Thomas Andrews (managing director of Harland & Wolff, shipbuilders of Belfast).

"God Himself could not sink this ship," said one wit.

You couldn't blame them. That's how people thought those days. Some things were dead certs. God was in his heaven, *Titanic* was unsinkable, and steerage passengers belonged down below.

Where was I?

Well, that night it turned freezing, but the sky was starry, wonderful. The sea was almost a boating pond. The lights of the ship were ablaze. Steaming along with three chimneys pouring out smoke (the fourth was a dummy), it looked like Piccadilly Circus, with a cracking fire in three houses.

Up in the crow's nest, lookouts Lee and Fred Fleet came on duty at 10 pm. They didn't think too much of the wonderful view. There was just a bit of canvas behind them for shelter. Brr!

At about 11.30, the two men saw this black thing ahead. Huge. Straight in their path.

"Do you know what it is?" asks Fleet.

"I couldn't say," says Lee nervously.

They dithered, terrified, like. Precious seconds went past. My great-granddad could blame them for that. (Later, Fleet obviously blamed himself. It got to him. He said he couldn't sleep for years, thinking of that black thing. Same thing with Lee – drank himself to death.)

So eventually they telephoned the bridge. First Office Murdoch immediately rang Full Speed Astern, and turned the ship to port. He wanted to steer round "it". For 37 seconds, nothing happened. Then at the last minute the bows swung to port. Murdoch thought they'd get by.

Too late. There was a serious grinding noise that rattled the plates in the dining room. "It" turned out to be an iceberg, and it had hit the bows. It made a hole 300 foot long, in dear old *Titanic*'s first five watertight compartments.

So that was it, really. Doom. Kaputt! The clever chaps had allowed only for the possibility of holes in the first four compartments.

You can't blame Murdoch, can you? If you saw a mountain coming at you, you'd tried to steer round it, wouldn't you? Fact is, though, they'd have done better to hit it head on. Shame about the poor stokers snoozing in the bows, but the rest would have been saved.

Murdoch went down with the ship. Perhaps my great-granddad had a word with him down on the ocean bottom.

As I say, that was it. They kept going for a few minutes.

"Half-speed ahead!" says Captain Smith. Someone'd seen another ship not far off. Maybe they could reach it, was the idea.

Not such a good idea, though. Water was pouring in through the bows at a rate of 400 tons a minute. Crew scurried about trying to find out what had happened. The telegraphs started ringing furiously from below. The scale of the disaster was rung up to the bridge and orders were rung back. Rrrrr! Brrrr!! Clang!

They stopped. Just a matter of time now. Hours, if they were lucky. Less, if they were not. You gotta feel anxious for them.

Amazing, really. In that situation, I'd have been running round like a wet hen, clucking and screeching. On that sinking bucket, there was no panic. The crew all went calmly about their jobs, doing what the Captain told them. They say the crew on planes are just the same, when they think they're going to crash. Wonderful people. Not like yours truly.

Among the passengers, it took some time to sink in [ha-ha, no pun intended!] that there was any danger at all. On the top decks, people were up, milling around, joking about ice. Awaiting news, instructions.

Down below, Great-granddad was snoring. He could sleep anywhere. GG was dozing. It was very stuffy, and she couldn't sleep. Even so, she didn't know anything had happened. Then stewards came round, getting everyone up, telling them to put on their lifebelts. Great-granddad was hard to wake, but he wasn't the only one. Most people refused. They didn't know what was going on. Half of them couldn't speak English anyway.

Well, at five past midnight Thomas Andrews – he who built the ship, no less – turned up on the bridge, after a mosey round the ship. There's no hope, says he. "An hour, maybe." They couldn't conceal it any longer after that, could they? "Prepare the boats," says Captain Smith.

At that point, everyone got excited about the lights of the other ship someone'd seen. People trooped round to look. Right on! There they were! Stewards pointed them out, reassuring everyone. The other ship was close enough to signal with the Morse lamp.

"Tell him to come at once, we are sinking," says Captain Smith.

Flash, flash! Fourth Officer Boxhall sent the message. Some people thought they saw a reply, but old Boxhall didn't.

At 12.15 am, Sparks began calling for help on the wireless.

"CQD CQD CQD. Come at once. We have struck a berg."

At 12.25, the message was picked up by the *Carpathia*, 58 miles away. It stopped when it heard, and turned back at top speed towards *Titanic*. Good on 'em!

"We're coming hard," it signalled.

At about 12.45, Boxhall sent up the first rocket, a white one that exploded in a shower of stars. That's the international signal for a ship in distress. Up and up it went, 800 feet, and banged lustily. Very pretty, those distress signals. They sent up seven more over the next 35 minutes. Nothing like drawing attention to yourself, is there?

So they started herding everyone to the boats.

"Women and children first!" shouts Captain Smith through the megaphone. Always the gentleman.

Once the lifeboats were uncovered, some passengers were in them pretty quickly. Others were not so keen – it meant separation from their nearest and dearest, y' see.

The first boat hit the oggin at 12.45. By that time, old *Titanic* was listing pretty heavily. People didn't need encouraging.

On the port side, 2nd Officer Lightoller was in charge of the lifeboats. Now that was a real toughie.

"Two crewmen per boat, no men passengers, please," says Lightoller.

On starboard, Officer Murdoch was in charge – a bit of a softie, he was. Human nature being what it is, a lot of blokes got in. I expect you'd've seen me there with them.

"Sling 'em out!" comes the cry. That was the boats, not the men. Down went the boats. Some had only a few people on board. Stupid, when you think of it.

Was my great-granddad there, pushing with the best of them? Sort of. For a long time, they'd all been held back for fear of breaking the rules.

"We mustn't go up. It's Second Class up there."

I ask you! Great-granddad was ambitious, I must give him that. He wasn't going to die like a rat. He pushed GG – screaming and protesting about their bags – up the stairs to B Deck. You can't blame him. Unfortunately, he fetched up on Lightoller's side.

Big mistake. Even the nobs weren't rushing the boats that side. The crew wouldn't let them through. Women and children only. So Great-granddad pushed GG after some rich-looking dame and stood back in the shadows. That was the last she saw of him. That was about 1.50 am, she thought. She got into Boat 4.

She was lucky. By 2 am, there was only one boat left, with 47 seats. 1,600 people were still on board, just imagine!

Well, the rest you can read from the books about the *Titanic*. There are tons of them. As far as my fortune was concerned, that was it!

At 2.05, Captain Smith could see it was all up. He walked round the ship, telling his crew: "Men, you have done your duty. Now it's every man for himself." Most stayed with the ship, you gotta give them a big hand for that. They were hot on duty first.

By then, the bows were completely under water. The stern was rising out of the water. Everyone edged upwards. Some jumped overboard and swam towards the lifeboats. Others – they were either the fools or the geniuses – waited until the last minute.

Eventually, at around 2.20 am, up goes the stern, almost vertical, 150 feet in the air, lights still blazing. A pretty awesome sight, I'd say – if you were in the boats. A mighty wave washes over it, brushing off those still aboard. My great-granddad must have gone then. Sucked under with 1,501 others, as *Titanic* slid out of sight.

One feller kept his cool, though. The chief baker held his balance, standing on top of the stern. He stepped off just as it vanished into the water. Didn't even get his head wet.

It was pretty horrible out in the water, GG told me. People scrabbling to stay afloat, clinging to wreckage: chairs, doors, boxes, cushions, planks. Voices all around, people swimming and crying for help.

Unfortunately, those already on the boats – even the empty ones – were not too keen to help those who were not. One boat did go back to look for survivors.

"Shall we go back?" asks the crewman in GG's boat.

"It would be dangerous," says a plush-looking female. "The boat would be swamped." Always rely on the nobs for help, can't you? So they didn't stir. The boat was only half full.

Apparently, some strong swimmers did make it to safety. Two collapsible lifeboats had floated off the sinking ship. The swimmers nearby dragged themselves aboard. Once on, that was about all they could manage. They lay and froze at the bottom of the boats. The water was one degree below. Chilly!

Of course, in that sort of water nobody lasts long. Half an hour or so and all was quiet, GG said. The chief baker lasted longer, mind, being up to here with whisky! He clambered in their boat quite a lot later. Whisky's like a radiator, I'm told, I wouldn't know.

So what'd they do next, those eighteen little boats? Well, there was that ship on the horizon everyone had seen. Captain Smith had thought it was so close, he told Boat 8 to row over, dump its passengers and come back again. That was the obvious place to head now. So that's what they did: "Not far now!" they said to each other.

From time to time, Officer Boxhall in Boat 2 fired green flares, to catch the other ship's eye.

Seems no one out there was looking. The other boat didn't come, and so they gave up. You can't row round the Atlantic at night, looking for rescue boats.

They floated about aimlessly. Apparently everyone was quiet, trying hard not to freeze to death. You know, concentrating on staying alive. GG sat in a state of shock. She thought Great-granddad must be in one of the other boats, but didn't dare call out, in case he wasn't.

Then an unpleasant argument broke out between two of the women. GG was too embarrassed to say anything. No one argues in our family, ever.

I'm glad to report someone did see and do something about the green flares, however – the Cunard liner *Carpathia*. As it dodged through the ice at top speed, it saw the flares and fired rockets in answer. Pretty gallant stuff, that. They could easily have hit the bergs themselves. At 3.30, the passengers in the little boats noticed the rockets. Cheers began to go up.

At 4 am, just as dawn was breaking, *Carpathia* stopped her engines. Her captain thought he'd come to the wrong place. Fortunately, a green flare went up 300 yards ahead – Boat 2's last one, believe it or not. The *Carpathia* was absolutely on target. I'm definitely a pro-*Carpathia* man myself, otherwise I shouldn't be here!

GG's boat was one of the last to reach it, at around 8 am. An hour later, all 705 survivors were aboard.

So it was goodbye Great-granddad, the big American dream and all their belongings. GG had nothing, and I mean nothing. She got herself brought back to Southampton. Apparently my gran was on the way by then, though GG didn't know it. She blamed Fate for that, too.

She used to think about it a lot – whose fault it was. I mean. That got me interested too, young as I was. I blamed people for her. God, for example. Well, I know there's got to be disasters, history wouldn't be interesting otherwise – but why pick on us?

Then I thought, I'll read about it, make a Scientific Decision, based on the Facts. Being by then a teenager and a clever prat to boot, I got round to blaming more people than travelled on the *Titanic*, almost. Captain Smith, for example. Damn fool shouldn't have driven recklessly through the ice, says I.

Then I thought, Poor bloke, his last trip before retiring. Everyone worshipped him, then he gets a gnat like me biting at him.

After that I got hot about Thomas Andrews. It was all his fault for relying on only four watertight compartments. Why not five? Then I thought, he went down too.

Later I got really serious, studied the whole business. Read mounds of documents about *Titanic*. I reckon my Great-granddad and the other 1,501 had one serious piece of bad luck: Captain Stanley Lord was the captain of the steamer *Californian* that night.

Kindly elucidate, I hear you say. If it's real blaming you're about, let's have chapter and verse.

Hold it! I say. We have a mystery here. We think we know what happened; the why is a bit of a problem. The charge, milud, is that Captain Lord – did nothing. Why, we can only surmise.

Ho! says the cynic. How can doing nothing be a crime?

Captain Lord was the captain of an ordinary freighter, the *Californian*. It set sail from Liverpool on 5 April, a few days before the *Titanic*. Theirs were the lights they could see a few miles away from the *Titanic*. The *Titanic* saw the Californian, the *Californian* saw the *Titanic*. Howdy! Howdy! you'd think. No way! The *Titanic* sent wireless messages for two hours. Fired eight distress signals. The *Californian* did nothing.

How do we know they saw each other, pray? Captain Lord denies that ship he saw was the *Titanic*.

Consider the facts:

Sunday afternoon: *Californian* sees three icebergs, reports the fact to other shipping, by wireless. The *Titanic* hears the message, steams on.

10.30 pm: *Californian's* Third Officer Groves is on watch on the bridge, reports white patches ahead. Ice! Lord immediately orders Full Speed Astern. Within three minutes the ship hoves to, surrounded by field ice. That's it for tonight, decides our Cap'n, and goes to his cabin.

11.10 pm: Groves sees a steamer pounding up from behind, 10-12 miles away. As it gets nearer, he sees its lights more and more clearly. It is brilliantly lit. He goes below to tell Lord.

"A passenger steamer," says Groves.

11.40 pm: Lookout Fleet on the *Titanic* notices iceberg. The *Titanic* veers sharply to port, but still hits it. *Titanic* slows down rapidly, but for ten minutes holds way. The bows start to dip. She stops.

Soon after, people on the *Titanic* notice the lights of another steamer, 3 – 5 miles away. Fourth Officer Boxhall thinks she is near enough to see signals from the Morse lamp.

He signals, "Come at once, we're sinking."

On the *Californian,* Groves thinks the mystery ship has put her lights out suddenly. In fact, he can't see the lights because the *Titanic* has turned to port and stopped. She is almost end on to the *Californian.*

Lord arrives on the bridge soon after. Groves indicates the ship and says it's a passenger steamer. Lord says it's not.

"The only passenger steamer near us is the *Titanic*," says he, and goes below again.

12.10 am: Second Officer Stone comes up on the bridge, takes over from Groves. Groves tells him about the passenger steamer. Stone sees it, guesses it's about five miles away.

Groves goes down to talk to Evans, the wireless operator, Evans has just turned in for the night and is half asleep.

Up on the bridge with Stone, Apprentice Gibson comments on

the "glare of lights" on the mystery ship's stern.

12.15 am: On the *Titanic*, wireless operator Phillips has sent the first of many distress calls: "CQD, CQD, CQD. Struck berg. Come to our assistance at once." He sends the last call at 2.10.

Groves is trying to raise the mystery ship on Evans's wireless. He fails to notice that the clockwork has run down. (The wireless needs winding up.) He doesn't hear Phillips's call.

In later years, Groves blames himself for the death of 1,500 people.

12.45 am: On the *Titanic*, Boxhall sends up the first rocket – a white distress signal exploding in a shower of stars.

On the Californian, Stone, on the bridge, suddenly sees a white flash in the sky, from the direction of the mystery steamer. Clever boy, he realizes before long it's a white rocket.

12.50–1.25 am: *Titanic* fires seven more white rockets, at intervals of about five minutes. The last is around 1.25. The two stopped ships swing around, showing different lights to each other.

After seeing five rockets, Stone tells Lord via the speaking tube. Lord chooses to ignore them. He's more worried about the ice than about the other ship. He stays dozing on his settee.

Gibson returns to the bridge, sees the mystery ship still there, ablaze with lights. Three more white rockets go off, all exploding in stars. The last is around 1.25.

1.25 am: After the eighth rocket, Stone suddenly says,

"Look at her now. She looks very queer out of the water. Her lights look queer."

"She looks to have a big side out of the water," says Gibson. "She seems to be heavily listed."

On the *Titanic*, the crew and passengers are being told to stand on starboard, to correct the listing.

For half an hour, Gibson and Stone talk about what they have seen.

2.am: They can only see the stern light. By then, most of front part of the *Titanic* is under the sea.

Stone sends Gibson down to tell Lord, mentioning the eight rockets. Lord asks if the rockets were white. Gibson goes back upstairs.

2.20 am: The mystery boat vanishes, Stone makes one last report to Lord. Lord checks again – twice – that the rockets were white, then goes back to sleep. Neither he nor anyone else thinks of waking Evans. Evans could have raised the *Titanic* on the wireless. Phillips was putting out CQD calls until 2.10 am.

Well, you can see why, if there's blaming to be done, my Great-granddad might have a profound word with a certain Cap'n. Assuming they're now in the same place, of course. Thousands of people were in frightful danger, right in front of the Cap'n's eyes, a little way over the water. He did nothing.

I expect he was afraid of the ice, poor bloke.

He finally got up at 4.30 am, you'll be pleased to hear. By 5.40, it was fully light, and safe to go. Dawdling at a snail's pace because of the ice, *Californian* finally got there just before 8, six hours too late. All the survivors were on the *Carpathia*. Too bad, nothing left to rescue. My Great-granddad left just a few bits of wreckage, to mark the spot.

And here I am, seriously poor. I blame ...

Well, I think I'll buy a lottery ticket instead. My numbers? 1 for maiden voyage, 4 for the number of GG's lifeboat, 14 for 14 April, the day of the disaster, 18 for my Great-granddad's age and mine, 35 for the number of people in Boat 4.

A dead cert, I'd say.

CHAPTER 9
THE NEW BOAT

T he older man unzipped his anorak pocket and took out an
Ordnance Survey map.

"The map shows a sandbank. I think we ought to go out to
sea and round this spit here, Pete," he said uneasily, showing
the map to the lad who sat beside him.

"Yeah. I expect there'll be buoys marking the sandbank," said
Pete. He called to a third man, seated forward of them. "Dad!
Denis says there's a sandbank over there. Can you see any
buoys?"

The third man, Bob, shaded his eyes and looked out across the
estuary. The sea sparkled in the morning sunshine, beckoning.

"Seems a shame to take a long way round, son. Can't see any
sandbanks or buoys. Isn't there a channel across the sandbank, a
short cut? Save us several miles, if there were," he said, half-

rising and craning forward over Denis's map.

"I can see one buoy, anyway," said Pete, who had better eyesight. He nodded to port.

"Where?" said Bob. "Can't see it. Oh yeah." He sat back, took out his flask and poured himself some piping hot coffee.

"This could be a short cut, this channel here," said Denis, jabbing the map. "What d'you reckon, Bob?" Denis habitually deferred to his younger, more self-confident friend. "Shall we try it?"

Bob frowned at his coffee, as if there was something wrong with it.

"Yeah, why not? I reckon those buoys are for big boats, not for the likes of small fry like us. Why not?" he said. "Want some?" He waved the coffee at Denis and Pete.

"OK," said Denis.

"Yeah," said Pete.

They were not sure they were agreeing to the coffee or the short cut. Perhaps both.

The three men had bought and collected the 30-foot yacht only that morning, and were taking it back to their home town further up the coast. It was their first outing, a wonderful adventure. Bob and Denis had both been in other people's yachts before, and longed to have their own vessel.

"Seems OK, doesn't it, going this way?" said Denis. They had steered seaward of the buoy, and were making good speed along the channel in a stiff breeze.

"Yeah," said Bob. "You gotta know when to take short cuts."

Pete closed his eyes and enjoyed the smell of the sea.

There was a jolt, and the forward movement slowed suddenly, then petered out altogether.

"What we stopped for, Denis?" said Pete.

"Run into something," said Denis. "Sand, prob'ly."

"Got off the channel a bit, have you?" said Bob. Pete noticed that he said *you,* not *we.* "Don't worry, we can probably push her off."

He stood up to go aft. The boat tipped alarmingly, and settled further into the sand.

They tried poling off, to no avail. The boat was wedged fast. Bob said, "You got her stuck real deep, Den."

Denis said nothing. He resented the suggestion that it was all his fault.

"Can we get out and shove, Dad?" asked Pete anxiously. "I don't suppose it's very deep, if we're stuck."

Bob scratched his head. "Better not risk it, son. You never know, on sandbanks." He added optimistically, "If we wait a bit, a wave will float her off, I expect."

"Don't see how it can, Bob," said Denis. "The waves are pushing her towards the shore."

"Go on, you're just a pessimist, Den," said Bob. "Always were."

The big wave came and lifted the boat up.

"Whoops! Here we go!" said Bob cheerfully.

The boat lurched shoreward on the crest of the wave, then swooped downwards in its wake. There was a sharp crack as the hull hit the sandbank sidewards on, with enormous force.

"Jeez!" said Denis, staring at the floor.

The hull had split, and water was pouring in. He looked up and caught Bob's blank gaze. It seemed like an age before the older man's face registered any expression. Then he looked flustered, uncertain.

"You've sunk us, Den!" Bob said. "We gotta walk, or somep'n?"

Slowly Denis turned round and stared at the shore.

" 'Bout five, six hundred yards, I'd say," said Bob. He peered overboard. "Doesn't look too deep. Ugh! You got my new jeans wet!" Water sloshed about their feet.

"But – what about the boat?" said Denis. "We've only just bought it!" He seemed unable to take in what had happened.

"Yeah, well, it's insured, isn't it?" said Bill. "C'mon, Pete."

He stepped gingerly over the tilting gunwale.

"Gah! S'only a coupla feet deep! It's a doddle."

"Who's gonna take the lifebelt?" said Pete, rummaging in the locker. "There seems to be only one."

"Better give it to me, son," said Bob. "I'll go ahead, then if there's any trouble, I can stop you two getting out your depth."

Pete wondered if this was as self-sacrificing as it sounded.

"Better tie these round us, just in case, though, Dad," he said, picking up a plastic drum. There were three – one each.

Denis was last to leave the boat. As in a bad dream, he tied the drum to his waist, then stumbled overboard after the others.

"T'in't at all cold, is it?" called Bob, well ahead.

"How d'we know which way to go?" said Pete. "Can't see where the sandbank goes."

"Oh, just follow the tide, that's my advice."

To Denis, the sea water had come as a shock. The dunes along the shore suddenly seemed a long way away. He felt tired.

Indeed, the water didn't feel cold at first. Bob and Pete cracked jokes, and one joke even raised a smile from Denis.

Then the fog came down, and they lost sight of the dunes.

"Let's jus' keep following the tide," said Bob confidently. Denis could barely make out his bulky shape ahead.

They waded on, and gradually fell silent.

The noise of the water swirling about their legs seemed to get louder and louder. Denis's legs were numb with cold.

Bob kept changing direction and cursed frequently as he tried to work out which way the tide was going.

"You sure this is right, Dad?" asked Pete plaintively. "We were going in the other direction just now."

Behind them, Denis winced. A terrific weight constricted his chest.

"Don't keep asking questions, son," said Bob in irritation. "Just follow me."

His right foot sank in unexpectedly deep water, and he hastily stepped back.

"Sorry, lads! A bit off the mark, there," he shouted over his shoulder. "You alright, you two?"

"Yeah," said Pete. He was up to his waist, and shivering.

There was no answer from Denis.

"Denis?" said Bob sharply. He stopped and looked round. "God almighty!"

"What's the matter, Dad?" said Pete, and swivelled round.

Denis's body was floating just below the surface and drifting away into the mist.

"Quick, Pete, get him up!"

The two of them splashed backwards heavily and tried to raise the inert Denis upright. The body just sagged between them, and Pete let go, unable to sustain the weight.

"Can't hold him, Dad. What's the matter with him?" He sounded frightened.

"He's dead, that's what!" said Bob with a shrug. Don't let on you're upset, he told himself. Mustn't worry the boy.

Why's Dad angry? wondered Pete in a sudden daze of shock and cold. He couldn't grasp what had happened.

"Heart attack, probably," added Bob casually. "Always a bit soft that way, he was." He let go of the sodden clothing. The body splashed heavily into the sea. "C'mon, Pete, we gotta get ashore."

The corpse drifted under as they floundered blindly into the white dampness.

"Pete, I think we're nearly there. I think I kin hear breakers," said Bob. He was soaking from head to foot – they had both fallen headlong twice. "Pete? You hear that? That's the shore, sure as eggs is eggs."

He glanced over his shoulder.

"Pete?"

There was no answer. Pete was not to be seen. Bob stopped, terrified by the damp silence.

"Pete?" he screamed. "Pete! Stop fooling around, son, we're

nearly there. Pete!"

Even to himself, the screaming voice sounded detached, muffled.

"Oh Christ," he muttered. "Which way's he gone?" He stared wildly around him.

The mist rolled white and unrelieved in every direction.

"Got into trouble while swimming, did they?" said Harry, his glasses fixed on the wrecked yacht. Most of it was still visible above the sand, raked at a crazy angle.

The lifeboat headed back towards the harbour. At the back of the vessel, huddled in a blanket, sat Bob, pale as death. He had insisted on accompanying the search. He muttered incomprehensibly to himself. They hadn't been able to get much sense out of him.

"Much too cold for swimming," said coxswain Steve Martins, taking a wide course round of a buoy. "Seems they went aground on a sandbank and just abandoned the boat. Thought they could walk ashore."

"Who are they?" asked Harry.

"No idea. His son's name's Pete, that's all we know. Amateurs, for sure," said Steve contemptuously. "No radio, lifebelts, compass, charts – nothing! Just an Ordnance Survey map, so he said!"

"Funny guy," said Harry. "I talked to him just now. Says he's certain his son got ashore and will turn up. He says he's probably drying out at some cottage."

"No way. He'd've been reported by now," said Steve.

"We didn't find the other one, either, did we?" said Harry gloomily. "Not much to show for hours of looking."

"The sea will return its own in good time," said Steve with the cynicism of experience.

They passed between sand dunes into the river. Harry looked back. The sea glinted under an ice-blue sky.

LONDON

"Mountain honey," she thought, "and vine leaves... and ..."

The waiter came up, pad in hand. He looked enquiringly at them.

"Kebabs," said Kate aloud. She was still in her daydream. In fact, she was a dreamy sort of girl altogether.

What she dreamed of most was Greece and all things Greek. Her knowledge of Greece came not from geography – indeed, she had never been to Greece. It came from books of legends, guidebooks, mythical tales, and most of all, Homer. Odysseus stepped in and out of her dreams like a bus conductor collecting fares.

"You know what's wrong with you?" Kate's last boyfriend had yelled during their last quarrel. "You're seriously unreal. I can't see you. You're in another room with some other guy all the time!" At which he had banged the all-too-real door and quit her life. That was three weeks ago.

"I'm sorry," began the waiter, "we don't –"

Petros Stavropoulos interrupted him briskly.

"Miss Whale –," he said.

"Wall," said Kate. "Catherine Wall. Call me Kate."

"Of course. Er, Kate," said Petros in his brisk New York manner, "Giuseppe's doesn't do kebabs. It's an Italian restaurant."

"Did I say kebabs? I was only thinking about Greece," said Kate. "I've never had real Greek food."

How American he looks, thought Kate. I wonder if the whole family are like him.

"My father is looking for someone to give my sister some coaching in French and Latin while we're on board ship," said Petros. "I don't know if Judith mentioned that."

Judith had been at school with Kate, and had kept in touch. Judith was now the girlfriend of John, the young business partner of Petros's father. All very complicated, but that was how Kate came to be sitting in a London restaurant with a very handsome young American Greek.

"Yes, of course," said Kate aloud. "I thought that was the whole point of my coming on the cruise."

"Well, yes," said Petros. "So my father thought we could meet and I could, well ..."

He hesitated, embarrassed.

"... check me out," said Kate, not in the least embarrassed. "Go ahead."

"Not check you out," said Petros, reddening a little. "Just find out a bit more about the Latin and French. It's pretty important Sissy should have the best. She's one very bright kid, is our Sissy. Full of high spirits. I'm sure you'll get on with her like a house on fire."

"I'm sure I shall," said Kate politely. "About the French and Latin. I did both to A-Level. I got very good marks in both. I had a very good Latin teacher who was French. Didn't Judith say?"

"I expect she did."

Under Petros's inquisitive but casual gaze, Kate squirmed. She felt like one of the lobsters in the tank behind Petros – alive, and waiting to be served.

MANCHESTER

"Two months in the Aegean! Sailing round the Greek islands on a millionaire's yacht. I don't believe it," said Jill, the girl next door at college. "You lucky cow! Envy envy! How on earth did you get the job?"

"Contacts," said Kate.

They were in the children's department of the bookshop. Kate took her brief seriously: ten-year-old Sissy was clearly going to be a demanding pupil, probably attended the best school in New York. She'd need entertaining as well as teaching.

"Have you got any French *Asterixes*?" she asked the assistant in the language-teaching department.

"They're upstairs with the gardening books in the adult section," said the assistant.

"Obviously," said Kate.

"Just a matter of size, I'm afraid," sighed the assistant. "That's the only shelf big enough."

Kate emerged from the bookshop clutching a whole pile of *Asterixes*, mostly in French but two in Latin as well. If she was as clever as her big brother said, Sissy might well have a voracious appetite for *Asterix*.

To offset the frivolity, Kate had also bought some grammars and study aids. Père Stavropoulos would expect results from her.

ATHENS

She met the family at a grand hotel, where they always lived when they were in Athens. Micky Stavropoulos was the millionaire concerned, a self-made man whose wealth came from running oil tankers. He was small and looked more Greek than American. Hungry for her Greek experience to begin, Kate was reassured.

"Hello, hello!" he said affably, with a thick Greek accent. "You are Kate. I am Micky."

He waved her to a seat, sat down, took out a fat cigar and lit it.

"You have good trip from Heathrow?" he enquired, blowing a tremendous gob of smoke in the air.

"Yes, thank you."

"You find your room?"

"Yes."

"Nice room, heh?"

He had not seen it, but it was a nice hotel.

"Yes, it's lovely."

The room looked out on to a back yard and a street full of beggars, but Kate had beautiful manners.

"Excuse me, I have to make telephone call," said Micky, rising to his feet. Clearly, he was a man who had many a stone to unturn. "We meet later, for dinner, yes?"

He hurried off, waving his cigar at someone who had just entered the lobby.

The next day's arrivals were less encouraging. Sissy arrived with two aunts. She was clad in blue jeans.

Her father introduced Kate. Sissy nodded a casual "Hi!", then addressed the older aunt – evidently her senior minder.

"Aunt Julia, I told Jake and Christos I'd be coming this afternoon. I'm going to my room to call them, OK?"

They did not see Sissy again until dinner.

The aunts were another matter. They were expensively dressed, heavily tanned, and could have stepped off the pages of *Vogue*. They looked critically at Kate, who was wearing a light summer frock.

Kate felt uncomfortable under their gaze. Her mother always insisted it is bad manners to stare at people. She resisted the temptation to stare back.

"She'd look OK if her hair were cut by Nico, don't you think, Tina?" remarked Aunt Julia to Aunt Tina, after staring at Kate. "Nico is our hairdresser in New York," she explained. "Such a marvellous cutter! He does Mrs Johnson when she's there."

Mrs Johnson was someone important, Kate supposed. She was not into politics, and did not keep track of First Ladies.

Tina consulted her gold watch. It was impressively small and expensive-looking. "Where's Petros?" she complained.

Kate was ignored for a day or so. The freedom was little use to her. Although dying to explore Athens, she had been rather nervous about straying far from the hotel – partly because she did not have much money, partly because the Stavropoulos party threatened to move off any moment.

Micky kept coming and going, and was constantly called to the telephone. The aunts popped in and out of the hotel lobby, carrying shopping parcels. Whenever they caught Sissy in the lobby, they tried to detain her, promising that her father would be ready to go any moment.

Sissy knew better. She found no trouble in outwitting her aunts. Quite often, a pair of teenagers carried her off. One of them was older and was supposed to be in charge. Kate found him a weedy sort.

"Can't see him flashing a protective sword," she thought. "What if a pair of sinister Trojans in dark glasses turns up, bent on kidnapping Sissy, the rich Greek princess?" Didn't seem likely in this comfortable hotel.

Occasionally Petros put in an appearance, and tried not to look part of the group. The beady eyes of his aunts never failed to notice him. A reluctant Petros was despatched on trivial errands, like a menial.

"A Persian slave," thought Kate. "He must be seething."

Finally, after about two days, a man in a sort of naval uniform appeared. Micky held an animated conversation with him. The uniform nodded, then went over to the phone. Micky bustled over to the aunts, who had been arguing with Sissy about a hat.

Kate was seated at a table in the cafe, writing postcards. She registered Micky's presence out of the corner of her eye, but was more interested in the scene outside.

Absorbed in this modern Greek drama, Kate did not notice that the Stavropouloses had gradually been drifting out of the hotel. It was the face of Sissy peering through the window from outside that brought her scrambling to her feet.

"Come on!" Sissy was mouthing.

The waiting was over.

A pair of chauffeur-driven Mercedes took them down to the port of Piraeus. It was almost a regal progress, despite the usual frantic Athens traffic jam.

It was certainly a relief to get out of the stifling heat of Athens. As they moved serenely down to the docks, a suspicion of a breeze could be felt.

ABOARD

The yacht was a splendid sight.

"There my li'l boat," said Micky, with some pride, pointing to a yacht moored some way off.

Little was not the word. For a private yacht, it was grand – a hundred feet long at least.

Kate was most struck by the colour of the hull – not your ordinary vulgar white such as lesser millionaires have. It was a wonderful deep blue.

"English boat," said Micky. "Name is *Dragon*. Like aarrrh!, you know," he added, clenching his hands to claws and roaring with commendable ferocity. "I 'ave bought it from friend in Lon'on. Ver' famous seagoer. John something. Ver' good friend."

He waved his cigar expansively. Being a good friend clearly did not mean remembering names.

A launch waited to take them out to the *Dragon*.

Kate stepped aboard. She looked around, and breathed a great romantic breath. The great adventure was beginning – her first encounter with the *thalassa,* the wine-dark sea roamed by Odysseus. She was sailing into the real Greece.

She peered over the side. The sea did not look too wine-dark – more bog-dark, in fact. Never mind, it could only get better.

The pilot of the launch had seen better days, but his vessel was spick and span, and evidently once intended for greatness. It revved away from the quay with a display of bravado and much smoke, in a sweeping arc. The pilot stared resolutely ahead.

Micky beamed, the aunts turned green and held tight, Sissy argued with the pilot. "Palinurus the Pilot," thought Kate, remembering her Virgil. "I hope he doesn't fall in the sea just yet."

She turned to watch the docks recede. The dingy dockside, warehouse and grubby ships did not quite tally with Pious Aeneas. More like Liverpool Docks.

"Perhaps Piraeus is the gateway to the real Greece," she mused. "Here we leave the ordinary world behind."

She turned to face the real Greece, in the shape of the *Dragon*. It was truly such a wonderful blue! Palinurus had taken a wide, theatrical curve to the far side of the yacht. Vvvrrm! He revved the engine to stop her shooting past. They drifted back past the huge eye painted on the prow and stopped alongside.

"The dragon's eye," thought Kate.

Micky emerged from the cloud of engine smoke, and was welcomed aboard ceremoniously. A solitary sailor played a Greek bagpipe.

"English tradition," Micky said jovially to Kate as he mounted the steps. "English Royal Navy play pipes when admiral come on ship."

As she clambered aboard somewhat unsteadily, Kate was taken aback. Instead of the functional metal and plastic superstructure she had expected, the only metal to be seen was gleaming brass. The fittings were finished in panelled oak, and polished to a high sheen.

The interior was equally magnificent, even opulent. As she took off her shoes and padded around the thick carpet of her cabin, Kate dug her toes deep into the green pile. The bowers of the blessed Hesperides could hardly have been more pleasant.

THE WINE-DARK SEA

They rode out of Piraeus in stately fashion, the *Dragon* cutting the water with a cool hiss. The bare hills behind Athens changed from brown to grey, then the Parthenon slowly faded from view. Bog-dark changed to blue-dark.

As night fell, the lights of an island passed to starboard.

"Where's that?" asked Kate, hoping to raise conversation from Sissy, who had a bottle of Coke and an English *Asterix* for entertainment.

"Where's what?" she asked, without looking up.

"The lights over there. Is that an island?"

Sissy managed to tear herself away from her book for a moment or two.

"Oh, that. That's Salamis," said Sissy.

Salamis! A magic name. The place where, in 480 BC, the small fleet of the Athenian Themistokles drove the huge lumbering fleet of King Xerxes's ships on the rocks and saved Greece from Persian slavery. Kate's hands gripped the arms of her chair: she imagined Xerxes seated on his throne of gold overlooking the cliffs. As certain as he had been of his victory, as spectacular was his defeat.

These were enchanted waters.

"Why aren't we stopping in Salamis?" she asked Sissy.

"I don't know," said Sissy. "We used to go there a lot, but Micky never talks about our friends there any more. I reckon he quarrelled with them. Pity. Johnny boy was a good friend of mine."

"Was he their son?" asked Kate.

"No, stupid, their dog."

Kate felt duly humbled.

Next morning, Kate woke and wondered where she was. The slight movement of the boat reminded her. She was in Elysium.

She leapt out of the bed and padded to the porthole. Land was visible three or four miles off. She put on jeans and a shirt, and rushed up on deck.

It was an island. At last, a Greek island almost within hailing distance. She took a deep breath. The air was like wine.

Sissy was sitting in the shade, smearing sun-oil on her exposed areas, which still bore an unhealthy New York pallor. She was determined to recapture their normal fried colour. Beside her stood a chair cluttered with a towel and an empty Coke can.

"Where's that?" asked Kate, nodding islandwards.

"Aegina. You coming swimming, Kate?" It was not a question, it was a demand.

"OK," said Kate, "I'll get changed."

By the time she came back, the bottle of Coke was alone. Splashing was audible above the faint humming of the ship's generator, somewhere out of sight. Kate made her way aft, past the crew's quarters. One of the crew leant against the rails, casually watching the water.

"Hi!"

The call came from the water, but Kate could only see a smart blue dinghy. She was baffled.

The crewman nodded at the dinghy. A turbulence made itself

evident behind it, and suddenly a body heaved itself out of the water and into the dinghy.

"I'll come and get you," shouted Sissy.

With commendable skill, she eased the dinghy back alongside. No doubt the crewman had been detailed to keep watch, in case she got into difficulty.

Very conscious of her pink condition, Kate descended warily and was rowed a few yards away from the ship.

They swam.

The sea was like a millpond. It was heaven to be in it.

Back on deck, Kate thought she ought to tackle the question of lessons with Sissy. It proved more difficult than she expected, but then Kate had no younger sisters.

She plunged straight in.

"Sissy, when are we going to have lessons?"

"Lessons? Oh, you mean French and that stuff. Dunno. You'd better ask Micky. His idea, not mine."

She turned up her cassette player full volume and listened to the Rolling Stones.

Micky was not to be found, so Kate decided she would tackle the aunts at lunch.

Nothing more happened that morning. A sea breeze made it very pleasant to sit out on deck with a glass of iced lemonade and various small nibbles. The nibbles might have been Danish, or American, or perhaps Athens supermarket.

Nonetheless... a little tongue of discontent wagged in Kate's ear.

It was wonderful, but was it Elysium? Was it Greece at all? Where were the stuffed vine-leaves and taramasalata? The black-shawled women and plangent musicians? The winged triremes? Was she just sitting in a holiday brochure, in fact?

She looked longingly over the water at Aegina. It was all over there, somewhere beyond the reach of Sissy's loudspeakers.

Lunch was served in the dining saloon.

Sissy gobbled down a hamburger and left, even before the rest of them had finished the first course. Micky ate in haste, then hurried off to endless telephone calls. Petros was nowhere to be seen. Perhaps he wasn't even aboard.

Kate was left with the waiter, in his starched white coat, and the aunts. Aunt Tina put on her sunglasses and stared at her.

"You ought to pluck your eyebrows," she said languidly, addressing Kate. She leaned forward to select a piece of Turkish delight. "They're bushy."

She popped the sweet in her mouth, and turned to Aunt Julia.

"Don't you agree, Julia?" she said. "She oughta pluck her eyebrows. Mary-Lou would do it just dandy."

She took off her glasses and stared again.

Kate squirmed. The prominent eyeballs made her feel uncomfortable. A vision of Aunt Julia inspecting the lobsters in the restaurant flashed through her mind. "Do you think I should give Sissy a lesson now?" she asked hastily. She thought she had better start earning her keep. "Do you think she'd like to do French first?"

Aunt Julia lifted her head from her cushion. She had moved to a reclining chair and was flicking through a fashion magazine.

"What was that?" she asked in a bored drawl. "Sissy? Aw, no. I think she's busy right now. Tomorrow morning, perhaps."

She turned round to peer into Kate's face. She was rather short-sighted.

"Mary-Lou? I do think you're right, Tina. Mary-Lou likes a challenge."

She went back to her magazine.

"I don't think these new Dior things would suit me, Tina," she said plaintively, "Remind me to ask Michel, next time we're in Paris."

An idea struck her. She twisted round, making her huge earrings swing violently. She made a warthog face and peered at Kate.

"They'd suit you, y'know. I tell you what – go see Michel. Say I sent you."

Pleased with the thought, she returned to her magazine.

Late afternoon, they did the landward spurt and rounded Cape Plakakia. A bit of temple ruin on bare hillside sent a thrill through Kate. Real Greece was in sight! She would roam the island in search of ancient columns and gods. The town of Aegina came into view, dominated by the church of St Nicholas.

Micky had been in no hurry to get to Aegina in the heat of the day, but now he was all rush. Friends were in port, and he buzzed around the radio in a frenzy of organization.

The setting sun cast a glow of fire over the island.

"Was this the fire caused by Hera's dragon?" wondered Kate, lost in the vision. Hera's dragon ravaged Aegina, so Zeus repopulated it with ants, which he then converted into people.

Kate's gaze keenly scanned the shore, seeking signs of life, human or insect. Seeing the baleful eye of *Dragon* in the bay, had the Aegineans taken alarm?

Dusk fell. All was calm.

They sailed into harbour and dropped anchor. Before the night was upon them, the first of numerous guests arrived.

Fortunately they were men, not ants. Zeus had done his stuff; indeed, very handsomely. Gold bracelets gleamed in the half light, diamond tiepins flashed.

The lights of Aegina were maddeningly close, and yet so far.

Kate leaned over the rail and yearned.

Behind her, a babble of Greek and American English conversation drifted over from the deck. Sissy was nowhere to be seen.

They went into dinner. The typewritten menu was undoubtedly in French, but the starched white tablecloths were more memorable than the food.

That was yesterday. Another day, another port.

The tiny harbour at Hydra seemed incredibly crowded with white-painted yachts as well as a number of traditional fishing vessels. How could they possibly fit another boat in? wondered Kate as they edged forwards.

The captain – the real captain, not Micky – was the man she had seen at the hotel in Athens. He was evidently a seaman of skill, since he had manoeuvred in the limited space with graceful ease.

Micky missed the lesson in navigation. He was busy calling up all his shore friends.

Another port, another vision. But where was the hydra, the monster with 100 heads? Perhaps even now, Hercules was struggling with it out of sight, beside some island lake. The fiery tinge still visible on the horizon came from Hercules's brand as he lopped off its numerous heads and staunched each new head that grew.

ASHORE IN HYDRA

"We go ashore, heh, Miz Whale?"

Hercules strode down the deck glowing with anticipation and turned into Micky. He had rounded up a large number of friends and acquaintances.

"We eat tonight real Greek meal. You like that, heh? Come."

He motioned to her to go with him. Kate followed him forward, where they could see the whole of the harbour.

"Hotel there, ver' good, food, ver' good, smashing, real Greek food, you like ver' much. Tiptop."

He made a ring with his thumb and forefinger, to emphasize the quality.

"You put on prettiest dress now, OK? Look smashing. Everyone ver' smart this evening."

It was a command.

Kate leaned over the rail, watching the sea somewhat glumly. She tried to forget the disaster of the previous evening.

She'd eaten a steak that had evidently come out of the freezer, and it had disagreed with her. She'd drunk one glass too many of wine, which made her sleepy.

The only Greek food had been a very sticky baclava, which her neighbour knocked into her lap with his elbow while gesticulating over the table. It stuck to her dress.

"Sorry," he'd said, and dropped it on the floor while trying to remove it. He shrugged and turned back to his conversation.

Micky and his friends had had a terrific time, and the conversation flowed over her head, behind her back and in front of her nose. None of it had concerned her. Most of it was about people they knew in New York. The women talked about clothes, the men talked about oil prices.

She had made her excuses and gone out for air. She thought she could just have a quick look around the town. By herself.

Outside, it was wonderfully noisy and full of exotic smells. The night was young, a hum of voices close at hand filled the corners and alleys.

She picked up a toy for a young boy coming out of a house.

"Evkaristo," he said.

She turned round the corner and bumped into Petros. She didn't even know he was in Aegina.

"Oh, Miss Whale!" he cheerfully, "We were just looking for you. Everyone's coming back with us to the *Dragon*."

He marched her to the quayside.

ABOARD AGAIN: A CHANGE IN THE WEATHER

Late afternoon. She shivered, the sun seemed less warm. Behind her she could hear raised voices. It was Micky, apparently arguing with the crew.

Beside her sat Sissy. Even she was disturbed.

"Is something wrong?" asked Kate.

"Dunno," said Sissy uncomfortably. "Maybe."

One of the aunts turned her head and looked towards the wheelhouse.

The arguing stopped. Micky seemed to have won the day.

The aunt lay back in her chair, reassured. Kate went back to her book.

The sky had lost its serene blue. Kate felt chilled. The argument in the wheelhouse suddenly broke out with renewed vigour. Nico the captain and Micky were now shouting at each other.

"What are they saying?" asked Kate anxiously.

"Oh... the captain says... I don't know," said Sissy crossly.

Certainly she knew, but was not saying.

Kate looked up at the wheelhouse. It sounded as if the knives might be out at any moment. She was beginning to feel very uneasy. She hated quarrels, and she feared things she did not understand. She lost her temper.

"Sissy, what are they quarrelling about, for heaven's sake?"

For the first time, Sissy stopped looking like a Hollywood brat and looked like a vulnerable young girl.

"Oh... the captain says there's a bad squall coming, and we should make for Spetsae. Somewhere safe, he says."

"What's Spetsae?"

"It's that island over there."

Kate followed Sissy's nod. There was a small smudge on the horizon. It might have been an island, or a dark cloud.

"What did your father say?"

"Oh, he said it's nonsense, the weather's completely clear, and anyway the boat can take anything."

The arguing stopped. Micky seemed to have won the day.

The aunt lay back on her cushion.

"Dad likes to win arguments," said Sissy.

Suddenly there was a terrific bang, as though someone in the wheelhouse had dropped something heavy. The captain emerged with a face like thunder and strode off towards the crew's quarters.

"What was that?" asked Kate.

"I guess Nico is not staying any longer, and is taking the other sailors with him," said Sissy, in a matter-of-fact voice.

Sure enough, five minutes later, the crew swung out one of the small motor launches. They clambered nimbly aboard, started the motor with a savage roar, and without further ado hurtled away towards the smudge.

Micky was left to handle the boat by himself.

"Sissy, don't you think you need a pullover on?" asked Kate. "Shall I get you one?"

"Don't hassle me! Oh, all right then," said Sissy, ungraciously. "It's in my cabin somewhere."

"Hey, where's Nico and the crew?"

Kate turned with astonishment. Petros and his girlfriend had just swung themselves on board, dripping. It seems they had been diving. A dinghy rocked at the stern, moored to the taffrail.

Before she could answer, there was a bellow from the wheelhouse.

"Petros, c'm here! I need you help me."

Petros pulled a face at Kate, then obeyed. The girl with him vanished down the companionway, no doubt to change.

"Petros won't be much help in an emergency," thought Kate. "He's strictly ornamental."

Micky had been busy on deck and in the wheelhouse for more than an hour, lashing things down and putting things away. Occasionally he muttered darkly when something went wrong. The mutterings seemed to get more and more frequent. Petros appeared occasionally, flushed and harassed.

He came out now, and stood with Kate, looking up at the masts.

"We oughta set sail for Spetsae," he said. "A storm's brewing, but Micky can't do the sails by himself." He added sheepishly, "Trouble is, I don't know much about it."

Most sails had been stowed away. Micky would certainly have

problems handling them alone.

"What about the engine?" Kate asked.

"That's just an auxiliary, for getting in and out of harbour."

Petros was silent for a moment.

"I guess we'll ride it out. Dad will do his best with the engine."

Things were getting worse by the minute.

Micky came up behind them. Shading his face against the sky, he studied the masts intently, then shrugged.

"Dad! We gonna be all right?" came a small voice behind him.

Micky wheeled round.

"Sissy! What you doin' up here? Down below, please!"

Micky was not someone Sissy would disobey. She went below, almost dejectedly. Micky went aft without further comment.

The sky was darkening rapidly. A strange yellow light spread over the sea. The wind picked up, white crests appeared on the waves. Kate, who never suffered from seasickness, started to feel ill.

The wheelhouse door opened.

"Kate! Miz Whale! Down b'low! Now! Shut whole the doors! Petros! Cm'ere! Quick, boy! Big wave coming, huge wave!"

Micky held the door open until Petros reached it, then wrestled to shut it again. It banged shut as a sharp gust caught it. The aunts were nowhere to be seen.

Perhaps they've fallen overboard, thought Kate.

She staggered down the steps, clutching the rail. She could hear the engine turning over desperately, but it was wholly inadequate for these rough seas. Micky was just trying to gain momentum so he could hold the bows facing into the waves.

Kate just made it to her cabin when the boat shuddered violently and lurched sideways. She was thrown against the wall, but luckily did not hit anything sharp. Slowly, the boat righted itself and resumed its unsteady motion, but she could not move. Momentarily stunned, she lay hunched on the floor. Somewhere on the boat, water was slopping about. A lot of it.

In the cabin, the noise of the wind sounded much more frightening than on deck, even though it was more muted.

"Uuughhh!"

She retched and tried to be sick into the sink, but nothing came up.

She crawled back to her bunk and lay down. Could anything be as bad as this? Her mind started gabbling in overdrive.

"Ohgod-ohgod-ohgod! Want-to-die. PleaseGoddon'tletmedrown, frightened-of-drowning .... whoops! .... upwe-goooooo ... ohgodohgodohgodnot ... d-row-n ... notdrown.... Aaahhhhh!"

Down they went again. Her suitcase fell open, and a pile of rumpled clothes tumbled out. She thought she giggled.

Good thing they were not made by Dior. No way to treat high fashion. Hahaha. Whoops.

"Oh! Ow!"

She was almost tossed out of her bunk. She pulled herself back in again, painfully. Limb hurts, can't think which one. Brain not working.

The pitching movement became more and more pronounced. It was more awful than the worst big dippers at the funfair, but strangely enough the feeling of nausea had eased.

She slept.

Fitfully. The wind roared brutally on and on and the timbers screeched. It was dreadful. She forced herself to stay asleep. From time to time, the sound of shouts above penetrated her consciousness, but did not wake her.

SHIPWRECKED!

When she finally woke, it was morning.

"I'm dead!" she thought dreamily. "The boat's not moving. We've sunk to Poseidon's watery underworld. I'm an infernal nereid!"

She found herself stuck in the corner between the bunk and the wall, held fast by gravity. The porthole was almost directly above her.

It was some minutes before she took it all in.

"Why are we flying in a boat?" she wondered. "Nereids don't fly, they swim."

Then she realized the boat must be lying on its side. She reached out a hand.

"Ouch!"

She caught her fingers in the folding table. Poseidon did not have folding tables. Not a nereid after all!

"I must get up. Perhaps we're floating and about to sink!"

Panic set in. She managed to pull herself up and haul herself out of the door and along the corridor. Climbing the steps was trickier, but fear drove her on.

She emerged into broad daylight and a serene blue sky. She was the only one on the boat, which was lying on its side on a rocky shore.

They had been shipwrecked on an uninhabited island! She was cast away!

Not quite uninhabited, at this moment. Her gaze swept the shore. There in the distance she could make out a small figure, waving his arms and talking to a tall, official-looking person. The small figure was Micky. Her gaze moved on. Sissy was sitting on a rock nearby, doing her best to get in the way. The aunts were not in sight.

The enormity of what had happened began to sink in.

They'd just left her on the wrecked ship, like a piece of flotsam. She might have been swept back into the sea for all they cared! A spasm of rage seized her. How dared they?

Her rage sustained her across the first two or three rocks. After that, getting on shore safely without falling in the sea concerned her more.

The glorious ultimate vision.

The sea, a beach, a shipwrecked vessel.

The distant figures of Micky and Sissy seemed to freeze. She stared at them with detachment, as if they were specimens in a museum. They were fixed, immobile, like shapes on a black Attic vase. They were figures from some distant past.

She took the band out of her long hair and shook it free. An Attic zephyr lifted it slightly.

"Please?"

She looked up. A tall figure loomed against the sun. She shaded her eyes and tried to see his face. He resembled the official-looking man she'd seen talking to Micky years and years ago, two minutes ago. He was astonishingly handsome. He was holding out his hand to help her.

The fog of misunderstanding in her brain cleared. This was not an uninhabited island! She had been shipwrecked in Ithaca, and this was Odysseus, home from his wanderings. He had come to conduct her personally to Hellas, the Real Greece, and tell her tales of adventure and the wine-dark sea.

She smiled and placed her hand in his.

"Evkaristo," she said. It was modern Greek, but he would understand.

"Welcome," he said gravely.

She leapt over the last rock and was ashore.

CHAPTER 11

THE CONGREGATION

With his usual grave expression, Parson Trenowth went over to the lectern and began his sermon. The clifftop church of the remote Cornish fishing village was crowded, as usual.

"My text for today is 'Be not drunk with wine, wherein is excess'."

The congregation sat back comfortably, at ease with their consciences. They never drank wine, only the best French brandy. The local smuggler, Whorwell, hid it in kegs under the tower stairs of the church, as almost everyone knew – except apparently the parson.

He was a sweet old man, the parson, mild as milk; it seems incredible he should not know about the kegs. The fact is, he never said a word.

Soon after the parson began his sermon, there was a buzz in the porch. One by one, worshippers began to slide out of the pews and go out. At last, there were only three people left in the church, including the parson's wife.

The parson looked up from his lectern and said amiably to the clerk, "There is surely something amiss."

Of course there was. When the clerk and the parson went out, they found the congregation assembled on the cliff, looking out to sea. The two men joined them, the wind swirling about the parson's cassock. Hundreds of feet below, an excise cutter was engaged in a mad chase to catch Whorwell's boat, the *Black Prince*. The whole congregation watched with bated breath as the drama unfolded.

In the end, it was local knowledge that saved Whorwell. Just as the cutter closed in behind him to make the kill, he made a hair-raising turn towards a craggy stack called Gull Rock. The currents and rocks at Gull Rock are so dangerous that only the experienced – or foolhardy – go there. The excise captain knew this, and sheered away to save his ship. There was no further hope of his catching Whorwell red-handed on that rugged coast.

When the congregation saw that Whorwell was safe, off went the hats. Three rousing cheers were heard.

After the tumult had calmed down, the parson said, "And now, my friends, let us return and proceed with divine service."

The congregation duly filed back into church and sat back easily.

Parson Trenowth returned to the lectern and intoned benignly, as though nothing had happened: "The Book of Ecclesiastes, Chapter Seven. Go thy way, eat thy bread with joy, ..."

CHAPTER 12

THE NOBLE CORPSE

It was a tradition in those parts. Whenever the equinoctial winds started to blow, some of the older men would go to the cliffs. There, with a commanding view of the sea, they would watch and wait from sunrise to sunset. The eccentric vicar, the Rev. Robert Hawker, had built them a shelter to sit in, and was there himself not infrequently.

In the days before railways, nearly all freight went by water. Thus, thousands of vessels passed up and down the coast, carrying cargo of all kinds, day and night. In good weather, scores of sails could be seen from the cliff. In bad weather, some skippers still braved it.

The coast from Morwenstow to Hartland Point is dramatic – and horribly inhospitable to seamen.

Huge cliffs rise directly out of the sea, exposing raw geological strata like bleeding flesh. Massive chunks of hard rock have tumbled into the sea, often worn into strange shapes by wind, water and ice. Treacherous underwater ledges of rock reach out underwater, invisible to the layman's eye. They create terrible races and currents which sailing ships cannot cope with.

Even to be on solid land on the cliff top, and look down, brings the heart to the mouth. How much more terrible to be up there and see seamen far below, struggling to save their precious vessels from the rocks!

Yet the watchers persisted, partly from duty, partly from a morbid fascination with disaster. Ships were wrecked quite often – and someone had to deal with the bodies that floated ashore.

One autumn day old Peter Burrow sat in the hut. Wild gusts of icy wind blowing straight in his face apparently left him unmoved. He was gazing intently out to sea.

Fortunately, the gale was coming from the sea. Otherwise it seemed so fierce that hut and human must surely have been blown over the edge and dashed to pieces in the foaming seas, hundreds of feet below.

"Someone in trouble?"

Burrow heard the words but could not see the speaker.

The face of the vicar peered through the opening. The face turned to follow the line of Burrow's gaze, and made out a small brig about three miles offshore.

Hawker slipped into the shelter beside Burrow. He was dressed in a yellow blanket with a hole in the top for his head. Despite this, he was not in the least uncomfortable.

"What's she doing?" he shouted.

"She coom down at first light, Reverend. Coom round from Bideford way, she have."

Boats from the north all have to negotiate the notorious rocky Hartland Point between Bideford Bay and Lundy Island. The area is racked by a number of fierce currents.

As they watched, the brig changed tack, evidently trying to gain distance from the shore.

"That won't do 'er no good, neither," commented Peter gloomily.

Nor did it. In the driving seas, tacking had little effect. The ship was being blown visibly closer inshore.

"She've been beating to and fro since I been watching, more or less," shouted Peter. "Got caught by the Harty Race, I doan doubt." The Harty Race is a notorious current near Hartland Point. "All the tackin' in the world won't do her no good now."

A natural pessimist, Burrow expected things to go wrong, especially around the equinox, and they often did. His presence seemed to bring bad luck to passing ships. Hawker felt almost inclined to drag him away, just for the ship's sake.

"Oh, I hope not, Peter. Those poor men out there. They must be in fear of their lives."

Hawker was a professional optimist, but he had no illusions. In his time, he had conducted burial services for more than forty bodies cast up by the sea.

Despite his respect for a man of the cloth, Burrow relished the bone of doom, and would not stop gnawing it.

"Well, Reverend, tis said among us," and he burst into a doleful tone, raised his arm like a prophet and swept the coast from extreme south to north,

From Padstow Point to Lundy Light,
Tis a watery grave, by day or night.

Tis like the poor fellows out there will find it so."

Burrow had clearly written off the crew of the unknown vessel. In his eyes, they were dead men, even though they were still alive and fighting for their lives.

Accustomed to sudden death as much as his parishioners, the devout vicar felt a spasm of dissatisfaction. He longed for the day when the sea would provide a clue. A sign that, if men drowned, there was more to it than just fate snipping its scissors.

He sighed without hope.

"Nonsense, Peter. You will see. If they realize they can do no more, they will soon launch a boat and make for the shore."

Hawker's prophecy was almost too apt. As a gust of wind whipped his words away, activity could be seen on the little vessel wallowing in the distance.

"They'm trying to launch the boat," commented Peter.

Soon, figures could be descried climbing over the gunwales into the boat.

"One. Two, three. Four... Five or six. At least six on 'em, by my reckonin'," said Burrow. "Whoah, now!"

The last two fell apparently fell heavily as a huge wave suddenly swung the frail boat round.

"They woan never make it," added Burrow. "Wheer can they land safely along o' here?"

"They can do it with our help," said Hawker tartly. Such passivity infuriated him. "We've guided seamen in before now. If it comes to that, we shall need help, and lamps."

Silently, he raised a prayer for the jolly-boat floundering at the mercy of the waves.

They watched intently. Staring at such a small, uncertain point was a great strain in the grey afternoon light. Hawker found it hard to keep track of the jolly-boat. Sometimes it vanished from sight and seemed lost for ever. Then it would suddenly bob up again, carried high on a wave.

The boat covered about a mile towards the shore, then vanished from sight for good.

Silent, Hawker felt hope ebb away. "I must go," he said.

He had already left the shelter when a cry from Burrow brought him back.

"Folk's still aboard, Reverend!" called the old man, gesturing. Indeed, the brig was holding its course down towards Padstow, tacking with each change of the wind.

Unfortunately, it could no more escape the lee shore than before.

"They are in desperate straits, Peter," said Hawker briskly. "We must do something. If they are driven ashore or strike a reef, they will all be killed. We must be ready to signal where they may safely land, or prepare a boat to go out to rescue them. It will soon be getting dark."

With such words, Hawker bid Burrow remain where he was and keep track of the brig, and watch should the jolly-boat reappear. He himself hurried back to his vicarage.

He burst through his door with great vigour. He threw off the blanket and called for an extra fisherman's jersey. It would be cold riding along the cliffs.

"Trudy! Tell John to fetch my mule. And let Jacob know that help is wanted on the cliff. There's a vessel being driven on the rocks. Bring lights, tell him."

His mule was fetched. In haste, Hawker mounted, wheeled round and departed at a neat trot, back towards the cliff. Within five minutes, a motley collection of villagers appeared and followed him down the path.

Burrow was not to be seen at the shelter. The vicar waited impatiently for the leading villagers to come up.

"Peter Burrow has surely gone to investigate," he called. "Keep watch in case the boat reappears. In the meantime, I shall follow the brig." He turned his mule's head inland.

The brig was being blown steadily south, creeping ever nearer to the coast. A succession of bays and headlands made it difficult for Hawker on the coastal path to keep up.

Eventually the brig was so far inshore that he could not see it at all. A most unclerical word escaped his lips.

"Lost it!" he fumed inwardly.

He breasted a headland, and suddenly found himself high above a narrow inlet. In the gathering dusk, he stared down at the foaming sea, past the rocky bar. About a mile offshore, the brig was just visible.

It had gone aground in the sand, in the offing.

"If these winds continue, she will be broken up by the morning!" thought Hawker. "There must surely still be time!"

Action was needed. He turned fretfully toward the nearby village, where there were fishermen with boats.

A short lane took him fast into the twilight. His optimism waned with the failing light. He arrived in the village convinced there was nothing anyone could do. Could he even hope to persuade the fishermen, who knew what the sea was like?

They would have to try to launch their boats into heavy adverse seas, just as it was getting dark. No one could ask it of them.

And so it proved. He knocked at doors, and was met with gravely shaken heads.

A cluster of solemn villagers gathered around him, full of sympathy but unwilling to venture anything concrete. The village acted in unison in such life and death matters.

"Tis nigh-on impossible, Mr 'Awker," said their spokesman, a grizzled fisherman. "We should ne'er git beyond the bar, even if we could get un into the water." He nodded towards his boat, drawn up safely on the beach.

Disheartened, Hawker had to agree. He remounted, bade them good evening and took himself back towards Morwenstowe.

He reached home to dramatic news. Burrow had indeed seen something – an upturned boat drifting ashore on the waves, and assumed correctly it was the jolly boat from the stranded brig.

With help from other villagers, he had hauled the capsized boat on to the beach, clear of the tide. A name was written on its stern.

"She be from the *Alongzo*, Mr 'Awker, registered at Stockton-on-Tees."

With a heavy heart, the vicar sat down to the task that always fell to him on such occasions, of writing to the owners with news of the vessel. The letter was sent off with the evening's post.

The next day, the gales subsiding, a party of fishermen put off to investigate. The *Alonzo* had remained aground, even though the tide had risen. She leaned seaward at a crazy angle, though from sea-level it was impossible to see why. No holes were to be seen.

"Ahoy! Ahoy there!"

No answer from the ship.

"Seems sound enough," commented the senior fisherman, throwing a line over the rail.

A boarding party clambered aboard with difficulty and found no one. Two of them made their way along the sloping deck towards the wheelhouse.

It contained no living thing, dead or alive, though the log and other papers were there. Evidently the *Alonzo*'s last port of call had been Gloucester, and the boat had a crew of nine. It was carrying a cargo of iron for South Devon.

"Sailed hersel'" aground, like. Bain't no one here."

One of the fishermen peered into the hold.

"Hey, Taam, coom and look!"

Tom went and looked. The cargo of iron had shifted in the storm and was now lying halfway up the side of the hold. Its weight was what held the vessel pinned aground at such a rakish angle.

The owner's agent arrived that afternoon.

"I cannot understand why the captain deserted the ship," he said. "Fowler was a brave and trustworthy fellow. Dammit, I liked him. Excuse the language, Mr Hawker, but it shatters my belief in human beings. A captain's duty is to his ship."

The vicar nodded but made no answer. He had seen all types at sea. He wondered also what he would have done himself in the captain's position.

"It seems all nine abandoned ship," he observed. "When the *Alonzo* sailed on, she was a ghost ship."

"Or my belief in Henry Fowler is justified and he stayed on board," agreed the agent. "But then, why ain't he still on board?"

The sea provided a sort of answer. Bodies decompose in the sea, and after eight or nine days rise and are carried ashore by the current.

First to be washed up was the captain, a strong, tough-looking man. The agent identified him.

Grimacing with distaste at the rotting flesh, Hawker studied the lined face carefully.

"Am I right in thinking that is the face of an angry man?" he asked the agent, who had stayed on to deal with the wreck and the bodies.

"Certainly it looks so," exclaimed the agent. "Harry Fowler was a good-hearted lad, loved a joke." He looked intently at the face. "Something had enraged him, I guess."

"It could be, could it not, that the crew forced him to leave the ship?" suggested the vicar delicately.

"Could be," sighed the agent.

Some days later, four more bodies were washed up. Their faces wore expressions that the vicar described as 'reluctant agony'.

"I have seen it many times in the faces of drowned men," he

said quietly, noting the shudder of pity on the agent's face. "The sea is no kindly killer, even where it drowns rather than batters to death." He paced up and down the chapel where the bodies had been placed.

"It is very distressing. Many people drown on our coast. I wish that I might sometimes see on their faces that placid nobility which you see in those who die quietly in their beds. Then we might learn to accept these seemingly needless deaths as God's will."

Standing in earshot, old Peter Burrow was much struck by these words.

A day or two later, while Hawker was busy in the church, Peter Burrow burst into the porch with an expression of triumph on his face.

"Mr 'Awker sir, we do 'ave a noble corpse down on the beach."

If it had not been in the church, and such a grave piece of news, Hawker would have smiled at Burrow's turn of phrase.

He nonetheless hastened down to the beach. The storms were now over, and the waves lapped quietly at the stones.

Above the tide mark lay the body of a fine, strong fellow, over six foot tall, with an expression of peace on his face. His shirt had been torn to shreds by the sea, exposing a number of paintings on his skin.

"Unusual tattoos, are they not?" said Hawker to the agent, who had followed him down to the beach.

On the corpse's chest was a tattooed Crucifixion, flanked by figures of the Virgin Mary and St John. Below were the initials P.B.

"Peter Benson," said the agent, leafing through his list of crew names. "Let's see. Foreign fellow. No home address. Don't know where he's from, that means. We can't let his people know."

On the corpse's left arm was an anchor design.

"Probably represents hope, or safety, or some such idea," opined Hawker at his most vicar-like. "And this –" he pointed to the intertwined initials P.B. and E.M. on the other arm "– is a love affair, if I'm not mistaken, perhaps ancient. I wonder whether E.M. is still waiting for him. I do hope not."

The bodies were buried in the churchyard with all due reverence, and the jolly-boat placed alongside, keel upward, to show that its day was also done.

Hawker had to wait three years for an answer to his question about the initials.

One morning he received a letter forwarded by the Danish consul at a nearby port. It contained enquiries on behalf of a grief-stricken family in Denmark. Hawker replied offering what help he could, and received in reply a letter from a wealthy farmer, Karl Bengtsen, who was desperate to find his son Peder.

Peder had left home in a fury nearly five years earlier because his father had prevented him from marrying the girl of his choice. His father suspected he'd gone to sea, but was not sure. They had received no word from him for years.

Then one day someone reported seeing him on board a ship. The father made enquiries from shipping company to shipping company. Some companies knew the name or something like it. He never stayed long with one ship, he was too restless. Finally, the trail had gone dead with the *Alonzo*.

Hawker wrote of the ship and the discovery and subsequent burial of "Peter Benson". He received in return a dignified but grateful letter from the distressed father. With it was a brief note in Danish.

"She's asking to put five red roses on Peter's grave," noted Bengtsen in English in the margin of the note. It was signed "Elli Meyer".

The following morning, Hawker took five red roses, blessed them, and solemnly laid them on the grave of the "noble corpse."

"We do have our small victories over the sea," he wrote to the agent, "thank God!"

CHAPTER 13
THE END OF THE ADVENTURE

"**T**hey love it," said the Englishman. "The children love being at sea."

He was tall, dark-haired and looked fit. He probably had not worn a shirt for weeks.

In front of him, a golden-haired boy played among the ropes outside the marine shop on the quay. An olive-skinned boy of about the same age inside the shop watched him curiously.

"How old is he?" asked the man from the shop, with a strong Spanish accent.

"Four," said the Englishman proudly.

"Our Raimondo, he is also four," said the woman from the shop.

The Englishman went over to the boy, to stop him uncoiling the ropes.

"Hey, Charlie," he said to him, ruffling his hair affectionately, "you love the sea, don't you?"

"Muy bien," said the boy without looking up. "Sure do, Dad."

He put on an the exaggerated American accent. They'd spent a week with an American family in Bahia Blanca. The Americans were also touring the world in a yacht.

"Hey, he speak Spanish!" said the woman in the shop, beaming with pleasure. "Carlo, hablas espanol! You enjoy living on boat?"

"Si, señora," said the boy called Charlie.

"We called him Charlie because of Hurricane Charlie," said the father. "He was conceived during a storm off Jamaica."

"Por favor?" asked the woman. She did not understand.

The Englishman was embarrassed. It was not something to explain. He waved his hand vaguely with a smile. His Spanish was not up to it.

They had drifted down the coast of South America from little port to little port. Playing with other children here and there, Charlie had picked up a bit of Portuguese, and quite a lot of Spanish. His father had a smattering of Spanish, but it was never much. Just enough to get by. They came across so many different languages.

"Let's go, Charlie," said the father, picking up his purchases.

"Here, put your hat on. The sun's hotter than it looks," said the proud father. "Don't want you getting sunstroke, do we?"

When the boy took no notice, his father picked up the miniature stetson on the ground beside him and plonked it on Charlie's head. Charlie immediately tipped it backwards, off his forehead.

"Don't do that, Charlie," said his father, "there's a good boy. I don't want your ma screaming at me for not looking after you properly."

"Hazel's not here," said Charlie. "What she can't see, she won't scream about, Dad."

The wise words rang strange from young lips.

"What's wrong with the hat?" asked his father anxiously. "I got it specially for you. It's a cowboy hat."

"I know, Dad," said the boy patiently. "It makes my head itch."

"How can you tell? I only bought it five minutes ago," said the father indignantly. "You haven't worn it properly."

"It sits on my itch-line," said Charlie mysteriously.

A fat Argentine woman waddled over from the Cafe del Mar on the other side of the little harbour.

"Ola, Maria!" called the woman from the chandler's shop. "Es un hijo americano."

"English, not Americano," said the father. "Ingles."

He picked up his purchases again, and stretched out his free hand to his son. "C'mon, Hazel's expecting us. Adios!" he called the couple in the shop. "Say goodbye to Raimondo, Charlie."

"Adios!" said Charlie politely.

Hand in hand, man and boy strolled out into the sun, and down the jetty. Their 45-foot ketch *Adventure II* lay moored in the harbour, away from the channel where fishing boats entered and exited. Their dinghy was moored at the end of the jetty. Some little boys were taking turns to throw stones in it. They scampered off when they saw the Englishman and the blond boy approaching.

They got into the dinghy, placed the purchases in the middle, and cast off.

"Lovely!" Roger said with a sigh. "Smashing. One of your best, Haze. I'll do the dishes."

He leaned back against the bench seat in the saloon while Hazel cleared the table and put the dirty plates on the draining board.

"Coffee?" she said.

"Why not?" he said. "Let's be devils. I saw you going into that wonderful food store. Mmm! Terrific smell. What was it?"

"Not coffee. Stew, maybe," said Hazel. "Someone was cooking out at the back. I heard her singing to a child she had with her. Sounded vaguely familiar. Like a hymn."

"Welsh hymn, maybe," said Roger. "Lot of Welsh down this part of Argentina. Miners. I read about it in that guidebook I picked up in Bahia."

"Never knew that," said Hazel, pouring out two thimblefuls of coffee. They'd acquired foreign tastes in coffee. Roger had never been one for the jar of instant. He liked it black, small and strong. "You learn something every day."

She sat down opposite him.

The ketch had a large central saloon, with a galley attached. The children had a little double-bunk cabin in the bows, while Mum and Dad occupied the larger cabin aft.

That was their little world below deck. Above deck, of course, they had as much space again, when the weather allowed it or they were in port. They had to be careful with the children on deck. They were still very young.

"What was in that casserole, Haze? New taste to me," said Roger.

"Don't know what it's called – a vegetable I found down at the market. It did all right, didn't it? I baked it with some of that funny cheese you wanted to throw away. Never throw anything away, I say. You never know when you'll need it."

Hazel was an excellent cook. They took it in turns to cook and look after the children, but undoubtedly Hazel's meals were better. She knew how to make the most of the local foods. She had been down to the market while Roger was in the chandler's.

Roger was the dab hand at catching food from the sea. He'd taught Charlie a trick or two, but three-year-old Sandra was a bit small yet.

"Children OK?"

"Yup. They had some fruit and cheese. I put Sandra down for an hour. Charles is in our cabin. He's building a spaceship with the Lego your mother sent him."

"Does he understand the instructions?"

"I think so. It's all pictures. Anyway, bright boy, our Charles."

Roger put down the copy of the local newspaper he'd bought. He got out a large-scale map from a fitted drawer, and began to study it.

The ketch was beautifully fitted out. It had been their house and home for nearly seven years. They'd spent a fortune on it.

"I reckon we'll gradually head for the Falklands, then," said Roger after lunch. "What d'you think?"

Hazel pondered.

"Sounds good to me. We're following the coast a bit further south, though, aren't we? That was the plan. What's the weather for this week?"

"Forecast seems OK, as far as I can make out." He gestured at the newspaper. "I've been listening to the radio, too. Bit of a gale due here by Thursday, but we should be well out of the way by then."

He went back to his map, measuring distances.

"I think we should make Stanley by next month. We'll stop at Rawson and Puerto Deseado on the way to stock up. Spend a little time there."

"What about Tierra del Fuego?"

"Do that on the way back to Cape Horn. It'll be mid-summer by then."

Summer comes in December in the southern hemisphere. They planned to spend some time in the Falklands, then return to the mainland and sail north up the coast of Chile.

Port Stanley, the capital of the Falklands, lay 600 miles or so to the south-east. The ship could make 7-8 knots in fair weather.

But they were in no hurry. They wanted to see the south of Patagonia. Hazel took terrific photographs of animals and scenery. The snow-capped Andes made some marvellous shots, and from Puerto Deseado they thought they might take a trip inland, to get closer. Hazel was getting material for a book of photographs.

Also, Hazel had promised the children they'd see penguins. Roger thought there were some in southern Patagonia, but if not, there were certainly penguins in the Falklands.

In any case, they did not want to stray too far from the coast before setting out across the open sea to the Falklands.

"Goodnight, pet, God bless," said Hazel as she tucked Sandra up. "No, it's lights out for both of you, Charlie. Sandra can't get to sleep if you have your light on. It's been a long day."

"I'm not sleepy," protested Charlie. "The wind's too loud."

It was their third day out from Puerto Deseado. A stiff breeze was making itself heard outside. A murky evening light had faded into darkness.

The movement of the boat had taken on a peculiar roll as a distinct swell developed. Down in the cabin, the noise of the wind was muffled but irritating. The children were used to the pitching.

"You've slept through worse than this," said Hazel. "C'mon, Charlie, let's not argue. I've got things to do."

She leant across and gave them both a final hug. Dutifully, Charlie turned out his reading light, put away the picture book he had been looking at and turned over on his side. Hazel switched out the central light.

"Night-night!"

"G'night, Mum," came a dozy voice. Sandra was already asleep. Hazel shut the door behind her.

Roger came down into the saloon, in search of a chart. It lay on top of a cupboard, under a wedding photo. He glanced at the photo, then picked up the chart.

"Reliving happier days, Haze?" he asked teasingly.

"I'm perfectly happy now, thank you, Roger," said Hazel with dignity. She meant it.

The photo showed the two of them on their wedding day. What made it unusual was the location: the former rubber capital of the world, Manaus, in the heart of the Amazon region of Brazil. Roger had been delivering a boat there, Hazel had been working for an American oil company in Manaus. They met, and got married on impulse.

That was nearly seven years ago. They had never regretted it. They had a lot in common. Not least, both felt more at home on water than on land.

"Wind's picking up," said Hazel. "Hope it doesn't get worse."

"We'll sit it out," said Roger, without looking up. "I'll let out the storm anchor. Can you give me a hand with the sails, love?"

"Sure," said Hazel. "I meant, if it gets worse, it'll keep Charlie awake. He'll be very ratty tomorrow."

"Force 9 gale promised later," said Roger. "No rain, though."

"Think you'll be all right by yourself?"

"Yup, no sweat," said Roger. "You get some sleep. I'll wake you if I want help."

Hazel sat down instead of going aft to the cabin.

"Roger."

"Uhuh?"

"I've been thinking. Watching Charlie, really. Do you think he's missing anything?"

"Like what?" said Roger.

"Well, school. Other kids."

"Naah, don't worry about that," said Roger. "Plenty of time for that. What did anybody ever learn at school? Charlie knows more about life than any four-year-old at school, I can tell you. He's seeing the world. Don't you worry."

"I do worry, Roger," said Hazel. "He's got to be able to read and write, and do maths. I do my best to teach him things, but we just haven't got the books. Nor the other kids."

"Look, I'd better go on deck," said Roger rather crossly. He knew that Hazel was right, but it was no simple matter. School meant staying in one place. For the last six or seven years, they had not stayed in one place for more than a week or two. Roger got bored if he was not on the move. "We'll get him a computer or something. There's lots of good educational software. Don't worry. Meanwhile – let's have a good time, shall we? We're on our way to the Falklands. They'll see living history there."

Hazel went out, dissatisfied. She knew there was a problem ahead, but did not see how it could be solved.

The weather lived up to its promise. When dawn broke, there was a howling gale. It woke the children at daybreak, but did not disturb them too much. Their parents had expected it, and were prepared for it, although at the back of Roger's mind there was always a small worry corner marked "What if...?"

What if the storm got worse? What if the mast broke? What if the radio were broken?

He shook his head. No point in getting alarmed needlessly. They'd be all right. They'd always been all right.

The day began early at sea. The children were used to spending all the hours of darkness in bed and being up at first light. However, Hazel usually waited an hour or two before giving them breakfast. It was not as if they had to be anywhere. By seven or so, they generally had a good appetite.

In the galley, Hazel hummed as she prepared breakfast for the children. Sandra was a fussy eater. Hazel was careful to give them a lot of different foods, fresh wherever possible. Sandra was a problem. There were few things she would eat, and certainly not any strange new foods.

"Ugh!" was her usual opinion when Hazel brought something new on board from a local market. The things she really did like – cream cheese and bananas – were not readily available fresh.

"Singing Welsh hymns again?" came a voice from behind. She

felt the gust of draught as Roger opened the door from the cockpit and entered.

"What?" called Hazel without turning round. The gale made it difficult to hear what he said. She never noticed that she hummed. She must have been humming quite loudly for him to hear it.

"That Welsh hymn you heard in Puerto Madryn. You were humming it!" he shouted accusingly.

Hazel laughed. She put a plate in front of each of the children. They grimaced.

"I don't want a word from either of you," she said. "That's your breakfast."

They were quite unprepared for what happened next.

There was a terrific bang, and everything was thrown sideways. The plates of food slid off the table and crashed on the floor. The other crockery and cutlery was in the cupboards. At the violence of the shock, the doors flew wide and the contents were disgorged on the worktop and floor, where the china broke to smithereens with a frightening crash.

Then, suddenly, the door burst open. A huge torrent of seawater poured in.

At first, they were too shocked to say anything.

Slowly, the boat righted itself as the keel regained depth. At the first impact, Charlie and Sandra had been thrust under the table. The subsequent rush of water had flooded after them. It carried a melee of maps, charts, souvenirs, photos and kitchen equipment. The children were sitting in water, soaked through.

Hazel's mind took some seconds to register the scene. Later, she found the picture burned indelibly in her memory.

It was Sandra's crying that brought her to her senses, but Charlie spoke first.

"Lord save us!" he said.

Hazel had no time to wonder at the simple magnificence of her son's instinctive words. She rushed forward to pick them both up.

As she did so, she heard Roger calling from the deck.

"Hazel! Hazel! Come up here!"

Even over the shrieking of the wind, she could hear the tone of urgency.

"Coming!"

She searched impatiently for a dry towel or blanket to wipe the bench seats and table, so that the children could sit there out of the water.

"Now sit there, you two," she said, "and hold tight, in case it happens again." She went to the cupboard. Luckily, their life-jackets were still inside. "Now put this on, Charlie. Do it up. Now you, Sandra. Don't grizzle, petal, everything's going to be all right. You know how to inflate them."

She saw the anxiety on their faces, and gave both of them a quick hug.

"Everything's going to be all right. You're only wearing these just in case," she said. Mentally she blessed Roger for having made them practise putting on life-jackets before they left Puerto Deseado. "I'm just going outside to see what's happened."

"Mum, don't go," said Charlie.

"I'll only be a minute, Charlie. Roger needs my help."

"Can we come too?"

"No, it's pretty windy out there, children. You be brave and stay here. I'll only be a minute or two."

The strain in her voice must have showed. She could see Sandra was about to burst into tears. Charlie was white-faced but showed no anxiety. He was determined to be brave.

"Hazel? You coming?" Roger shouted.

It was very difficult to walk, so violent was the pitching motion of the sea. She managed to get to the door and open it. A great gust of wind blew in.

Just then, she realised she was barefoot. She banged the door shut, then scrabbled through the soaking piles of garments, looking for a pair of trainers. She had to force her feet into them.

"Ugh!"

Roger was in the cockpit, peering aft. She went over to him and saw what he was looking at. The mast was down, the furled sail had been torn away and was trailing over the rail in the sea. It flapped helplessly, like a dying monster.

"What happened?" said Hazel.

"What's that?" shouted Roger. Hazel had spoken into the wind. He could not hear her. She turned to face him.

"What happened?" she shouted at him.

"No need to shout!" he yelled. "Dunno. I just nipped down to the cabin when it hit us. I reckon it was a wave."

"Must have been some wave!"

"Kids OK?" asked Roger. She lip-read him.

"Yeah, they're all right. A bit stunned!" she shouted.

"Aren't we all?" said Roger.

"Think we can do something about it?" asked Hazel anxiously.

"Well," said Roger, "we can try to rig something up when the gale's died down a bit." He sounded rather uncertain. "Don't worry, Haze. The main mast's fine. We can make Stanley OK."

"I'd better be getting back to the kids," said Hazel. "We'll try and get things straight. Hang a few things up to dry."

Things were starting to look normal in the saloon.

"There's a bit of your breakfast, Charlie," said Sandra. An apple was rolling to and fro in a cupboard, following the motion of the sea.

"I'm not eating that," said Charlie, eyeing it with horror. It came to rest against a sodden piece of bread and butter. "I'm not hungry any more."

Hazel couldn't make an issue of it. Breakfast was out of the question at the moment. She went outside again.

"How's it doing?" she asked.

"Managed to find most things OK," said Roger. "I think the wind's down a bit. Probably safe to get the kids up here now. They can make themselves useful, and dry out a bit at the same time."

Hazel went below to get them. Hazel hummed as she went. Cheerfulness had returned.

"I want to do that," said Sandra. She tried to push Charlie off the rope he was furling.

"I'm doing this one. You go and do it somewhere else."

"Stop squabbling, you two," came a voice from round the hatch. "Come inside and help me, Sandra. Hold on, I'll come and get you."

She called to Roger.

"I'm taking her below, Rog. It's too rough outside."

Roger did not hear. He was upwind.

She clambered on deck, collected Sandra and took her below. They walked along the corridor.

That was when the second huge wave hit them.

It came up without warning, finding them quite unprepared.

The yacht heeled over until the main mast was submerged in the mountain of water.

Roger had had a moment's notice before the wall of grey water was upon them. He seized hold of Charlie's harness, and they slid down the deck together as the water washed over them. Somehow, Roger managed to cling on to Charlie, and they both found themselves sprawling against the side of the cockpit.

Hazel did not see the water coming until it poured along the corridor and the floor rose sideways beneath her. As she was thrown against the wall, she screamed. She tried to leap forward to grab Sandra. As she did so, the water swept both of them off their feet.

"Sandra!" she shrieked. Her eyes and ears were filled with water, and she thought she was drowning. She could not breathe, and everything went black for a moment.

Then the water receded, and she found herself pinned against the door of the saloon. She was unable to move or speak.

"Sandra!" she screamed. Her lips moved, but no noise came out.

The scream was in her head.

Then, all to slowly, the ketch righted itself.

"Sandra!" This time she did scream. Even Roger heard it. "Sandra! Where are you?" She panicked. She got up and went to the cockpit. "Roger, where's Sandra? She's gone!"

She rushed back inside.

Charlie was crying, frightened by the panic in Hazel's voice and the roaring of the wind.

"Come on, Charlie, let's get up," said Roger. He removed some weed from his mouth which the sea had deposited, and lifted himself to his feet, clutching the rail. He could hear Hazel below, shrieking out "Sandra!" She went through the saloon, into the corridor, opened the lavatory door and into the children's cabin. She was nowhere.

Hazel looked round desperately.

"Our cabin. She must be in our cabin!" She hurried down the corridor to the after cabin. Sandra was not there.

"Sandra! Sandra!"

Tears were rolling down her face, though she did not notice them. "Roger, I can't find her!"

A sudden draught from above made her look up. The hatch was wide open. Dark, scudding cloud was visible. The cabin was open to the world. Sandra had been swept overboard!

Hazel sat down, unable to think, with her face in her hands. Her mind was full of jumbled images: Sandra terrified; Sandra falling overboard; Sandra drowning; Sandra drowning; Sandra drowning....

"Have you found her, Hazel?" The panic had got to Roger now.

"What?" said Hazel dully. "What's that?"

"I said, have you found her?" came the voice. It had an edge in it. There was a silence.

"She's been swept overboard," said Hazel numbly.

There was no reply from Roger. Then, as if in a dream, Hazel heard his footsteps as he lurched away down the corridor.

"Sandra! Sandra!"

As if in a daydream, Hazel went up on deck and looked round. Ropes, books, maps from the yacht and many other treasures from their little world were drifting away on the wave. Charlie's rabbit. Sandra's teddy bear. Somewhere beneath them her little daughter was drifting away from them too.

Hazel clutched the rail. The knuckles of her damp hands were white from the intensity of her grip.

"Hazel! Hazel! Come here! Quick!"

Roger's voice snapped her out of her sombre daydream. She hurried forward as best as she could. The floor heaved and rolled.

"Roger? Where are you?"

"Down here, in the bilges," came a muffled voice. 'She's down here, Haze. She's OK."

Incredibly, the water had swept Sandra with such force against the bilges that she was wedged there.

"She's stuck fast. Careful now, we mustn't hurt her," said Roger.

Hazel said to Sandra, to reassure her: "Don't worry, pet. We'll soon have you dry again."

Sandra was up to her waist in water, but otherwise unharmed.

Hazel was almost manic in her cheerfulness. It was only when they were back in the saloon again that her emotions caught up with her brain. She burst into tears.

"We'd better go and inspect the damage," said Roger.

"D'you think it might happen again," asked Hazel.

"Can't tell," said Roger. They emerged into daylight.

Disaster!

Now the main mast had snapped off too, leaving a short stump about as tall as Roger. The dinghies had gone. Even a long section of the guard rails had vanished. On deck, they could be swept overboard by any sudden gust of wind or mighty wave. The little auxiliary engine could not cope with these mountainous seas, and in any case it had been swamped in the wave. Roger could not start it. They had just one emergency life-raft left.

The storm had them wholly in its power.

Down below, a myriad of loose objects rolled backwards and forwards with the sea. As a particularly big wave hit them, a CD player fell off a shelf, missing Sandra by inches.

"I'll set off the emergency beacon," said Roger.

"Is that necessary?" asked Hazel. She hated to admit defeat. "Can't we manage?"

"How?" said Roger bleakly. We've no mast. I'll try to fix the radio, as soon as I've set off the beacon."

He got up and went out.

"Can you fix the hatch somehow?" Hazel called after him. "The children are getting cold."

"What do we do now, Mum?" asked Charlie.

"We have to wait," said Hazel. "I expect they'll send a helicopter. Now, where's that book?"

A hundred miles away, in Port Stanley, the RAF station did indeed pick up their distress call.

"Who is it?" asked the duty officer.

"Can't tell," said the radio operator. "Could be a fishing vessel. Or a yacht. Not a very strong signal. Can we do anything?" he asked.

"Wind's too strong at the moment for the Sea Kings," said the duty officer. "Not safe. The Hercules can do a sweep over the area though, see if it can trace them. Can you see who else is in the area?"

The radio operator searched for other signals, and located the fisheries patrol boat.

"Hello, *Cordelia*. Where are you?"

The fisheries patrol boat gave its exact bearings.

"Why?" came the crackling voice from 60 miles away. The storm was producing some interesting interference in the airwaves.

"Distress call received from unknown vessel. About 100 miles west-north-west of Stanley. Can you proceed to the area, please."

"Roger."

For the rest of the day, the stricken yacht drifted with currents and the wind.

Inside, the family made themselves as comfortable as they could. Hazel sat reading to the children, to take their minds off the storm. With her spare hand, she operated the pump, trying to reduce the level of water in the cabin.

They had to stay where they were. Nowhere else was dry enough to sit.

"I'm hungry," said Sandra.

"There's only a biscuit, I'm afraid, pet," said Hazel. "I can't cook you anything. Our gas bottles were swept overboard."

"When's the helicopter coming?" asked Sandra for the umpteenth time.

"Soon."

Roger was bent over the radio, seeing if he could restore contact with the outside world. He'd given up trying to restart the engine.

Darkness fell.

"Move over this way, Charlie," said Hazel. "It won't drip on you so much then."

Water was seeping in from above, as the spray washed over the hatches. Roger had boarded them up as best he could, but they were not watertight. The saloon looked a little less like a ruin than it had, but it was still a mess.

Roger came in. He had been round to check that everything they had left was lashed securely to the boat.

"Wind's dropping."

The frown on Hazel's face eased a little, but she gestured upwards.

Roger looked concerned.

"Can't do anything now, it's too dark," he said. "We'll have to hope it doesn't get worse."

"Try stretching out on the bench," Hazel said to Sandra. She put her daughter's head in her lap, using a dryish folded shirt as a cushion. Charlie leaned against her on the other side.

Hazel had stopped reading. Her shoulder hurt too much, and anyway Charlie had had enough. Sandra had lost interest some time ago.

The two adults made occasional remarks to each other. They were struck numb by the disaster that had hit their little world. They did not feel like chatting.

Undefined objects rolled backwards and forwards somewhere on the boat, or knocked against the bilges. Occasionally, there was a thump as flotsam hit the sides. Waves broke against the side and sprayed over the deck.

"What'll we do about the *Adventure*?" said Hazel. "There'll be no one aboard if they take us off. We can't just leave it. It's our home!"

The same thought was worrying Roger. The boat was not insured. After their first boat, also called *Adventure*, had been wrecked in Australia, the insurance had become too expensive. They had trusted to fortune. They could not afford to lose it.

"We'll think about that when the time comes," said Roger. "Let's get these two safe first."

Somehow the hours passed, with Charlie and Sandra dozing fitfully. Around midnight, Hazel thought she heard the sound of an aircraft. Roger went on deck, but there was no sign of anything in the dark sky. He returned.

"See anything?" said Hazel.

Roger shook his hand.

"Next time take a torch, to attract their attention," said Hazel.

About two hours later, Charlie woke up.

"I can hear a plane," he said. They all strained their ears to listen. Neither Hazel nor Roger could hear anything but the wind.

Then, a few minutes later, Charlie opened his eyes again.

"There's the plane again."

This time, the sound was unmistakable. Roger had his torch ready, and rushed on deck, waving it. Hazel could not contain herself. She followed him outside, streaming a large yellow towel, which thought would show up in the darkness.

The plane swooped low overhead and disappeared. The markings were quite clear, even in the dark.

"It's the RAF! They've come!"

The sounds of the plane were soon swallowed up in the wind. When it failed to return, they were devastated.

"What are they doing?" said Hazel.

"They must have seen us," said Roger, uncertainly.

"You don't think they were travelling too fast to see us?" asked Hazel, nearly in tears.

The two adults returned below to the cabin, half elated that someone had found them, half terrified that someone had not found them. As the minutes ticked away, the second seemed more likely – the plane had been travelling too fast to see them.

Thirty minutes passed.

Then, out of the darkness, they heard the deep churning noise of a Sea King. Soon its powerful headlights played around them on the sea, and finally homed in on them.

"They're here, children! They're here!" Hazel would have danced if she had been able, but the slippery, storm-tossed deck was definitely not the place for that.

The big helicopter held steady over the yacht – a feat of skill in that gale. One of the RAF crew, a flight sergeant, was slowly winched down as Roger held the line below. The flight sergeant's feet touched.

"Hello, there!" he said with a broad grin. "Want a lift home?"

At this sally, Hazel felt a warm rush of gratitude to these men who had risked their lives for strangers out in the South Atlantic.

"'Fraid it's home we're leaving," said Roger.

"What happened?" said the flight sergeant. Roger gestured at the two broken masts.

"Wow!" said the RAF pilot. "Some storm, eh? Must have been pretty rough for the children. Who's first?"

Roger pushed Charlie forward.

"He heard you first," he said with a wry grin. "He can have first look at the helicopter."

Up went Charlie with the flight sergeant. Sandra, Hazel and finally Roger followed.

There was not a sound from the four of them as the helicopter hovered over their home for the last time.

In the end it was too much for Charlie, and he burst into tears.

"When are we coming back, Dad? I left Bacon in the saloon. You will get it back, won't you Dad?" Bacon was his rabbit. It wasn't clear whether it was *Adventure II* or the rabbit he was referring to.

———

They were all calmer by the time they reached Stanley. Roger and Hazel were somewhat subdued, realizing the huge effort that he been put into rescuing them.

Charlie was excited, looking on the whole thing as a new adventure. Sandra was cooed and fussed over, and took it all in her stride.

They were all taken to the Memorial Hospital, but only Hazel needed treatment, for her bruised and injured shoulder.

Roger looked out of the window while he waited for Hazel to come out of the doctor's room. Charlie stood beside him.

"Thinking about the boat, Dad?"

"Yup," said Roger. He was grateful that Charlie understood so much.

"It's not the end of the adventure, is it, Dad?"

Roger looked at him. "You mean the boat, Charlie?"

"Not just the boat, Dad."

The southerly wind lashed the sea into waves fifteen, twenty, twenty-five feet high. The sky was heavy with the dark clouds that had scudded towards the little vessel from the south. The bamboo walls of the cabin shook, and the rigging shuddered and howled in the storm.

This was no modern ship weathering a storm. This was a seemingly frail craft with only six men aboard. It was a raft made of balsa wood, with a big, rectangular sail. It was a craft the like of which hadn't been seen on the Pacific Ocean for hundreds of years. And the men aboard weren't there for a pleasure cruise, or even because it was a cheap and cheerful way to get to the other side. No, these were men with something to prove. This voyage was a scientific expedition.

The captain of this odd-looking craft was the Norwegian explorer, Thor Heyerdahl. And this raft, which rode out the storm with ease, was the *Kon-tiki*.

The idea for this voyage – an absurd, dangerous and impossible voyage according to the experts – had been planted in Thor's head years before. He had gone to live on a tropical island in Polynesia as a very young man. And what he found there convinced him that the Polynesian islands had been settled centuries before by people from South America. From Peru.

The route of the *Kon-tiki* across some two thousand miles of open Southern Pacific Ocean was not new. Generations of sailors have sailed across from east to west using the Mendana Route. Strong currents are helped by strong prevailing winds, blowing sailing vessels across the ocean to the tropical islands of the Melanesia and Polynesia. The weather on this route is nearly always good, and it was the route sailed by Magellan, Drake, Cook and many others.

What was startling about Thor Heyerdahl's idea was that earlier people might have made that crossing. Not in galleons or clippers, but on primitive rafts. How else could such a suggestion be proved right or wrong, except by building a replica of one of those early boats and making the crossing?

Thor set to work. He had no money and no crew. He was living in America at this time, and he tried to interest people at the universities and in business. By Boxing Day 1946, he had almost given up. He wrote in his diary that he had followed his beliefs, overcome obstacle after obstacle, and still didn't have the money to fund the expedition.

The day after he wrote this, he had a phone call from the Norwegian military attaché at the Norwegian Embassy. The attaché listened attentively as Thor outlined his plan – then wrote him a cheque for $500. They were on their way!

First, Thor had to find a crew. He had earlier met a Norwegian engineer called Herman Watzinger, and he offered him a place on the boat. Then he wrote to old friends and acquaintances: "I am going to cross the Pacific on a wooden raft to support a theory that the South Sea islands were populated by Peruvians. Will you come?"

Astonishingly, despite the risks they all did.

Thor's next task was to build the raft – of balsa wood.

"Balsa wood?" said the experts. "You must be mad."

Balsa has one weakness which apparently makes it useless for building boats: it soaks up water so quickly that it becomes waterlogged.

"No boat built with balsa wood will float for long," they asserted confidently.

Thor disregarded their defeatist advice. He knew that the ancient boats were built of balsa wood, and that was what he was going to use. And he was going to build his raft entirely in the old way, without nails or wire. The only concession he made to the doom-mongers was in deciding to use newly-felled balsa trees. If the logs were full of sap, they might be more water-resistant.

Thor and Herman set off for South America, to Ecuador. After a difficult journey to Quivedo, where the logging camps were, they were within sight of the great balsa trees they would need. Together with a plantation owner called Don Federico, they set out into the jungle. Don Federico led them towards a huge old tree in a clearing, with a trunk nearly a metre across. Before they cut the tree down, the explorers gave it a name, as was the custom of the Polynesians. They called the great tree Ku, after a Polynesian god.

In all, twelve huge balsa trees were felled and dragged to the River Palenque, where two sets of six logs were lashed together into temporary rafts. Not ones to waste transport, the locals loaded the rafts with bananas and lianas (a kind of tropical plant) and set off to Guayaquil, a port in Southern Ecuador. From there, Herman would take the logs to Peru by steamer.

Thor flew to Lima, the capital of Peru, to meet him; three other members of the crew joined them there later. And it was in Lima that, by chance, they found their sixth crew member – a Swede called Bengt. "I've heard about the raft and your plans," he told Thor, "and I want to come with you."

Now began the building of the raft, in the naval dockyard in Callao near Lima. They chose nine of the thickest logs and floated them to see how they lay in the water naturally. Then they lashed them together in those positions. The longest log was put in the middle; it was forty-five feet long. Shorter logs were laid on either side, so that the raft had a blunt point; at the rear end it was straight. That's where the steering oar went.

They used hemp rope to lash the logs together, and then laid smaller, lighter balsa logs crosswise on top. Over that was a deck made of split bamboos and covered with plaited bamboo-reed mats. Then they put up the bamboo cabin, and two masts made of mangrove wood – mangrove is extremely hard. The masts were set up side by side, leaning against each other, so that they could be lashed together at the top. Finally, they pushed five solid fir planks down between some of the logs, to act as little centre-boards. All the old Inca rafts had centreboards like this, and they helped to stop the rafts going sideways.

They worked on. They loaded supplies of food and fifty-six cans of water. Finally, they acquired a bright green parrot ... and they were ready to go!

They left Peru on an unusually cold April morning, pulled out into the open sea by a tug. The tow rope was cast off, and they were left alone, bobbing up and down in the fierce Humboldt Current. This sweeps icy water from the Antarctic up the coast of South America before turning away from the coast near the Equator.

Old pictures had shown Thor what the rafts made by the ancient shipbuilders looked like. Unfortunately, they hadn't told him how to steer the raft. So the explorers began their great voyage – by going round and round in circles! They struggled and fought with the steering oar; it was to be some time before they got the hang of how to steer the raft. Meanwhile, the wind was blowing more and more strongly as they were swept out to the open sea. There was no turning back.

Old hands back at the naval dockyard in Callao had been very pessimistic. They repeated the Americans' gloomy warnings about balsa wood quickly becoming water-logged. They said the raft would be unmanageable in high seas and gales. The crew would be wet all the time, and their food would become uneatable. An admiral had said that the voyage was so foolhardy that they must sign a document saying that the Peruvian Navy weren't responsible for the disaster that would certainly happen.

Old seadogs shook their heads and said the sail was completely wrong, and even if the raft could get across the ocean, it would take at least two years. Another sailor told them that the movement of the raft would cause the logs to rub against the lashings – so that all the ropes would be worn through before they'd been at sea a fortnight.

Now, out at sea, Thor and his crew discovered that the raft worked in a way they hadn't expected. The water flowed over the balsa logs and ran out through all the gaps in the floor. That seemed all right. But what would happen if the logs became water-logged? For the first week or so, as they each secretly watched the balsa logs becoming more and more sodden, they remembered what the experts had said.

They snapped off small pieces of the wet wood and threw them into the sea, then watched them sink. At night, when they were trying to sleep, they would lie on the cabin floor, feeling the logs heaving under them. It was uncomfortable to lie across the logs because of this movement. They also knew, as they lay there, that the logs were rubbing up and down. The ropes were under severe friction. How long could they last?

Strangely, there seemed to be little sign of wear. As the days and nights passed, the raft stayed afloat, the ropes still doing their job. They were a long way into their voyage before they discovered why the ropes hadn't worn through. It was because the balsa logs were so soft. The ropes had worn into the wood and sat in the grooves they had made, protected from the constant movement and friction of the logs.

It was an extraordinary journey. The ocean current did its work, drawing the raft on its course across the Pacific. By day, they watched dolphins and pilot fish and sharks; by night, they could look at the astonishingly bright stars and the glowing phosphorescence of the plankton in the sea. They saw giant squids floating on the surface, and the gleaming eyes of deepwater fish come up to the surface to have a look.

They had to fend off a whale shark, a creature big enough to have flipped the raft over if they hadn't frightened it away with a harpoon. These creatures can be fifty feet long and weigh fifteen tons. When its head peered at them from one side of the raft, its tail was rising out of the water on the other side. Very scary!

The raft bobbed on and on, while the crew carried on with their daily routine of steering, looking after the ropes, cooking, sleeping. Bengt, the Swede, spent hours reading the seventy-three books he'd brought in his box. Herman would as like as not be diving under the raft to check it, or hard at work with some piece of equipment to enable him to take weather observations and gather hydrographic information.

Every noon Erik took the sextant reading, which told them where they were and how far they'd travelled in the previous twenty-four hours. When he was off duty, he drew sketches of the crew, the raft and the creatures around them. The two wireless operators, Knut and Torstein, sent daily reports and weather information by radio. Radio hams passed the information on to Washington and elsewhere. As for Thor, he was kept very busy making his film record of the voyage, fishing and keeping the logbook up to date.

The raft had a little rubber dinghy which was towed along behind, but they soon learned not to row off in it without a line attached to the raft. Blown by the winds and carried by the great ocean currents, it was all too likely that the little dinghy – and whoever happened to be in it – would be left drifting far behind. They learned how impossible it was to turn back for anything when a big wave washed their green parrot off its perch on the mast and the bird was lost overboard. A member of the crew, alone on the night watch, could vanish just as easily. So – out came the lifeline for the night watch.

All should have been well, but one day, when Herman was measuring the wind speed in a storm, he saw Torstein's sleeping bag go overboard. He leant out to grab it, and fell overboard himself. A strong swimmer, he did his best against the high seas, but it was hopeless. He couldn't keep up with the raft, and fell back until he was level with the stern. Desperate, he tried to swim towards the steering oar; if he could only reach it and hang on to it, he might be all right.

It was no good, it slipped away. He was out of the other crew members' reach, and in that wind they couldn't throw him the lifebelt – the wind blew the lifebelt straight back on to the raft. There was nothing the others could do.

It was a terrible situation. At great risk to himself, Knut dived into the swelling seas. In one hand he carried the lifebelt, which was attached to a life-line. The rest of the crew watched in agonized suspense as he battled through the waves towards Herman. Would he reach him?

Herman struggled to reach the lifebelt, and at last, as they surfaced on a wave, they were both seen clinging to the lifebelt. The other four took hold of the lifeline and slowly pulled them back to the raft and safety.

In New York, they had worked out that ninety-seven days was the least time in which they could make the crossing to the Polynesian islands. That would be with perfect weather and winds and currents.

So it was with amazement that, on 30 July, they were overwhelmed by the sound of seabirds overhead. They gazed and gazed eastwards towards the horizon. If there was land, that was where it should be. And there, in the red light of dawn, they could see a thin, dark line.

Land!

But how could they get to it? During the night, they had been caught up in one of the northward currents which flowed around these islands. There was no way they could sail the raft towards the island they could see. And how were they going to land on any of the islands, even if they didn't just drift past all of them?

Everybody has seen pictures of idyllic Pacific islands. As likely as not, the island in the picture is protected by a coral reef, against which the great Pacific rollers break. Within the reef is a calm lagoon, and then a sloping white beach against a backdrop of palm trees.

Maybe you've seen a documentary film on television about the Polynesians. Skilful fishermen ride the surf before bringing their big canoes safely in through the narrow gaps in the reef to the still waters within.

Great, but what do you do with a raft like the *Kon-tiki*? It was too big to go through the gaps, even if they could manage to manoeuvre it that closely without being dashed on to the reefs. The only chance was help from the people living on these islands.

Having sailed past the first island, they soon spotted the next one. Erik told them that it was Angatau. By now it was evening, but there was enough light for the inhabitants to see the raft, and they came running down on to the beach. Soon a canoe was launched and expertly brought out through the reef. The two men on board paddled towards the raft, smiling.

Four more canoes followed. Soon numerous Polynesians were clambering on to the raft to shake hands and be given cigarettes. The crew's spirits rose, since these men would show them how to get to land.

The canoes were attached with ropes to *Kon-tiki*'s bows, and Knut, sitting in the dinghy, joined the canoes. It was no good. The *Kon-tiki* had been blown across the Pacific by the east wind; now, in order to reach land, she had to sail against it. It couldn't be done.

Knut rowed ashore, but he couldn't explain to the Polynesians that the *Kon-tiki* had no engine. The Polynesians were longing to make the raft and her crew welcome, but they didn't understand that it was impossible for her to come any nearer. Knut nearly got stranded on the island, but he just managed to get back aboard the raft before it floated on its way, further and further from Angatau.

They sailed on for three more days, watching and waiting. Then they saw another line of surf, and another. They couldn't be in a worse place; they were heading for the awesome and dangerous reefs of Takume and Raroia. Reefs fifty miles long lay ahead of them. There was no stopping, no going back, and no way they could sail round the barrier.

Crunch time, in other words.

The crew rushed to do what they could. The centreboard planks were drawn up, in case it helped the raft to ride over the top of the reef. Film and papers were stowed away in waterproof bags. They found their passports and put them in their pockets. Lastly, they put on their shoes – for the first time in over three months – and seized a lifebelt each.

The lifebelts would be of little real use, because anyone who went overboard would be crushed against the reef. Still, they might just help.

Without the centreboards in place, the *Kon-tiki* rode sideways on. When the first great wave hit it, it lifted the raft up and hurled it down into the valley between it and the following wave. Somehow they survived that tremendous sea, but they were dazed and disoriented by the force of water.

"Hold on!" yelled Thor to the others. "Hold on!" He could see the next huge wall of water advancing towards them. It picked up the raft and smashed it across the reef. The *Kon-tiki*, which had so bravely sailed its way across half the world, was unrecognizable; no longer a craft of any kind, it was simply a shattered wreck.

Miraculously, the crew were all there, holding on, as more waves rolled over them. Shaking the water out of their eyes they could see the reef stretching southwards towards a long island. But to the north, only six or seven hundred yards away, was a smaller island. Serene in the quiet waters of the lagoon, it was a little bit of paradise, with its white sandy beaches and tall palms. On the trees coconuts were visible, and heavy blossom gleamed white on leafy bushes.

To reach the shore, they had to wade across the reef. Once on dry land, they took off their shoes and felt the hot sand under their feet. The ground seemed uneven, and their legs unsteady as they always are after a long voyage.

They had done it. They had crossed the ocean on a raft.

CHAPTER 15

THE SURGEON'S BOY

"**G**et a move on, boy! Hurry up! You'll be dawdling when the last trump sounds."

It was true, Lars was dawdling. Lars was always reluctant to get below deck to his duties as a cabin boy. It was much better, in his opinion, to be up on deck, exchanging jokes and rude comments with a couple of powder boys. From the deck, you could see the huge and surely invincible fleet of Swedish warships, flags fluttering, waiting to go into battle.

It was 1676, and Lars was fourteen. It was May, the weather wasn't too bad, and there was excitement in the air. For a moment Lars forgot the tangy smell of the sea, remembering instead the stink of hide in Per Gullsteg's workshop. Per might be the best cobbler in town, but he was also a hard taskmaster. Nobody envied his apprentices, and no father who cared for his sons would choose to apprentice one of them to Per.

Lars had no father: he had died when Lars was eleven. He had been a seaman all his short working life. He rarely came home, and when nothing was heard of him for several months, his family weren't particularly worried – except that the money was running out, and he had never been away as long as this before.

Then Anders, Lars's father's best friend, limped back into town. He had seen one action too many, had had his leg amputated and his career at sea cut short: a cannon ball had hit a spar next to him and driven it through his leg. The cannon ball had then scored a direct hit on Lars's father.

So all at once Lars's mother was a widow, with no means of support. She did what she could for her son but, when Per told her he would take Lars on as an apprentice, they had no choice.

Lars hated the work. He had to get up long before dawn and work a fourteen-hour day for little food and practically no time off. After a while he got used to the regular beatings which Per used to administer on Sundays before hauling him off to church, but he always swore to himself that he was going to run away.

And one day, when Per had been especially hard with the whip, that's what he did. He'd gone that very night, slipped out of the window of the cobbler's house where he lived. He took his few miserable possessions wrapped in a cloth. He left a message for his mother with a friend, another apprentice, although he didn't know whether she'd get it or not.

It took him six days to reach Stockholm. He slept under hedges or in barns. Before he did his midnight flit, he had stolen a hunk of bread from the cobbler; when that was finished, he earned himself a meal or two by helping on a farm. He stole food where he could, but by the time he got to Stockholm, he was hungry, tired and dirty.

Still, at least he knew what he would do. He had the name of an old mate of his father's, now retired from the sea, who kept a tavern in a street near Skeppesholm. He made his bedraggled way there, and stumbled through the door to be greeted with cuffs and oaths from the landlord and sympathy and food from his wife.

"Running away from a good apprenticeship, on dry land?" roared the landlord. "Stupid boy!"

Lars grinned at him. The landlord might sound fierce, but Lars had been trained in a hard school. "I want to go to sea," he announced. "Like my father."

"And look where it got your father," said the landlord's wife. "Sixty feet down at the bottom of the sea, food for fishes."

"I shan't be food for fishes," said Lars boldly.

"No, born to be hanged, I'd say," grumbled the landlord.

After a good night's sleep and a large breakfast, Lars was very happy to wander round the docks. Merchantmen from all over Europe were docked, discharging cargoes, loading timber and leather to take on the return voyage. Ships were in from the Indies, with spices and rare cloths, and there were even boats which had sailed to China and back.

Lars could have watched the busy, constantly changing scene for ever. He heard a dozen strange languages spoken, saw men with swarthy faces, quite different from his pale-skinned fellow countrymen. There were tall, red-faced men from England, neat

Frenchmen sauntering along together in tight little groups, visitors from Germany and Russia. Some of the Russians looked very dangerous with their high cheekbones and dark, slanted, savage eyes. Like the Finns, thought Lars, slipping out of the way of a pair of officers who were eyeing him with interest.

Back at the inn, the landlord advised him to sign on for a merchant ship. "If you *must* go to sea," he added.

Lars set his chin at an obstinate angle. "It's the navy for me," he cried. "I want to go into battle, see some action."

"See?" The landlord was scornful. "You won't hear or see anything, boy. You'll be deafened by the roar of the cannon, and blinded by the blood flying in your eyes. Someone else's blood if you're lucky, your own if you aren't. No, no, get this itch for the sea out of your bones by sailing with a merchantman to India. There's enough adventure for anyone."

Lars was adamant, and he got his way. The landlord reluctantly took him down to the naval recruiters.

"He's small for a lad of fourteen," said one of the men there.

"Good thing too," said another. "Take up less room below decks."

"Your father would never forgive me for this," said the landlord, shaking his head as he showed Lars how to sign the papers.

"I can't write my name," whispered Lars.

"It doesn't matter. Just mark here with a cross."

It was done. Lars was signed up as a cabin boy.

"On the *Kronan*," said the man.

The landlord was impressed. "That's the flagship. She's the most powerful warship afloat."

Lars didn't care. The *Kronan*, which means the Crown, was a ship of the fleet, and that was all that mattered.

"You're to work for Gustav Svensson, an officer," said the landlord. "That's what they said. A surgeon. Maybe that's good, maybe not. At least you aren't a powder monkey, to get blown to bits as soon as the guns start firing. Hope you aren't queasy, because I can tell you, when a ship's under fire, the decks run with blood. You'll see terrible wounds, men blown to pieces, their guts hanging out. Nothing the surgeon can do for most of them except chuck them overboard."

Lars was silent for a moment. "Is that what happened to my father?"

The landlord gave a growling, embarrassed noise. "No, lad, from what I heard – and I do hear mostly when I want to know what's what – your father was killed instantly. Now, you just keep your wits about you. Remember that on board a warship you carry out orders quicker than they can give them. Otherwise you'll feel the rope's end, and you won't like that too much."

"Can't be worse than what my old master used to give me, with his whip."

"Don't you be so sure," said the landlord grimly. "There's little to match a piece of rope applied by one as knows how."

There was no chance of Lars slipping away, however grim the landlord's tales were. He was pushed on to a big cart pulled by two heavy horses.

"Going to Dalarö," the landlord managed to tell him, as he scrabbled to find a few inches of space to sit down.

"That's where the war fleet is," the landlord said, waving him goodbye as the cart lurched forward.

Lars looked around him. He was travelling to the *Kronan* in the company of a bad-tempered officer and a motley crew of men who had volunteered or been rounded up and pressed into service. Most of them would rather have been elsewhere. One of them, a cheerful ruffian with hardly a tooth in his head, jostled Lars along the rough seat before telling him that he'd picked a bad time, a very bad time to join the navy.

"Why?" asked Lars.

"Why, boy, don't ye know? The Danes, God rot 'em all, have joined forces with the Dutchies, may their bones lie at the bottom of the ocean. They hopes ter drive us out of our provinces along the Baltic, them as we took fair and square some twenty years ago. And what business is it of they Dutch, I'd like to know, apoking of their noses in where they have no reason to be?"

Lars's eyes widened. "Do you mean there's going to be a battle? At sea?"

"Why, bless you, boy, of course there is. More than one, I dare say. What d'ye think all these warships are for? Just for the officers to stand about in their fine clothes speaking lah-di-dah? They are not. They are for blowing the enemy out of the sea, and the sooner the better, says I. On the other hand," he went on, lowering his voice, "I'd as soon not be present on that happy occasion, and the first chance I sees to be elsewhere, why, I shall tekk it. And you heed my advice, boy, and do the same."

"Not I," said Lars. "My father was a sailor, and died in battle."

"Then more fool he," cried the ruffian.

———————————

Lars couldn't believe his eyes. He, Lars, was going to be on board that towering palace of a ship?

The sailor in charge of the boat heading out to where the *Kronan* was moored noticed the look of wonder in the boy's eyes.

"Isn't she a beauty?" he said with satisfaction. "No one can't touch her. Pride of the Baltic, she is. The biggest vessel in all Sweden, the *Kronan*, and the flagship of the fleet. A fine ship, and you're honoured to be serving on her, eh?"

"Yes, sir," said Lars in a whisper. She seemed huge. How could anything so big stay afloat? She rode high in the water, with the top deck so far up he had to crane his neck to see it. Above that soared her huge masts and a great mesh of rigging.

"Wait until you see her under sail," said the sailor.

"She's made of gold," said Lars, staring at the great crest on her forecastle and the lights gleaming out of the windows at the stern.

"Paint," said the sailor, concentrating on steering his way through the forest of ships and boats dotted around the great fleet of battle ships. "Them's the Royal Arms, you should know that. There's the crown, see? That's what the ship's named after."

"Guns," said Lars, noticing for the first time the cannon in their gun ports.

"126 guns, she carries," said the sailor with satisfaction. "That's 240 tons weight. She's a yard short of 200 feet, in case you was going to ask, and she took seven years to build. Nothing to touch her. Fit for a king, she is, and the King's been aboard her, too."

"The King?" said Lars, bemused.

"The King, boy. 'Is Majesty King Karl XI. They gave a great reception for him – oh, must've been two years ago. Brilliant affair, all the nobs aboard, 'is Majesty sitting up there on his throne, musicians – the lot!"

Lars gave a great sigh. This was a very different world from the small town and the cobbler's workshop which he was used to. The sailor was telling him the names of some of the furled-up sails as they passed under another warship. Lars knew some of them from his father's talk, but he kept his mouth shut and listened.

"You goin' to be a powder monkey?" asked the sailor.

"Cabin boy," said Lars.

"You'll get to see action just the same," prophesied the sailor. "All hands on deck, come a battle."

"I'm working for a surgeon."

The sailor pulled a face. "Butchers, that's what they is. Whip off yer leg or arm off as soon as look at ye. There's yer livelihood gone in a flash. 'F yer too far gone, they throws you overboard for the fishes to finish off."

"Still alive?" said Lars. "Wounded?"

"Yup. If they can't do nothing for you – it's over the side with ye, make room for the next wretch."

"You could swim ashore," said Lars hopefully.

"In the middle of a battle? Don't be daft, lad. 'Sides, sailors can't swim, most on 'em. Makes no sense, learning to swim. If you's goin' to drown, drown quick, that's what most of us reckon."

Lars soon forgot the chilling realism of the sailor's words. Right now he was alive, with the regular number of arms and legs about him. Let tomorrow look after itself. He'd been on board a week now, getting his sea legs, finding his way around the great vessel, getting to know some of the other boys on board.

Life was tough in the navy, there was no denying that. But Lars had been brought up tough, what with one thing and another, especially the business end of Per's whip. He was quick on his feet, quick enough to be gone when oaths and abuse turned to cuffs and blows.

His master was quite different from Per. He was a gentleman, to start with. He could read – there were several books in his cabin. Lars had searched his wooden sea chest while he was about his duties, just to find out what was what. Good things this officer had, thought Lars, turning over a belt made of silk and leather. Good quality leather; Lars knew about leather. There were gloves, too, and a heavy glass liquor bottle. Only an officer could have that – an ordinary seaman would be flogged for possessing it.

Lars looked with surprise at some of the other things in the chest. The silk ribbon adorned with a flower didn't interest him. Soppy, he thought; a memento from some girl. But why had he packed cloves of garlic, peppercorns ... and what was this? It smelt like ginger. Not that Lars had ever had much to do with ginger, but he remembered that smell from somewhere.

Lars wasn't to know that these were old and valued remedies, such as any old hand would take to sea: garlic and pepper would treat a cold, ginger would cure seasickness. These were clearly for his master's personal use, unlike the items in the wooden medical chest. Lars didn't want to look at these too carefully. There were porcelain jars, and others made of glass and pewter; a brass spoon, juniper berries... No knives and saws, though. Lars knew where those were: ready in the cockpit, together with tourniquets, sponges, basin and other gloomy items.

Lars knew about these because he had helped his master to

check through his surgeon's equipment, making sure blades were sharp, bandages ready. Ugh, thought he, recalling the scene. He much preferred to be cleaning the cabin or helping on deck, out in the fresh, salty air and sunshine

The *Kronan* carried a huge number of men – 550 crew and 300 troops. It was a little world of its own, and Lars very soon felt part of it. None too soon, because word was flying round the ship: they were going into action.

That was something new, something stupendous, and such a glory as he would never see again: sixty great warships under sail, heading down the coast of Sweden to show the Danes and the Dutch just who did rule the Baltic.

An hour afterwards, Lars could hardly remember the details of that first battle despite the noise, the air black with smoke, the thunder of the guns, the juddering of the great ship as the cannons launched their broadside.

The *Kronan* had been quickly engaged. She manoeuvred herself astern of the Dutch admiral's flagship and with a single shot tore a huge gaping hole in the Dutch ship's forecastle. "Ye can drive a coach and four through it!" one of the Swedish gunners yelled in triumph. "There's a ship as won't see no more action for many a month, even if she do keep afloat!"

Casualties aboard the *Kronan* were few, and the surgeon only had a handful of wounded or bruised men to deal with. One poor powder monkey was badly injured; gunpowder had exploded in his face. He was blinded, but it wasn't going to matter for him; he died in the night. Otherwise, Lars felt it wasn't too bad. If this was what action at sea was like, then he could cope.

Little did he know.

The fleets chased each other back up the coast, and lined up for battle again on 1 June, off Öland. In charge of the Swedish fleet was Admiral Creutz, a nobleman who was aboard the flagship

Kronan. The admiral wasn't experienced in naval battles; incredibly, this was his first spell of sea-duty after years of being a civil adviser to King Karl XI. He was sixty years old.

Of course, he was commander of the fleet, not of the *Kronan.* There were three working captains aboard the *Kronan,* and they should have known how to handle the great warship. But it wasn't their fault that the ship was so gravely overloaded, with its huge tonnage of guns and its complement of nearly a thousand men.

The *Kronan* wasn't designed to carry the heavy armament that she had aboard, and she was thus dangerously top-heavy. The admiralty had no excuse for not knowing how perilous this was, because within living memory, in 1628, another Swedish warship, the *Vasa,* had capsized and sunk on her maiden voyage out of Stockholm. She had had only a small crew on board, a fraction of the number aboard the *Kronan,* yet fifty men lost their lives. And the *Vasa* wasn't taking part in any battle when she went down, let alone a battle as crucial to Sweden as the one the *Kronan* was now engaged in.

Creutz had shown himself to be an aggressive commander. Lars had heard how he had urged his admirals to attack in earlier actions. But now he was too quick off the mark, and as soon as he gave the order, some of the more experienced men aboard knew it. Lars heard his master utter an oath, unusual for him, and shake his head as the warship began to swing round to confront her enemy.

Lars should have been in the cockpit with the surgeon, but hearing the order for action, he had slipped away to where he could see more of what was going on. Plenty of time to get back down to the cockpit once the battle got going. Or so he thought, not knowing that this act of indiscipline, which could have earned him a flogging, would, in fact, save his life.

Lars heard a great shout echoing across the deck. It was the voice of Admiral Creutz.

"In the name of Jesus, make sure that the cannon ports are

closed and the cannon made fast, so that we don't go down like the *Vasa!*"

Too late. The Master Gunner hurried below desks to make fast the cannon, only to find that they had already had their muzzles down in the water. The weight of them was helping to drag the ship further and further over. They hauled at the guns, pulling them up almost vertically to counteract the heeling of the ship.

At that moment, fate took a hand, and the ship was struck by a squall. It was so strong that it blew the ship flat over; her masts and sails were touching the water.

It was all happening too quickly for Lars to feel afraid. Numbly, he clung to the rigging, feeling the deck fall away from him as the great vessel keeled over into the sea. Then came the loudest noise that Lars had ever heard, and he was in the air, blown clean off his feet by an immense explosion.

He was flying out over the waves and then was flung into the seething water. He could hear nothing, see nothing. He reached out by instinct and clung to a plank which was drifting past. He blinked, wiped his eyes and looked back to where the *Kronan* should be.

All that remained of the huge flagship was a great ball of fire. The explosion which had ripped through the ship – probably caused by a lighted linstock (a wooden stick they used to hold the fuses that set off the guns) falling into the ship's main magazine – had not only destroyed the ship and eight hundred men, but had also cost Sweden control of the Southern Baltic. It was a catastrophe.

Unlike most of the sailors, Lars could swim. He hadn't been brought up near all those lakes for nothing, and he had been in and out of the water every summer since he was tiny. As soon as he had recovered his breath and his wits, he struck out for the shore. He didn't want to be hauled aboard any other of the fighting ships; he wanted out. Lars didn't know how many men had lost their lives that day, nor that he would be numbered among them. He did know that the paper he had signed with a cross bound him to the navy far more securely than his indentures to Per.

Nevertheless, he had escaped from Per, and he was going to escape from this. Never, ever again was he going aboard a ship or into battle. He knew then that this was probably how his father had died, in this scene from hell. Lars wanted to live, not to die like that.

Would the landlord take him in? Or would he do his duty and take him back to be lashed before being sent back to sea? Could he risk it?

Lars was lucky. The landlord was away on business for a day or two, and his wife was in charge. She washed the smoke from Lars, fed him, soothed him and tucked him up in bed, where he slept for nearly twenty-four hours. Then she woke him, gave him food and money, promised to somehow let his mother know he was alive and well, and bade him go on his way to do what he could.

Lars knew exactly what he was going to do. He reckoned that one of the farms he had stopped at on his first escape would be glad of a strong lad to help with the harvest. And after that? Well, who could tell? One thing Lars knew for sure. He was never going near the sea or any boat again as long as he lived.

CHAPTER 16

THE SEARCH FOR THE LUSITANIA

THE SEARCH FOR THE LUSITANIA

The scene of the crime (almost)

They turned off the lane. The track past the ruined fort was bumpy.

"Slow down, Donna," said Carl. "You'll damage the springs."

Donna braked and stopped.

"We can't go any further," said Donna. "It says No Entry. The road's closed for building works."

She got out of the car and went to have a closer look at the notice.

"They're building a golf course and leisure centre," she said. She walked over to the ruined fort beside the track and peered inside. It was overgrown. The sky gleamed through gaps in the masonry. A mossy stairway beckoned invitingly to the first floor. "This is an old British guardhouse, probably. Coming up?" she called to the car.

Donna loved old buildings.

Reluctantly, Carl got out of the car and came over. He looked up inside the ruined building. There was no first floor, just a narrow ledge.

"No way," he said. "My devotion to history is purely in the mind. I don't intend to break my neck falling down historic buildings."

"Let's go on the cliff and look around," said Donna gaily.

Donna and Carl were doing a history project for high school in Indiana. The subject: Why the USA entered the First World War. They had been to France with their parents for a summer vacation.

"Visit Ireland on the way back," their teacher had urged. "Get some first hand information on the *Lusitania*. It'll really bring history to life."

So here they were. Donna had read up a lot about the subject before they left Chicago. Carl had done some reading, in a desultory sort of way. He was content to let Donna do most of the work.

It made Donna feel queer, being near the site of a great disaster. She had become very involved in the subject. War was a subject that hit her in the stomach rather than the brain. Now, she had to apply only a little information and the thing would unfold before her eyes.

Carl was less involved. He was enjoying the sightseeing, which made history mildly more interesting. In any case, his great-grandfather was German, and had emigrated to the US just before the First World War. He was unsure what he was expected to think about the *Lusitania*. Still, there was nothing Donna would do he wouldn't do.

"OK," he said doubtfully. "Let's go."

The guardhouse is part of an old military wall across the narrow neck of cliff that joins the Old Head of Kinsale to the mainland. Everyone entering or leaving the Old Head has to pass that way. From the guardhouse, you can see the sea in almost every direction.

They pushed past the flimsy barrier across the track. Somewhere at the end of the track, a mile or so away, was the lighthouse. They had come to see it.

"Shall we walk there?"

"Take too long," said Carl with a lazy smile. "Let's look from here. We can see just as far."

"I'm going to look over the edge," called Donna.

She padded down the slope in the thick spar grass, to the edge of the cliff. She peered over.

"Oo-er!" she said, and hastily beat a retreat. The sea lapped gently at the rocks some hundreds of feet below.

"Watch it!" said Carl, noting irregular hollows in the ground. He studied the map. "You're now looking down into Holeopen Bay East. I guess that means you'll probably fall down a hole under all that grass."

He grinned as she scrambled back to safety, covering her jeans with green stains in the process.

"Come over and look, at least, Carl," she said impatiently.

They stood on the narrow neck of land and looked round. On each side of them, the rocky coast of southern Ireland stretched into the distance. It was a series of bays and coves, backed by green fields and very few other signs of human habitation. It was very peaceful and very lovely.

The sea was calm, the sky cloudy but bright, the temperature mild. Patches of glassy sea showed the sun trying to break through. They were looking at what they had come to see.

"It was a day like this, you know, when it happened," said Carl suddenly. "A bright, calm, warmish day. Somewhere out there."

"May 7, 1915," said Donna sombrely. "About 2 in the afternoon."

They knew the bare facts. They gazed out to sea.

The bare facts

On 1 May, 1915, the British passenger liner *Lusitania*, the fastest and most luxurious passenger liner in the world, set sail from New York, bound for Liverpool. It was a massive ship – 780 feet long, 88 feet wide, 60 feet high. With sixteen boilers, its revolutionary coal-fired steam turbines could generate 70,000 horsepower, giving it a normal peace-time speed of 25.5 knots.

This was the Cunard liner's 201st trip across the Atlantic. On board were 1,257 passengers and a crew of 702. They included 129 children and 159 Americans.

Britain and Germany were at war, and because of this speed on the voyage was restricted, to save fuel. The voyage was nonetheless comfortable, and passengers ate and drank and slept and enjoyed the incredible luxury of the ship. They talked about what they would do in England.

Early on the morning of May 7, the ship ran into thick fog about 75 miles west of Fastnet Rock, which is off the southernmost tip of Ireland. Submarines had been reported in that very area the previous evening. Admiralty warnings about the submarines had been repeated all through the night. It was a very worrying place to be.

The world becomes a different place in fog. Passengers woke early to the deep, repeated blast of the horns as the ship groped its way into the invisible at reduced speed. They looked out of the portholes and saw nothing. The rumble of the turbines was less insistent than usual.

By about 10.30 am, they were, they guessed, about twenty miles south of Fastnet, though they could not see it.

On deck, on the bridge, people walked up and down and stared into the mist, hoping for a landfall. It was an anxious time. On the bridge, all thoughts were on the German submarines.

At 11 the fog rolled away, much to everyone's relief. The weather turned bright and warm. No land was in sight, nor any other shipping.

The lack of friendly shipping worried the Captain. Because of the war, an escort of naval ships might have been expected. In fact, the British Admiralty had no ships to spare. The liner was on its own.

"Land to port!"

Shortly before noon, a shadowy patch of land was seen to port. Captain Turner studied it and decided it was Brow Head, which is eight miles west-north-west of Fastnet Rock. He had expected to be much further east. He was not even past Fastnet Rock yet after all.

It would be safer to steer closer to the coast.

Course was changed to take the ship north-west towards Queenstown. Passengers noted the change as they stood and watched the wake at the stern.

At 1 pm, passengers were having lunch. The lookout on the bridge reported another landfall, this time more clearly visible. The captain stared at it and identified it as Galley Head. Brow Head could not have been Brow Head after all – it must have been Toe Head, about 45 miles further east. He was well past Fastnet.

Individual features on the shore became distinct. Anxious passengers could saunter on deck after lunch and watch the green and friendly coast of Ireland as they travelled. Churches, houses and trees could be seen. It was rather comforting.

At 1.50 pm, the helmsman swung the wheel once more, and the huge ship turned east again, to resume her earlier course. The ship was too close to the shore. The coast of Ireland began to recede a little.

The familiar feature of the Old Head of Kinsale came into view. Captain Turner felt he needed to take a bearing, to know exactly where he was. To do this, the ship would have to hold an absolutely straight course for forty minutes past the Old Head. Speed must remain completely constant.

It was a fatal decision.

For a slow underwater vessel to be able to target a fast-moving surface craft, it had to get itself into a particular position to one side of the target. It had also to be able to predict the course of the ship for some minutes ahead.

It could not have been an easier target for Kapitänleutnant Schwieger, commander of submarine *U-20*. The ship had just altered course to get right in his sights. He took up a position 750 yards away, 35 feet down. The *Lusitania* held its course rock-steady ahead of him.

"Torpedoes coming on the starboard side!"

There was a hoarse cry from the starboard bow of the *Lusitania*. It came from Leslie Morton, the eighteen-year-old lookout. He bellowed panic-stricken through a megaphone but no one on the bridge heard him. He had seen some 500 yards away a crest of foam, caused by bubbles from the torpedo. It was travelling at a speed of 22 knots under the water, and would hit the ship in about a minute's time.

Instead of continuing to shout, Morton put down his megaphone and rushed below to get his brother, who was asleep. It was half a minute before another lookout, Thomas Quinn, noticed the foaming streak from the crow's nest, 125 feet above the water. He immediately notified the bridge through the voice tube.

Captain Turner had been below, probably in the toilet. Hearing the alarm, he hurried up, and was on the bridge just in time to see the white trail.

At 2.10 pm, the one-ton torpedo plunged at right angles into the ship. The point of impact was just behind the bridge, below the first funnel, about ten feet below the waterline. The torpedo entered one of the long coal bunkers, now nearly empty except for a lot of volatile coal dust.

It was the costliest torpedo Schwieger ever dispatched. It caused a massive explosion not only in the ship but across the world.

What Schwieger saw

Kapitänleutnant Schwieger had the cool eye of a recording machine. He described the scene in his diary, using the present tense like a video camera. His clock is set for German time, an hour ahead of British time.

3.10 pm The result is an exceptionally powerful detonation. A huge explosive cloud envelops the first funnel. In addition to the detonation caused by the torpedo, there must have been a second explosion, caused by a boiler or coal or gunpowder.

The superstructures above the point of impact and the bridge are torn apart. Fire breaks out, and thick smoke engulfs the top of the bridge. The vessel stops immediately, and develops a heavy list to starboard, sinking at the bow. She seems likely to capsize.

The Kapitänleutnant had some criticism for the way the people on board tried to save their lives.

Great confusion develops on board. Lifeboats are cleared, and some of them lowered into the water. In many cases, senseless things are being done. Some lifeboats are released fully occupied, hit the water hard and immediately fill with water. Because of the list, fewer boats are cleared on the port side than on the starboard side.

Only now, Schwieger suggests, does he discover the name of the boat he has torpedoed.

The steamer blows off. At the front, the name Lusitania becomes visible in golden letters. The funnels are painted black. No colours are hoisted at the stern.

The funnels were indeed painted black, instead of the normal red and black of the Cunard Line. Also, no flag was flying. Both these measures were ordered by the Admiralty for all ships. However, names were also painted over black, on Admiralty orders. Perhaps wind and sea had washed the paint off the brass letters, or perhaps the letters looked gold in the bright light.

3.25 pm As the steamer can remain above the surface only for a short time, we submerge to 24 metres and run out to sea.

He adds, apparently at a much later date after he had returned to Germany, to show that he too is a human being,

Also, I would have been unable to shoot a second torpedo into the crowd of people trying to save their lives.

The ship sank three minutes after. Schwieger stuck his head up again only fifty minutes later.

4 15 pm Rose to 11 metres and took a look round by periscope. Far away astern, a number of lifeboats are drifting. Nothing can be seen any more of the Lusitania. The wreck must be lying off the Old Head of Kinsale.

Five minutes later, the trigger-happy captain has spotted another ship to take a potshot at. He fires another torpedo. Conditions for firing are excellent, he says. Failure is impossible. Unfortunately, the torpedo misses. It must be the machinery's fault, says Schwieger.

The cause of the failure could not be discovered. It is not possible the settings of the torpedo tube were incorrect. The torpedo officer was at the stern to supervise it.

Human mistakes didn't happen in German submarines.

The lucky ship was the tank steamer *Narragansett*. It had heard the distress calls from the *Lusitania* and had been steaming to the rescue. The torpedo was seen from the bridge. There was absolutely nothing they could do about it. No time to change course.

The torpedo passed a few feet astern of the ship.

As Captain Harwood mopped his brow, he thought about the incident. Obviously the SOS had been a decoy signal from the Germans, to lure surface ship into a submarine trap.

He changed the ship's course, away from the *Lusitania*.

Schwieger would no doubt have been happy to know his torpedo was not wasted after all.

What they saw from the cliffs

"Where did it happen?" asked Carl, shading his eyes to look.

"Out there, about twelve miles off shore."

"Can we see so far?"

Gazing out on the shimmering ocean hundreds of feet below, it was impossible to guess how far the horizon was.

"They must have been able to see it, because people were up

here and all along the shore, watching it happen."

"Really? Gee, that's extraordinary," said Carl. "I don't recall reading that."

He was being thrifty with the truth. There was in fact little he recalled at all, at this moment. He was waiting for Donna to tell him.

"Yes, schools were excused their classes to come and watch, even before it happened. Everybody knew there were German submarines in the area. A couple of days before, everyone turned out to watch another boat, a bacon-carrying schooner called the *Earl of Latham*, sunk close off the Old Head. They knew a big passenger ship was due on May 7. They sat on the stone walls round the lighthouse, which we can't see from here."

"Sounds pretty macabre, coming to watch people being killed."

"It's no more macabre than us watching disasters on the TV news."

"What did they see?"

"The *Lusitania* appeared from behind the next headland, Seven Heads Point, trailing smoke, it was unmistakable. It had four black funnels. At 1.45, just south of the Old Head, the ship changed course, away from the coast. Then it seems they heard the torpedo, a 'sort of heavy rumble like a distant foghorn', was how one fifteen-year-old boy described it.

"Then there was terrific explosion on the ship – they must have been able to hear it from here. It sent a column of steam 160 feet in the air, and the ship listed heavily to starboard.

"The liner sank in 18 minutes in 280 feet of water, sinking by the bows. The bows hit the bottom, breaking the hull but leaving the stern projecting high in the air. Hundreds of those on board climbed the steep slopes to the stern, too scared to jump.

"What would people here have seen?" asked Carl, trying to stir his idle imagination into action.

"The stern," said Donna. "The stern was pointing towards the shore. And then she went down sideways, taking most people with her. From here, they must have seen a number of lifeboats with people in them, but I don't suppose they could have seen all the people in the water. The wreckage and people spread across the sea for about half a mile. They would have looked like black dots, probably."

She shuddered.

"I can't imagine what the people in the water would have thought."

Carl said nothing. Donna was flushed. She had immersed her imagination in a scene of carnage. He could not follow her.

Presently he said,

"Wouldn't they have heard something from the shore?"

"Sure. Apparently there was a terrific explosion as she sank. Something to do with the air in the boilers coming to the surface. One man heard a 'long lingering moan', like "those who were lost calling from the deep.'"

Donna fell silent.

"Didn't anyone go out to rescue them? Did they just stand and watch?" asked Carl.

"As I remember it, it took some time for anyone to come. The Marconi operator on the ship kept on tapping out the message: 'Come at once. Big list. Ten miles south Old Head of Kinsale.' It took some time for the message to reach the right people. A lot of the bigger boats were scared of the submarines.

"Then, towards evening, there was a sudden surge: rowing boats, trawlers, tugs, ferries, a paddleboat. Everyone who had a boat put to sea. It must have been incredible to see.

"The first boat to arrive was a fishing smack called the *Wanderer,* from the Isle of Man. There was a brave Greek vessel too, the *Katerina.* And lots of local boats. It was a matter of pride. People from Kinsale wanted to have the honour of rescuing survivors ahead of Queenstown."

Carl could see Donna was worked up.

The accusation

"How could they do it, Carl?" she burst out. "I know it was war, but to torpedo a passenger ship like that, in cold blood..."

Carl protested. "Didn't the Germans publish a warning in the newspapers, in New York, before it sailed? I seem to remember reading something about that. The German Embassy warned passengers not to sail on British ships."

His memory was not as faulty as he supposed.

"If I warn you I may steal your computer because the cops are on strike, does that give me the right to do it?" asked Donna indignantly.

"Anyway, the British were blockading Germany," said Carl, in equal dudgeon, "so the Germans were only fighting back. For God's sake, Donna, it was war! The ship was carrying contraband."

"If you call food and clothing contraband, I don't," said Donna hotly.

"I'd call rifle ammunition and shrapnel shells and fuses contraband," said Carl, growing equally hot. It was amazing how well his memory worked when called on.

"They were all empty shells and fuses," stormed Donna. "I'm sure what the ship was carrying made no difference to the submarine anyway. It sank just about every boat it saw, without asking. And I don't call a few shrapnel shells a reason for murdering thousands of innocent civilians in cold blood!"

There! The word was out. She had been brooding on it for hours. She would not withdraw it, even if she realized that in war ordinary rules do not apply.

"They were under orders to do it," said Carl sharply. "It was their duty."

"They enjoyed doing it! It gave them a buzz to fire that torpedo and see it smash into the ship. I bet you afterwards they clapped each other on the back and said 'Well done!' while people were dying horribly just above them."

1198 people, all civilians, died with the ship. Their number included 123 Americans and 94 children. The dead included famous people such as the millionaire Alfred Vanderbilt and the theatre producer Charles Frohman. Many of the dead were flung into the sea along with the living, and picked up by a host of small rescue vessels.

Survivors and corpses were landed at Kinsale and Queenstown.

The memorial

"Let's go," said Donna. She felt out of charity with Carl, as if it had been his fault in some way. She didn't want to think about all the people floundering in the water, twelve miles from land. "Let's go back to Kinsale. I want to look at the market hall in Kinsale."

"What's special about that?"

"That's where they held the coroner's inquest."

They got back into the car and turned back on to the lane.

"Stop!" said Donna. "What's the stone over there?"

Just by the bend in the road was a newly carved piece of stone, set in a semi-circle of seats made of the same stone. It was obviously a memorial.

They got out to look. Carl read out the inscription.

IN MEMORY OF
THE 1198 CIVILIAN
LIVES LOST ON THE
LUSITANIA 7TH MAY
1915 OFF THE OLD
HEAD OF KINSALE.

"What does the picture show?"

"Difficult to say. I guess it's a woman and child trying to get on a rescue boat."

"Strange place for the memorial. It's not even on the Old Head."

"It suppose it would have been in the way of the golf course."

"You gotta be joking!"

"I'm not. Life goes on. Anyway, I guess there weren't many Irish folk on board."

They got back into the car in silence.

The Market House

"It says 'Museum' – is that what we want?"

"Yeah. Kinda ancient-looking, isn't it?"

The barred metal gate creaked as they opened it and went in. They passed through the open loggia at the entrance and climbed the old wooden staircase to the first floor. Various museum exhibits were set out in the long antechamber.

There was no one else in the ancient Market House, which was in fact a place of public business now used as a museum.

They stopped to peer at the exhibits. They included a wicker deck chair and US mailbags recovered from the *Lusitania*. The chair had been picked up with corpses. The mailbags hung in the corner.

A soft-spoken voice came from behind them. It was the curator.

"They were completely dry inside when they were opened after the disaster," he said. "The mail was forwarded to the correct addresses."

"Gee, that's weird," said Donna. "I guess I'd think twice about opening a letter sent to me on a torpedoed ship. It might be a sign of bad luck."

"That's superstitious," said Carl.

"No, it isn't," said Donna. "Things are touched by horrible experiences, just like people."

She pictured herself holding a letter from the mailbag and reading the address. It was her name. She mentally put it down hastily, as if it were alive.

"I don't know that I could even hold it," she said.

"The inquest was in there," said the curator laconically. He opened the door into the main chamber, a rectangular hall with a raised dais at one end.

"The coroner, Mr Horgan, sat in the middle, under the canopy at the end," said the curator. "The twelve members of the jury sat beside him. They were shopkeepers and fishermen. The witnesses sat at the side."

There was room for six or seven witnesses on each side, seated on wooden benches. It was all very simple and austere.

The coroner had opened the inquest the day after the disaster – a Saturday. The five deceased from the *Lusitania* were George Craduck, Richard Chamberlain, an unknown victim and a young couple who were on their honeymoon.

"The captain sat over there," said the curator. "He was wearing a shabby old suit that didn't fit. He didn't have any other clothes. They'd all been lost."

The captain had been among the survivors, but the loss of his ship had aged him overnight. He looked grey and shattered.

The court was packed with reporters, who had hurried over in great number by every available ship and train. It was surprising how they knew where to come, since no notice had been given.

The hearing lasted less than an hour.

"What was the coroner's verdict?" asked Carl.

"Mr Horgan told them what to say," said the curator. He showed them a small display with the verdict written out.

We find that the deceased died from prolonged immersion and exhaustion in the sea. We find this appalling crime was contrary to international law and the conventions of all civilised nations. We therefore charge the officers of the said submarine and the Emperor and Government of Germany under whose orders they acted with their wilful and wholesale murder before the tribunal of the civilised world.

"The verdict in the New York court was much the same," said Donna. *"They said, The cause of the Lusitania sinking was the illegal act of the Imperial German government, through its instrument, the submarine commander. Something like that."*

The curator nodded, and added, "As the verdict was read, Captain Turner bowed his head and burst into tears."

Donna stared at him, wide-eyed. The human dimension said so much more than the legal formula. She turned slowly to look at the bench where the Captain had sat.

Donna breathed out as they reached the open air.

"That was a bit much for me," she said. "Do you want to go to the churchyard?"

The five victims were buried in the parish churchyard of St Multose, a couple of hundred yards away.

"No way," said Carl sombrely. "Let's get back to the books. This is all a bit too real for me."

"Let's go to Cork and look at the papers," said Donna.

What the world thought

Cork library had many books on the subject, and copies of newspapers from 1915. Bits of paper fell off as Donna and Carl slowly turned the yellowing pages, looking for reports about the *Lusitania*.

German papers were delighted with the news. The sinking was an 'extraordinary success'. Schwieger was a hero.

The death of non-combatants is a matter of no consequence, said the *Frankfurter Zeitung* on May 8th.

The city of Liverpool, the home port of the *Lusitania*, was devastated. Hundreds of crewmen came from its narrow Victorian streets. There was a violent anti-German reaction. Gangs roamed the streets looking for shops with German names. Windows were smashed. Dozens of pork butchers' shops had to close.

British papers were predictably outraged. It was the first time in the history of war that an unarmed passenger ship had been attacked without warning. Civilized nations did not do that.

Americans had been even more shocked. The war did not concern them, they had thought. It was a European war.

The outcry had been immediate – and huge. PRESIDENT

STUNNED, said the *New York World*. WASHINGTON, SILENT, AWAITS ADVICE ON AMERICANS' FATE.

LUSITANIA SUNK! screamed huge headlines in the *Boston Evening Globe*. NOT KNOWN HOW MANY PASSENGERS SAVED.

NEWS SHOCKS THE PRESIDENT, said the *New York Times*. WASHINGTON BELIEVES THAT A GRAVE CRISIS IS AT HAND.

WASHINGTON DEEPLY STIRRED BY THE LOSS OF AMERICAN LIVES. PRESIDENT WILSON READS THE BULLETINS CLOSELY, BUT IS SILENT ON THE NATION'S COURSE.

It was the end of America's innocence. Its own citizens – many of them women and children, none of them involved in the combat – had been killed. Americans were shocked, and then enraged. A wave of fury across the nation led to demands that something be done.

The slow build-up to war began, although it was nearly two years – and more American lives lost to the torpedoes – before President Wilson actually made the reluctant decision to declare war.

"Expensive torpedo, that one of Schwieger's," said Carl reflectively. "It brought America into the war."

"The Germans obviously thought it might," said Donna, looking up from a book she was studying. "It says here that Schwieger was summoned to Berlin and forbidden to sink any more large passenger ships. It didn't stop him – five months later he sank the *Hesperian* with 600 passengers aboard, also without warning. They really hauled him over the carpet for that."

"The guy was trigger-happy," said Carl.

"'Only doing his duty,' you said," replied Donna mischievously. She shut the book.

"I need fresh air. Let's go and look at Queenstown. We can catch a train, someone said. I've had enough of bumpy roads for a day."

Queenstown

Kent Station was thronging. A train had just arrived from Dublin. Donna went over to the timetable on the wall and looked for Queenstown.

"Can't find it," said Donna. "Where is it?"

"It's not called Queenstown any more. It's called Cove. It's the 'cove', the harbour of Cork," said Carl pedantically.

Donna searched again.

"Can't find that either, Superman. Where is it?"

Carl leaned over and stabbed a finger.

"There. Cove."

"That's Cobb."

"Cove. The Irish spell it C-o-b-h, just to show it's an Irish cove."

"Why didn't you say? It leaves at 25 past."

They boarded the shiny new Japanese-built railcar.

Living and dead were brought ashore in the myriad of small boats after dark. Most of them came to Queenstown. In they came, the tug *Stormcock,* the steamer *Bluebell*, the Isle of Man fishing smack *Wanderer*, number 12 trawler from Peel and hundreds of others. The *Stormcock* was almost sinking under the weight of bodies and survivors.

The boats had picked up people from the sea, from the lifeboats, floating on bits of wreckage or swimming. Some were in the water for seven hours before they were found.

Two people, a man and a woman, had been found floating in a wooden lifebelt locker. Lady Mackworth, the young daughter of a Welsh MP and a militant suffragette, had drifted unconscious on a wicker chair and was picked up for dead. Captain Turner had been in the water for three hours. In the gathering dusk, it had only been his gold braid which was noticed from the *Bluebell*. Officer Bestic had scrambled from piece to piece of wreckage until his uniform had also been noticed.

A woman was plucked out of the sea when her diamond ring flashed in the dark. She was dead.

Another woman had drifted unconscious on an oar. She had been picked up by the trawler *Julia* as it got dark and placed with the dead. It was only later they looked again and found life in her.

Yet another survived by floating on top of the corpse of a large man.

Many of the survivors from the lifeboat transferred to a rickety paddleboat called the *Flying Fish*.

At Queenstown, some survivors crawled ashore, unable to stand. Others had to be carried. Many of them were naked, having lost their clothes in the water. Captain Turner stepped ashore wrapped in a blanket.

The American consul in Queenstown, Wesley Frost, was on the spot to report the terrible scene.

A ghastly procession of rescue ships landed the living and dead under the flaring gas torches along the waterfront. The arrivals began soon after 8 o'clock and continued at close intervals until about 11 o'clock. Ship after ship came up out of the darkness... to discharge bruised and shuddering women, crippled and half-clothed men and a few wide-eyed little children. Piles of corpses began to appear...

Desperate survivors went round plucking at the sleeves of strangers, hoping for information about family members they had lost. All night the searches went on. One survivor, Oliver Bernard, scenic director of the Boston Opera House, went to the morgue, where bodies were piled high.

Mothers, wives and daughters lay in a row all round the shed, in sodden garments, not believably human persons of the day before.... it was difficult to believe that these effigies had ever lived.

Donna sat on a bollard on the peaceful quayside and gazed at the tranquil harbour scene.

"My imagination can't cope," she said, shaking her head. "I haven't seen a single dead body in my life. How can I now think of hundreds? There are three boats here at the quayside. My mind boggles at the thought of hundreds."

"You're suffering from mental overload," said Carl, severely practical. "I think we've had enough real history. I think we'd better go to the bar over the road and have a coffee and talk football. Let the dead bury their dead."

"That's not possible," said Donna flatly. "Not for me, anyway. But I sure could do with that coffee."

She shouldered her bag and they walked across the road.

"But Carl, this is history, too – the two of us crossing the road."

"I don't think anyone's going to write a thesis about it in fifty years' time."

"Don't be too sure, kiddo. I'm going for the big time."

They laughed.

Aftermath

Donna looked out of the aircraft window. It was a cloudless day. Below, the rocky coast of Ireland was set out like a jewelled map. Down below somewhere, she and Carl had stood on a headland and looked out to sea.

Then a detail suddenly came to mind, one she'd read but only just remembered.

One of the survivors from the *Lusitania*, a nurse, had been sucked under by the sinking ship. She surfaced, to find a woman in the water beside her, struggling in childbirth.

It was horrible. The nurse could do nothing to help her.

Donna made as if to wipe the scene from her mind, but for the next ten minutes it went round and round in her fertile imagination. She thought she would go mad.

"Let me tell you about the Bears...," said a voice. It was Carl. He slid back into the seat beside her.

She squeezed his arm with exaggerated affection. There was something about Carl that dispelled horrors. Especially historical ones.

CHAPTER 17

CAST ADRIFT
BY MUTINEERS

"**Y**ou'll die if you speak, or cry out, or make the least noise!"

Christian Fletcher directed Thomas Burkitt to seize the captain, who had been asleep when the three men stormed his cabin.

"Tie his hands behind his back," ordered Christian.

Bemused at being woken up like this, Captain Bligh took no notice of Fletcher's threat, but shouted out for help.

It was no use. The officers on board the *Bounty* who were loyal to Captain Bligh had already been taken and tied up. Bligh was at the mercy of his senior officer and his fellow conspirators. Fletcher Christian had a cutlass; the others, who included the master at arms and the gunner's mate, had muskets or bayonets.

And so began one of the most famous mutinies in naval history: the mutiny on the *Bounty*. Down the centuries, people have argued the rights and wrongs of the case. Generally, Fletcher Christian has had the better press. Films and popular books show him as the oppressed hero refusing to submit to the cruel and tyrannical demands of wicked Captain Bligh.

But is this a true picture? While everyone knows about the mutiny, how many are aware of the remarkable voyage made by Captain Bligh and the unfortunate members of his crew cast adrift by the mutineers? This was a journey of nearly 4,000 miles, undertaken in an open boat, in appalling conditions. Only a born leader, a man who knew how to command and how to cope in a crisis could have brought so many men to safety.

The year was 1789, and it was Tuesday 28 April. The *Bounty*, under the command of Captain Bligh, was sailing to the south of Tofua, on its way back to England from Tahiti.

The island paradise of Tahiti was where the trouble had begun. Captain Bligh was there to collect samples of the bread-fruit plant. Planned as a short stay, their visit there dragged out for five months. During this time, instead of keeping his men occupied, Bligh allowed his crew of forty-four men to do pretty much as they liked.

This was disastrous. Life under naval command wasn't easy, wasn't relaxed, and wasn't very pleasant. Life on a south sea island was. So when the *Bounty* set sail again, it had quite a number of disgruntled men on board. They hadn't in the least wanted to leave Tahiti, with its sunshine, pretty women and generally idle way of life.

Was life at sea really so harsh in those days? Yes, it was, and there were reasons for it. Even ratings then accepted that life at sea was dangerous, and that a rigid discipline was necessary if men's lives were not to be lost. Bad seamanship could be fatal, and so could not be allowed.

Order and efficient working were maintained by a system of severe punishments, including flogging. A man could be ordered to receive between half a dozen and five hundred lashes. A deserter would be punished by being flogged through the fleet. He was carried tied to a mast on every ship in the fleet and then given a dozen lashes at each one. Not many lived to talk about this punishment. Other offences were punished by keel-hauling, running the gauntlet or, in the case of swearing and lesser crimes, fines.

And mutiny? That was punishable by death. Mutineers were hanged from the yardarm, a form of execution which had to be carried out by the mutineer's own shipmates, lest they had any rebellious ideas of their own.

It wasn't an easy life for either officers or men, but Bligh had a better record than most as far as looking after his men was concerned. He had served with distinction under the famous Captain Cook, and had learned from him to treat his men in a more considerate way than was usual at the time. He made sure they had suitable clothing for the weather, whether in the tropics or in a cold climate. He kept a fire going on board in wet weather, and he used a three-watch system of duty on board.

Ship's companies were more usually divided into two watches, with four hours on duty and four hours off. With a three-watch system, men were on duty for four hours out of twelve, so they had more rest time.

Bligh wasn't known as a flogging captain, either. There were only two punishments by flogging on the journey to Tahiti. Nevertheless, he was far from perfect, being very prone to swear at his men and abuse them roundly in foul language. His meanest trick was to cut rations to punish the men – that could be very hard on seamen indeed, and at the least made them very bad-tempered.

This was not Fletcher Christian's first voyage under Captain Bligh. He had accompanied him on the two earlier *Britannia* voyages to the West Indies – as gunner on the first voyage, and then as a more senior second mate on the second. When Bligh was given the command of the *HMS Bounty* he chose his crew himself, and one of the men he sent for was Fletcher Christian, to serve as master's mate.

So there they were, Captain Bligh and forty-four men, of whom nineteen were soon going to be turned loose on a vast and empty ocean.

Bligh was hauled out of bed and forced on deck in his shirt, enduring great pain from the tightness of the ropes used to tie his wrists.

"Why are you treating me with this violence?" he shouted.

Mr Haywood, one of the midshipmen supporting Christian, was quick to respond, abusing him and telling him to hold his tongue.

Bligh quickly realized that the mutiny wasn't complete, but he watched with horror as the boatswain was ordered, with threats, to hoist the launch out.

Bligh appealed to the people guarding him, warning them not to commit any violence.

"Hold your tongue, Sir, or you are dead this instant!" was the reply.

At this Christian, now holding a bayonet, stepped forward.

"I'll kill you, immediately, if you won't be silent!" he yelled in Bligh's face.

The captain's dismay grew as more men were hauled up on

deck and hurried over the side into the small boat.

"By God, man!" he protested. "You can't set these men adrift in such a boat!"

"I can, Sir, and I will, and you will go with them," answered Christian, greatly perturbed. "And you'll do as we say, or your brains will be blown out, and they'll be adrift without a captain."

The boatswain and the seamen who were to be cast adrift with the others in the boat were allowed to collect some things from the ship. They included twine, canvas, lines, sails, cordage, and a cask with twenty-eight gallons of water in it. Mr Samuel, the clerk, got 150lbs of bread, and a small quantity of rum and wine. He also managed to take a quadrant and compass, but they refused to let him take a map or sextant, a time-piece or any of the surveys or drawings belonging to Captain Bligh.

"Not that," said Haywood.

"That is all my work from fifteen years of surveying," said Bligh in despair.

"And it goes to the bottom of the ocean, where you should be," said Mr Haywood. As the clerk hesitated, he was given a hefty shove. "Damn your eyes, you are well off to get what you have!" said one of the midshipmen.

Bligh stood helpless as those seamen the mutineers wanted to be rid of were pushed into the boat. Then Christian served his own men a dram of rum, to stiffen their nerve. Bligh knew it was useless to try and recover the ship, as no one would come forward to help him.

The officers who had not been drawn into the mutiny were now brought up and thrust over the side into the boat. Meanwhile Captain Bligh was kept to one side, under close guard, by men who had their guns cocked and ready to fire.

"Fire then," said Bligh defiantly. "Go on, fire on me, a Captain in His Majesty's navy. Good God, do you know the punishment for what you are doing?"

The men uncocked their guns, and one of them, Isaac Martin, gave Bligh a shaddock, which is a kind of tropical grapefruit. He wanted to help Bligh, but the others noticed and dragged him away. He then asked to go in the boat, but the mutineers would not let him. He had to stay with the armourer and two of the carpenters, who also wanted to go on the boat but were made to stay.

Christian hesitated. He was unsure about which men to keep and which to force overboard. He wasn't sure whether to keep the carpenter or his mates, but in the end the carpenter was ordered into the boat.

"Sir, I need my tool chest," he protested. "It must go with me."

"It must not," roared Haywood. "I'll be damned if Bligh does not find his way home if he has anything with him."

"Let him have his chest," said another of the mutineers. "It's heavy, it will make the boat sink more quickly when they are all drowning."

"Damn my eyes! He will have a vessel built in a month," said someone else, looking over the side into the little boat bobbing on the waves. He called to his fellows to come and see how crowded it was, and how little room there was on it for all the men they had crammed into it. This they found very funny.

Christian didn't join in the laughter, but he was roused to temper when Bligh asked him for arms.

"Ho!" said Haywood. "Don't you know these fine fellows in the boat well enough? Why should you need arms? Do you need to defend yourself against them?"

This caused more mirth and merriment.

"All aboard now, Sir," said the master at arms, coming over to Christian, who turned and spoke to Bligh.

"Come, Captain Bligh. Your officers and men are now in the boat, and you must go with them."

Bligh struggled to turn his head round to face Christian. "Is this the way you treat someone who was a friend?"

Christian was clearly agitated, and answered in an emotional way, "That, Captain Bligh – that is the thing: I am in hell, in hell."

"Then let me go."

"No, no; if you attempt to make the least resistance, you will instantly be put to death."

Resistance? What resistance could Bligh put up, as, hustled over the side by a tribe of armed ruffians, he was thrown into the boat?

The launch was towed along behind the *Bounty* by a rope, while a few pieces of pork were thrown in, together with some clothes and, as an afterthought, four cutlasses.

"Sir, remember we have had no hand in this," cried the armourer, darting forward on the deck. "Nor us," shouted the the carpenters. "We wanted none of this."

The mutineers didn't cast the boat adrift at once, choosing instead to shout insults at the men in the boat and make fun of them. Finally, they grew weary of their sport, and cast off the rope, leaving Bligh and eighteen men adrift on the open ocean .

"Well, Mr Samuel," said Bligh. "The first thing we must do is check our provisions."

Mr Samuel, an orderly man, had already sorted out the food and drink which the mutineers had tossed into the boat.

"We have 150 pounds of bread, and 16 pieces of pork, each weighing two pounds or so.

"And to drink?"

"28 gallons of water, six quarts of rum and six bottles of wine."

This may seem quite a lot of food and drink, but it wasn't going to last nineteen men for very long.

Bligh had already decided on his plan. They would go to Tofua, to pick up some bread-fruit and more water – they had four empty barrecoes (small casks) on board. Then they would sail on to Tongatapu, and ask King Pulaho to equip the boat and give them enough water and provisions to last them on the voyage to the East Indies.

It was a good plan, except that it didn't work. They reached Tofua all right, and found it a desolate, rocky island with few springs and a limited number of coconuts. The crew spent a night ashore, plagued by flies and mosquitoes, and woke thirsty and longing for water.

The islanders now appeared on the scene, and the crew were able to barter for some provisions and water. The islanders wanted to know where their ship was, and Bligh instructed his men to tell the truth. The islanders listened without showing any emotion, and went on finding provisions for the crew.

Another night passed. The next day the chief, Eefow, appeared. He asked after Captain Cook, and said he had heard of Captain Bligh. He offered to go with Bligh to Tongatapu, as long as Bligh would wait on Tofua for better weather. So far, so good.

"He's a very helpful and affable fellow, this Eefow," Bligh remarked to Nelson, the ship's botanist who was with him.

"I'm not so sure," said Nelson. "There's something here which makes me uneasy."

"Nonsense, man!" said Bligh dismissively.

"Then why are there so many of them gathering here?" said Nelson.

"Ah," said Bligh, growing thoughtful. "Nelson, you may be right."

Nelson began to move towards the crowd of islanders, and then broke into a run. "Sir, they are trying to haul our boat ashore."

"By God, they shall not do so!" cried Bligh, drawing his cutlass. "Eefow, tell your people to stop that."

Bligh was now thoroughly alarmed, and he ordered his men to try and load up what they could. He became more uneasy at the line of islanders on the beach.

"Sir," exclaimed Nelson, "they're knocking stones together!"

"It means they're planning to attack," muttered Bligh shortly.

Time passed uncomfortably. Eefow still seemed friendly and shared a meal with them, but Bligh's suspicions continued to mount. Finally, the evidence was overwhelming. He made up his mind.

"Every man to the boat!" shouted Bligh. "Norton! Come back, man!"

This vain order was directed at his quarter-master, John Norton, who had run up the beach to cast off.

It was too late. About two hundred men started pelting Norton with stones; he didn't stand a chance. The rest of them nearly suffered the same fate, as the islanders came chasing after them in canoes.

"Quick, Mr Samuel, throw some clothes overboard."

"Clothes, sir?"

"Yes, clothes. Any clothes, and be quick about it."

Samuel did as Bligh said. The trick worked; the islanders in the canoes stopped to pick them up, letting the boat get away in the growing darkness.

It was a narrow escape – and at what cost! A man had been lost, and they now had less food and drink on board, after spilling some overboard in the panic-stricken jostling and confusion.

Bligh took stock. He could see no point in continuing with his original plan.

"If we go to Tongatapu, we will receive the same welcome as on Tofua," he explained to the men. "Once Pulaho knows we have no fire-arms, he'll take our boat and all our possessions from us."

"And then probably kill us for good measure," added Nelson.

"Exactly."

"What is to become of us, then?" asked one of the younger men. "We shall never see our homes and families again."

"Sir, let us sail for home," said another.

"Aye, and so we should if it were not so many thousands of miles to England."

"Sail for home," agreed another. "Waste no more time on these islands and their devil-driven inhabitants."

"That's right," cried several others. "Home!"

"We can't sail for England," said Bligh. "Let there be no thought of it! From the South Seas to Europe in an open boat not above twenty-three feet in length from stem to stern? It is impossible."

"Then we are doomed," cried the carpenter.

"We have no hope of relief until we come to Timor," said Bligh firmly. "There is a Dutch settlement there. We will be safe if we can reach Timor."

Hayward frowned. "That's a long voyage, sir. 1200 leagues, I reckon."

"It is indeed," said Bligh. "But what choice do we have?"

The discipline of the navy worked on board the little boat as it had on their ship – or had until the mutineers broke ranks. Bligh was the captain, and captain he stayed. The men and the safety of the ship were his responsibility. If harm came to the men, that would be his fault – of that Bligh had no doubts.

First he divided the men into watches and got the boat into some order. Then he led the crew in prayer, thanking God for their miraculous survival so far. He felt more at ease, and so did the men, now it was decided that they were going to sail on. However, any feelings of hope were quickly put to the test, as the sun rose on the boat the next morning a fiery red colour.

"That's a sure indication of a severe gale of wind," Bligh remarked to Mr Hallet, one of the two midshipmen aboard.

By eight o'clock, they were in the middle of a violent storm, bucketing about on high seas and bailing desperately in an attempt to keep the boat afloat. Bligh could see that the bread was likely to get wet, and if this happened, then they would all starve to death.

"Examine the clothes, Mr Hallet," ordered Bligh. "Two suits per person, and send the rest overboard."

Some rope and spare sails followed the clothes, and this lightened the boat considerably. It also gave the crew more room to bail the water out. Then they cleared out the carpenter's chest, and stored the bread in it.

"A ration of rum, Mr Ledward," ordered Bligh. "A teaspoonful to each person, and a quarter of bread-fruit."

Mr Ledward was the surgeon. "This is a small ration," he said. "Our provisions must last eight weeks," was the reply.

The terrible weather was to torment them for days. Winds gave way to rain, with thunder and lightning. That was good in one way, because they were able to store twenty gallons of rain water, but the men couldn't sleep from the wet and cold.

The crew suffered dreadfully, developing aches and pains from never getting dry, and some of them developed terrible stomach ache. Captain Bligh ordered everyone to strip and wring their clothes out with sea water. It sounds strange, but it left the men warmer than they were when wet from rainwater.

Day after day, Bligh doled out the meagre ration of food he had allowed for each man, and also a tiny amount of rum, which always raised their spirits. On and on the boat sailed, despite wind and rain, for more than a fortnight. Bailing had to continued night and day, and by this time some of the men looked half dead. They were starving, and had had little sleep. How could you sleep in an open boat, inches deep in water, with your bones and muscles aching from the cold, the water and the lack of exercise?

At last the wind dropped, the rain stopped, and the sun came out. They stripped off and dried their clothes, which were completely threadbare by now. Captain Bligh sat back and reviewed the food situation. He reckoned they should reach Timor in twenty-nine days. But what if they didn't? If they had to sail on as far as Java, this would take another six weeks.

"Our stock must last us for six weeks," he told the men. 'So we should eat less every day than we have so far."

"Sir, you ask too much of them," said the surgeon in a low voice. "You cannot cut their rations further."

"I must," said Bligh. "We may meet contrary winds or other setbacks. If we make good time, then we can increase the allowance as we get nearer to our destination."

Fortunately, they began to catch birds, which they divided up and ate raw, wolfing the pieces down. It sounds disgusting, but if you'd been at sea for nearly a month and were starving, you'd probably be as overjoyed at this extra for your dinner as the men on board were.

At the beginning of their voyage, the men had suffered from the cold, the wet, and the terrible storms. Now the weather was calm and serene – but that was no fun on board an open boat, either. The heat of the sun was strong enough to make several of the crew ill with sun or heat-stroke; they had no protection for their heads or bodies.

It was now a month exactly since they had been set adrift from the *Bounty*. The day passed uneventfully, with two birds being caught and divided up, to add to the basic ration of a 25th of a pound of bread for breakfast and the same for dinner, together with a very little water. Then, in the evening, a cry went up.

"A gannet! That was a gannet."

"No, no, you are mistaken."

Other voices took up the argument. "It was a gannet, I swear."

"Aye, do you think I don't know a gannet when I see one? And I never did see one out to sea. That means we're near land."

Bligh looked towards the western horizon, and what he saw there he found very interesting.

"Those clouds are fixed, Nelson," he said. "I have little doubt of our being near land."

The crew turned in for the night, except for the watch. Then, at one in the morning, the man at the helm let out a cry. "Breakers, I hear breakers!"

Bligh was awake at once, looking out to sea. There they were, the telltale white crests, not more than a quarter of a mile away. "Change course to the north-north-east!" he commanded.

The next morning, everyone could see the reefs, with the sea breaking furiously over them. Beyond them lay smooth water. It was an alarming situation for them: they were too weak from hardship to make any headway with the oars, and the east wind was blowing against them.

Tense, Bligh scoured the reefs with his eyes, and then relaxed. He had found what he was looking for. About a mile away there was a break in the reef, and through it he could see an island. As they drew slowly nearer, the break turned out to be wide, with a deep channel. They were able to steer through the reefs unharmed, despite their lack of strength. The tide carried them on, and Bligh promised them that they would land at the first convenient spot they could find. Dinner that night was lean rations as usual, but eaten in quite a different spirit. Their hardships seemed already to be behind them.

The boat edged along the coast, the crew looking out for somewhere to land.

"There," said Bligh, nodding shorewards. "A fine sandy point. We will land there."

"I can see the remains of fireplaces, sir," said Mr Hayward.

"Old ones," said Bligh.

Staggering ashore on legs made unsteady by their time at sea, the men eagerly hunted for food. They found a few miserable oysters but little more before night put an end to further searching. Bligh commanded half the men to sleep on the boat and half on land.

The next day foraging parties found plenty of oysters and fresh water. The captain had managed to make a fire, using a small magnifying glass, and, with the help of a copper pot which someone had intelligently brought with him from the *Bounty*, they had their first cooked meal since the mutiny.

They were sick men that sat to eat. Nobody could walk off a boat after such a journey, and in a state of near starvation, and be fit. They felt dizzy, their joints ached and were very weak, many of them shook uncontrollably, and they all had severe stomach pains – they were very constipated, apart from anything else.

Bligh felt it wouldn't do to linger, so he ordered the men to collect oysters and make the boat ready for sailing. It was none too soon: the local inhabitants were beginning to appear, twenty or so of them carrying spears. Many more were visible on the tops of the hills. It was time to beat a quick retreat: they had to get beyond the range of the canoes.

They saw many other inhabitants in the next few days as they sailed along the coast. After a day or so, they landed again, to look for supplies. Some men were detailed to go off and hunt, others had to stay to guard the boat. Weakened by fatigue and lack of food, members of the foraging party began to complain.

"Why should we do all the work?"

"I'd rather go without my dinner than have to go and search for it."

"You'll do as you're bid," said Bligh.

"And who says?" said one bold spirit. "In this place, I'm as good a man as you. Why should I take orders?"

Bligh wasn't putting up with that. He seized a cutlass. "Take up another, and defend yourself!" he called in a ringing voice.

The man had no stomach for a fight. "Don't kill me, sir, I beg of you. I'll go and find food. I spoke out of turn."

The boat sailed on, the men landing where they could to find food and water. An unfortunate find was a kind of wild bean that, eaten raw, gave some of them really bad stomach pains.

After that, Bligh directed their course out into the open sea again. The men were in better heart because Bligh had increased the food rations – he knew they were nearing the end of their voyage.

It was only a brief respite. Their sufferings were by no means over. Heavy seas and rain brought further misery and, as the days passed, many of them became seriously ill. Bligh doled out a teaspoonful of wine to the weakest, worried by the men's swollen legs, their inability to sleep, the extreme pallor of their faces and, worst of all, touches of delirium. Had they travelled this far to die almost within sight of safety?

"Well," remarked the boatswain, "you give wine to the men, Captain, but I think you need it yourself, for truly you look worse than any one."

At three o'clock on the morning of 12 June came the most wonderful sight they could imagine. A mere two leagues away to the west lay Timor.

They had done it!

It was forty-one days after leaving Tofua, and they had sailed 3,618 miles. Captain Bligh had managed to navigate the boat and keep his full load of eighteen men alive – a feat of leadership and seamanship which still seems incredible today.

On Sunday 14 June 1789, Bligh and his men stepped ashore at Kupang. The people of Timor gazed at the skeletal, sore-ridden, rag-covered apparitions with a mixture of horror, surprise and pity.

The journey was over.

CHAPTER 18

THE MIDGETS AND THE MIGHTY

Wars are fought between ideas as much as men. It is brave men and women who carry them out, often knowing they may be killed in doing so. This is not just because the enemy may kill them. Often, there is no time to test the ideas or the equipment properly, and everything goes wrong.

The Italian Navy was full of clever ideas. In 1940, one of these was the "pig", a midget submarine. Everything went wrong at first with the "pig". It looked like a giant torpedo and was about seven metres long. Its purpose was to get frogmen into an enemy harbour without being observed. Once inside, they would attach charges to enemy ships, set the fuse and retire. If they could.

As it was too small to get inside, the two-man crew rode on top of it, sitting on seats, like on a motorbike. Courage was essential.

Underwater, the pig was very slow, with a speed of about three knots. Still, it was quicker than swimming.

Pigs were used to attack Gibraltar in 1940 and 1941, and Malta in 1941. Each time the attack failed, and the enemy – the British – discovered what the Italians were about.

The Italian Navy persisted, and in December 1941, six men were chosen for an attack on two ancient British battleships in Alexandria, the *Valiant* and the *Queen Elizabeth*. They were Britain's last battleships in the Mediterranean fleet. The volunteers chosen had to accept that they would probably be killed or, at best, be captured and spend the rest of the war in a prison camp. Before they left on the job, they were told to put their affairs in order, in case they never came back.

Once in Alexandria, the men on the midgets succeeded in laying their charges. Two of them, Penne and Bianchi, were picked up and taken ashore for questioning. The others were discovered by Egyptian police trying to escape. They were handed over to the British military.

In a room on shore, a British officer interrogated Penne.

"Where did you lay the charges?" he asked.

Penne remained silent. He stole a look at his watch. The explosion was not yet due.

"We have ways of making you talk," said the officer, waving a gun vaguely. He clearly didn't have a clue how to make anyone talk.

Baffled by Penne's silence, the officer sent him off to the *Valiant*. Valuable time was passing.

"Where did you lay the charges?" asked Captain Morgan.

No answer. Penne looked at the wall clock and imagined it had a second hand ticking away the time.

"Take him below!"

Captain Morgan at least had a clue what to do. If there were a charge under the ship, let the Italians be near it, he reasoned. "Might help them to talk," he said to the duty officer.

It did, in a way.

Penne kept looking at his watch. Shortly before the explosion was due, he gestured to the armed marine that he wanted to speak to the Captain. He was taken up to the deck.

"Where are they?" asked Captain Morgan, gratified that the strategy had apparently worked.

"Captain, the charges will go off any minute. You cannot stop them now. Please get your men off the ship."

Morgan's brow darkened. This was not the answer he wanted.

"Where are the charges?" he said sharply.

Penne said nothing.

"Take him below again," barked Morgan.

As he was hustled from the room, Penne took another stealthy look at his watch. It was nearly time.

Soon after, an explosion rocked the ship. The power failed and water entered the ship below the waterline. The *Valiant* settled on the bottom of the harbour. The ship was disabled.

The attack had worked.

The six men spent the rest of the war as British prisoners. At the end of the war, Penne was awarded the Italian gold medal for bravery.

At the award ceremony, the man who handed it to him was Admiral Sir Charles Morgan, one-time commander of the *Valiant*.

Ideas travel easily. British naval men had monitored the activities of the Italian frogmen and greatly admired their bravery.

The midget idea was posted away in the back of their minds for future use. Apart from anything else, they noted that it required a lot of effort to prevent attacks from midgets.

The first British attempts to make strict copies of the pigs were lamentable failures. In any case, they were no use for what the British navy had in mind. The water was altogether too cold, in the locations where they were considering using them.

It was an ongoing headache called the *Tirpitz* that was exercising them.

The *Tirpitz* was Germany's biggest battleship, sister to the *Bismarck*. It was more or less permanently holed up in a fjord in northern Norway called Altenfjord. Admiral Doenitz did not want to put it at risk by sending it out in a confrontation with Britain's Home Fleet.

It was really as much a problem for Doenitz as for Britain. Either he could use it and lose it, or he could keep it and not use it. It was a problem he never solved.

With the *Tirpitz* in Altenfjord were a battlecruiser, the *Scharnhorst*, and a pocket battleship called the *Lützow*.

For the Allies, the *Tirpitz* threat was simple: if the battleship broke out, it could do a lot of damage to Allied convoys bringing supplies to Russia via Murmansk. It was therefore assigned a permanent guard of battleships and aircraft carriers to keep it in port.

Because of this guard, in the end the *Tirpitz* fired hardly a shot in anger. Its most notable success was achieved by staying in the fjord.

In July 1942, First Sea Lord Sir Dudley Pound had to decide what to do about convoy PQ-17, which was taking much-needed supplies to the Russians. It was rumoured that the German navy was about to launch Operation Knight's Move – the word was, the *Tirpitz*, *Lützow* and other ships were poised to attack an Arctic convoy at any moment.

No one in London knew if Operation Knight's Move had begun. If it had, it could destroy the whole PQ-17 convoy.

Pound called a meeting to discuss tactics. The British Home Fleet had escorted PQ-17 as far as Spitzbergen, north of Norway. The convoy was still there, awaiting orders.

"Is the German fleet still in Altenfjord?" he asked. "We must know."

No one knew.

"Very well, we must proceed as if it isn't," said Pound. "If the *Tirpitz* is on the loose, it could sink the whole convoy. Order the merchantmen to scatter. Each ship must try to reach a Russian port as best it can."

The convoy scattered. It was a big mistake. The *Tirpitz* was still in the fjord but there were plenty of other German forces around – U-boats and planes – willing to do the job instead. Scattered, the convoy had no defence against them.

Over the next three days, the Germans sank 23 of the 36 merchant ships and one of the three rescue ships.

It was the *Tirpitz*'s biggest success, and it had not even started its engines.

The German battleship remained a thorn in the side of the Home Fleet for over a year, tying up valuable ships on guard duty.

At the end of 1942, the Italian frogmen mounted on pigs sank two merchant ships in Algiers. This struck a chord at a naval experimental centre in Hamble, on the Solent.

"Midget submarines! The very thing to deal with the *Tirpitz*!"

Not much success had been had so far with air strikes and

other attempts to settle the *Tirpitz*'s hash.

What Hamble had in mind was something much bigger than the Italian model. The pig concept was soon dismissed.

"Can't ride into an Arctic fjord riding on a torpedo tube," said an engineer darkly.

The Hamble version carried a crew of four – inside. It was 51 feet long and could dive to 300 feet. In diameter, it was just about high enough for one short person to stand upright. Just one person would have to wear special diving equipment, and then only if he needed to get out and cut the midget free of nets during an attack.

Hamble was very proud of its new gadget, and built six production units, numbered X5 to X10.

"How do we get them to Norway?" was the next question.

"Sail them there, like any other submarine," was the jovial answer.

"What, a lightning strike 1,200 miles away, at four knots?" Rapid calculations were done. How long would that take? Three weeks? Four weeks? Absurd. "The war'll be over by then."

Not to mention the crew would be dead on their feet by the time they got there. For one thing, they wouldn't be able to stand up for weeks on end.

"Get midget crews," contributed a wag.

"Tow them," came the sober voice of experience.

And that's what they did. Six conventional S-class and T-class submarines were detailed for the tow. Once they reached Norway, the crews would be changed for a fresh crew.

"By which you mean a live crew," jested a Hamble wit. "The first lot would be dead from breathing foul air. It's not exactly roomy inside, y'know."

The six midgets were duly delivered to a Scottish loch for crew training. Loch a' Chairn Bhain is in the wilds of Sutherland, in one of the least populated parts of Europe. The main settlement, Kylestrome, consists of a few scattered houses.

"When's our next leave?" asked a fresh-faced innocent after

they had practised getting in and out of the midgets for the umpteenth time.

"Ye mean, in the nightspots of Kylestrome?" said a Glaswegian. "I hear the hotel's got a wild-looking fishin' rod."

"You'll get leave when you've sunk the *Tirpitz*," commented the duty officer .

"Oh, 'tis hard," grumbled a seaman.

"It is indeed hard for a sailor to keep his mouth shut," said the officer unkindly. "Especially a drunken one. This is a highly secret operation."

Security was strict. No one was allowed in or out of the base until the submarines had departed for the Arctic.

Practice during training showed that there was indeed a serious problem with long periods of confinement in the cramped quarters of the midgets.

In the end, it was agreed that the crews of the midget submarines needed fresh air occasionally. The good news was that they would surface during the voyage several times during the night, to replenish the air. The bad news was that each breather would last only a quarter of an hour.

"Lucky so-and-sos," grumbled a seaman to his operational counterpart. He had been detailed to crew for the voyage section. The operational crew would travel 'on the cushions' on the conventional submarine.

———————

Late on 11 September, the odd flotilla slipped away from the loch, bound for the North Sea and northern Norway. Despite the precautions, the air in the midgets grew predictably foul. Attention wandered occasionally, especially during the day, when it was less easy to surface.

Combined with the strains of travelling in bad weather, it was surprising that the tow lines broke only three times while the midgets were under water.

Sometimes the parent submarine ploughed on, not realizing

that it had lost its protégé. On one such occasion, X9 vanished for good, presumed sunk. In the case of X8, the tow-line parted and it was left behind, after jettisoning its charges. However, by extraordinary good luck, another submarine running behind the rest came across X8 in the darkness some time later and took it in tow.

On one occasion X6 rose to the surface, and found a German mine had got caught on it.

"Stand back!" said the midget's commander, Lieutenant Godfrey Place, "I'll deal with it."

He inspected the lethal object, then calmly proceeded to give it a firm shove with his foot. They watched the mine drift away without protest.

It was the stuff of legends, and made good telling afterwards – for those that were alive to tell it.

X10 got to Norway under the command an an Australian, Lieutenant Hudspeth, but a fire broke out on board. As her target had been the *Scharnhorst*, which had now left Altenfjord, she decided to turn back.

The remaining three all had been allocated the *Tirpitz* as their target. All had to pierce a succession of nets. These stood between the open sea and the battleship deep in the fjord, to protect it from stealthy underwater attacks. Just to make sure, shore-based batteries and searchlights stoody ready to blast any surface attacker off the water. At night, hydrophones were switched on to listen for any alien engine noises.

To complete the armed guard, anti-aircraft guns were ever on the alert for the drone of bombers, though so far none had reached this far.

The three midgets left their big brothers before first light on the morning of 22 September, just as the day watch began on the battleship. During the day, the boat-gates in the torpedo nets were opened for surface traffic to come and go. The hydrophones were accordingly shut down.

Nonetheless, the midgets got out their diving suits, just in case they got caught in the nets. They were to need them.

X7 did have trouble with the nets and was some time getting through. Muted swearing accompanied attempts to deal with the problem.

"I hope the Huns don't have their hydrophones on," whispered the crewman working alongside. "They'll blush at every word you say."

"They've heerd far worse, I've na doot," came the subdued reply.

"Quiet!" said Lieutenant Place. "Everything can be heard under water."

Eventually they broke through and laid their charges. It was nerve-racking work. Yet the real test of their nerve came when they tried to get out again.

They turned to leave as quickly and unobtrusively as possible, sinking to a depth of 100 feet. Alas, there did not seem to be a gap under the nets as expected! Each time they tried to break out, the midget got caught in the net. They were left struggling.

Meanwhile, Cameron in X6 had also pierced the defences, but he was no sooner through the outer net than he was beset by problems. In the dive, his periscope had become flooded and was out of action for the rest of the attack.

"We'll go in on the surface," he decided.

"Won't they spot us at once?" came the anxious query.

Above them, they heard the chugging of a tug moving slowly into the inner fjord.

"We'll follow that tug," he said quietly. "In its wake, no one will notice us." He laughed. "They can show us the way."

So they passed through the next boom on the trail of the tug.

The trouble with new ideas is that they have to be tested on the job. X6's periscope had already revealed a fault. Now the mines showed another. One of the charges flooded with water. The weight of the water unbalanced the submarine, upsetting the submarine's all-important trimming, which is its balance. Unbalanced, the vessel risks getting out of control.

Unable to see ahead because of the periscope, they passed blindly through the inner defences, which were open, and then ran aground on a sandbank inside. The compass was faulty as well!

They froze. It was a terrifying moment. For a moment they hardly dared moved inside.

Their alarm was fully justified. The black shape of the midget had been seen from above by the watch on the battleship. Fortunately, the watch failed to identify the shape.

Recovering from their momentary paralysis, Cameron's crew made frantic attempts to backtrack and dislodge the midget from the sand before they were discovered.

"Thank God!"

The craft slid off the sandbank, and immediately triggered off a new panic by rising to the surface, little more than a length away from the mighty battleship. They heard the alarm go off on the ship.

"They've spotted us!"

They had indeed been seen. The only hope was to lay the charges as quickly as possible and run.

There was a burst of rifle fire from the battleship. Luckily they were too close for any of the ship's big guns to be trained on them. The only way out was down.

"Dive! We'll have to guess the distance."

The little craft submerged, listing, and then surged forward until they estimated that they were under the ship. An explosion not far away produced an uncomfortable tremor as they dived.

"They're dropping depth charges. Let's lay our stuff and get out of here."

"Abandon ship!" was now the only possible order. X6 had been recognized and was virtually disabled – but it had done what it set out to do.

The four-man crew clambered out, dispatched the midget to the bottom and swam to the surface, where they gave themselves up.

They were taken on board the *Tirpitz* for questioning.

It was not a pleasant experience. The interrogation was sharp and to the point. The Germans guessed that mines had been laid successfully: they were determined to find out where.

Cameron stole a look at his watch. It would be at least half an hour before the charges went off.

He answered the questions politely and vaguely, trying to avoid arousing the interrogator's ire. It was essential to spin out the time.

Meantime, preparations were evidently going on in the background to move the *Tirpitz* from her moorings.

A German officer entered the wardroom and said something in the interrogator's ear. He cast a glance towards Cameron as he spoke.

The interrogation was broken off. Cameron was given a cup of coffee.

Clearly X7 had also been noticed, and not long after that X5 as well. The order to move the *Tirpitz* was cancelled. There was no point in moving. There might be mines anywhere.

The prisoners could see uncertainty among the German officers as to the best course of action. They could not determine what might occur, or whether anything would occur at all.

Cameron's face was a study in unconcern.

The explosion was startling when it came, even though Cameron on the *Tirpitz* and Place in X7 were expecting it. Precisely how it might turn out was always unpredictable.

A huge blast lifted the *Tirpitz* six feet out of the water. The charges had succeeded! Cameron staggered slightly, but recovered his balance without spilling his coffee. Had they not been similarly pre-occupied, the German officers might have noticed a puckish twitch at the corner of his mouth. Damage to the keel rendered the mighty *Tirpitz* unfit for further active service, even though it did not sink.

The battleship settled back in the water with a list that was quite pronounced in the wardroom. From a chance remark heard through the open door, Cameron gathered that the engines had been seriously damaged.

He relaxed slightly, and sipped his coffee. It felt odd, drinking coffee with the floor sloping at 15 degrees.

The explosion blew X7 through the security net and up to the surface. The crew scrambled to find their feet and regain control. They must surely have been spotted!

"Dive! We'll go down to the seabed!" ordered Place at once as soon as his predicament became clear. The idea was to gain time and think about the next move.

There was another explosion, to one side. It reminded them how many perils beset them.

"A depth charge," said Place grimly. "Intended either for us or for Henty-Creer. Or both of us." Lieutenant Henty-Creer was the commander of X5.

They dived. Once they reached the seabed, Place had time to consider his options.

They were no real options. X7 was disabled by the explosion, and they could do no more damage to the *Tirpitz*. The best course was to surrender – but that in itself posed perils. How could they surrender without being shot to pieces?

"Have we got anything white?"

The first lieutenant pulled out a white Guernsey.

"Will this do, sir?" he asked.

The Guernsey looked very British and rather ridiculous in the circumstances. Lt Place smiled.

"That will do very well," he said, as if he were choreographing a school play. "OK, let's take her up. I shall go first when we surface."

It is the place of the commanding officer to offer the surrender.

A crackle of gunfire greeted them as the hatch broke the surface. Bullets could be heard striking the outer plating.

Place opened the hatch very cautiously, to give the Germans time to notice. The sweater preceded him. He waved it cautiously.

The shooting ceased.

He emerged from the hatch, astonished to find the rim barely above the water. This would require care.

He heaved himself up and stepped on to a floating target which was bumping alongside, to allow room for the next man to emerge.

Unhappily, the transfer of his weight pushed the bows under water, and the midget vessel started to flood. Within seconds it had sunk to the seabed, 120 feet below.

The three remaining crew were trapped inside.

Their only chance of survival was to use the escape apparatus, which contained a supply of pure oxygen. Unfortunately, it can be used at a depth only with caution. Used wrongly, it kills.

Like the periscope and the compass, it was another idea that could not be tested except on the job.

Only one of the men made the surface, and he was barely alive by the time he reached it.

A German motorboat roared alongside. The two survivors were dragged aboard and taken to the *Tirpitz* for questioning. Lieutenant Place was clad only in underwear, socks and boots. He felt more than a little uncomfortable when it came to the interrogation.

The German officer was brusque. He did not mince his words.

"Tell us the position of your mines, or we shall shoot you."

He made a gesture so there should be no doubt as to his meaning.

"I am a British officer. I demand to be treated with the respect due to my position," was Place's polite but unfaltering reply. He was not sure whether the earlier explosion had been his charges or Cameron's. Either way, he would say nothing.

It was the end of the adventure, for all of them. Damage to the keel from the explosion rendered the mighty *Tirpitz* unfit for further active service, even though it did not sink.

None of the six survivors took any further part in the war. The lessons to be learned, and the details of the individual heroism, were not passed on until they were repatriated at the end of the war.

The crew of X5 were the unlucky ones. Having reached Norway, they had indeed been hit by depth charges, and been sunk. Lieutenant Henty-Creer RNVR was ill-fated. He did not even to make it to that wardroom on the *Tirpitz*.

It was a long way from the adventure in Alexandria to the icy Arctic waters of Altenfjord, but the idea had travelled well. The midget submarines had done their job.

Yet, in a way, the *Tirpitz* remained an unsolved problem. The Germans patched her up. In reconnaissance photos, she looked as if she might still be a threat to Allied shipping. From outside, it could not be seen that the three main engines had been disabled and the keel damaged. She could still do her bit meanwhile.

Lieutenants Place and Cameron had already done their bit. Like Penne, they emerged from imprisonment to collect their country's highest award, in this case the VC.

The men who died were the losers. However good an idea, it is the losers who test its effects.

CHAPTER 19
THE DIARY

...th ... g ... th
passengers.
His majesty, and a prosperous new ye...

January 5th

I... do suspect that all ... elow deck
shouting a lot, and ... ch less
There may be some ... ny the m...

January 12th
We have reached

The diary lay under a heap of yellowing newspapers. Martha glanced at the newspapers, then put them on a pile, ready to be thrown away.

She coughed. Must be the dust in her throat, she thought. Really, what one did for a holiday job! Sitting in a library sorting out old newspapers and documents. She must have been mad to agree to her mother's suggestion. Well, dosh was dosh.

Anyway, before long she'd be sitting in a schoolroom doing exam papers. Would that be any better?

She picked up the diary and opened it casually, to check which pile it should go on.

It was old, much older than the newspapers, and full of entries in beautiful copper-plate handwriting.

She sighed. Teachers must have taught handwriting then. Not like her own unreadable scrawl. Her father said sarcastically a beetle dipped in ink could do better. Her teacher had characterized her writing style as: "These are my thoughts but they're private and I'm keeping them that way."

She leafed through the diary. The pages were thin but still quite white. Martha sighed again. Her father would say "they don't make paper like that any more", she was sure. She could almost hear him saying it. It was paper made to last, paper meant to be read in two hundred years' time.

Martha had just thrown away her own diary for last year. It had three words written in it, under January 1st: "Got up late." Obviously the owner of this diary had a more eventful life. It was about three-quarters full.

She was just about to put it aside, to have a look at later when she had more time, when a handwritten name caught her eye. The *Griffin*. Now where had she read that name before? Just recently, too.

She coughed again. Must go and get a glass of water.

She got up and went to the staff room for some water. On the way back, she poked her head into the reading room where today's newspapers were spread out.

Just have a quick look in the papers, to see if she could find the *Griffin*. No good trying the *Mirror*, they didn't use two-syllable words. She scudded through *The Times*. No, nothing there…. the *Telegraph*? No luck. Could it have been the local rag?

No joy. She gave up.

As she returned to the store room past the issuing desk, she caught sight of a small blue handbill on the noticeboard: "Treasures from the Griffin", it said. So that was what she'd seen! She went over to have a look.

> … *exhibition at the Town Hall. A unique chance to examine the 18th century treasures from the East Indiaman ship* Griffin, *which sank in 1761 off the Philippine Islands, carrying a fortune in Chinese porcelain. Thanks to modern diving technology and skills, much of this wonderful lost treasure has been recovered and is preserved.*

A treasure ship, of sorts, if you're a porcelain freak. Her ma would be fascinated. So would she, come to think of it. Think of all those dinner plates lying unused under the sea for two hundred years, then someone digging them up and eating off them! Weird.

She went back to her work table, suddenly interested. Whose diary was it, and why was it written?

She opened the first page and read.

It was not a calendar diary. In fact, it seemed to be a personal log of someone who had sailed on the *Griffin* – a member of the crew probably.

She looked at the dates. Whoever it was, he had not written every day, obviously only when time allowed or something momentous had happened. Maybe he worked too hard to write. All that climbing of masts and lashing down sails in a storm, no doubt.

It began at a house somewhere in England, in mid-sentence. The opening page or two was missing, perhaps torn out.

... Dethick arrived home from London late this afternoon. He was very cheerful and said, "Well, we're off to China again soon, Edward."

"Very good, sir," I said. "Shall I pack your chest?"

"No," said Captain Dethick, laughing.

He often laughs at what I say. "You're too serious, Edward," he often says, but I don't mind, I know he intends well. No-one could wish for a better master.

"No," he says, "what I mean is, we're preparing the Griffin for next year's China season. I suppose we'd better start looking for a crew."

"Well, I hope you'll consider me again as your steward, sir," I said. "It was an honour to be aboard such a fine ship under such a good master last year."

"Not to mention our little arrangement about the tea and the chinaware, eh, Edward?" he said with a wink.

The Captain was referring to my little consignment of China goods which I brought back from the voyage last year and which he sold so well for me. I'm happy to say I was able get married with the profit. I must say it was very generous of the Captain. He permitted me to use some of the cargo space which the Company allows him. There are not many captains who would do that. Most are too busy thinking about their own purses.

"So you want to go to China again, Edward?" asked the Captain. He had a twinkle in his eye, I could see.

"Yes, sir, certainly I do," I replied. I was very stiff.

When I first went aboard, on the last voyage, the chief mate Mr Dominicus told me I was lucky. It was rare to find such a happy ship as Captain Dethick's. I can believe him.

So Edward was a servant, thought Martha. He writes uncommonly well for a servant. Perhaps he had been a gentleman's son, come down in the world, or a poor relation. Martha's fertile imagination ran riot. She imagined a young Edward, proud with family consciousness, forcing himself to look humble and be grateful.

She turned the page. The date was indecipherable. It looked as though something had burnt a hole in it.

Perhaps ash from the writer's pipe, thought Martha. The rest was perfectly clear.

> August ..th
> Although the Company has not yet accepted the Griffin, Captain Dethick is quite confident that we shall be going. The ballot is next week, he says. He is already thinking what officers he wants to come with us. He frets when he is at home, and wants to be away. Mrs Dethick smiles at him, but I can see she takes it rather hard and is not looking forward to his going. He will be away for a year.

"So Edward is already accepted," thought Martha. "The good captain obviously thinks very highly of him. I wonder what company that was?"

She was seized with a desire to know. She got up and went to the information point.

"What shall I look under? .. Let's try *China*."

She found China on the microfiche. There was a subheading, "Trade with, 18th century". That would be it.

Mmm, quite a lot of books. Most of them mentioned the East India Company in the title. That must be it.

She went over to the encyclopedia and looked up *East India Company*. Screeds of text – oh dear! Then she found a bit about the ships:

> *Every year, the Company decided how many ships it needed for the China trade. Shipowners could put their names forward. The Company held a ballot to choose the ships. About 50 or 60 were chosen each year.*

Martha shut the encyclopedia with a bang, and sneezed. Dust again!

"Doesn't anybody use these books?" she thought indignantly.

August 12th

"I hope Mr Dominicus will be chief mate again," I said to the Captain when he called me in to talk about it. "The crew looked up to him. A very fair man, very fair. Never a word in anger that was not just."

"He's a good man, is he not?" sighed the Captain. "I'm afraid we cannot have him, however. His good fortune is our misfortune, alas. He has been given command of the Delaware and is gone to India, so I am told. A better companion I do not know."

He fiddled with the papers on his desk in front of him. I could see that the paperwork irked him.

"Can I assist you, sir?" I said, indicating the paperwork.

"Would you? I should be most grateful," said the Captain. He was clearly much relieved. "I have been thinking that perhaps Dominicus's son Robert may not have gone with him to Bombay, and that perhaps he may come with us as a midshipman. I took quite a shine to the boy last time, when he was his father's servant. 'There's someone you can trust in a tight spot,' I told Dominicus. 'Your boy's got the making of a first-class mate.'"

"Shall I ... ?" I asked. I meant, write a letter in the Captain's name, but he shook his head.

"Don't worry about him. I shall write to Mrs Dominicus this evening."

"What about Mr Harvey, sir, as chief mate?" I ventured to say.

"Funny thing. I asked about Harvey at the Company's office. They don't know where he's gone. Just vanished. Not sunk or anything, just not signed on for a ship."

He searched among the papers on his desk.

"Well, there's my first list, Edward," he said tersely, and handed me the paper.

I was somewhat doubtful whether I should take it from him. I sometimes write letters of a less personal nature for the Captain, but he generally writes his own letters to members of the crew. Those are not things that concern me.

"Go on, Edward, your opinion, please," urged the Captain rather roughly. I think he was embarrassed to be asking a servant for an opinion about the mates, but he knew that I heard about things that went on below decks.

The only name that struck me as odd was Charles Hudson as chief mate. The Captain saw my face.

"Well, go on, man! Which of the names offends you?" he asked.

I must have visibly bridled at his tone, because at once he became conciliatory.

"Now what is the name? I value your opinion," he said, less urgent but still very pressing.

"Well, Mr Hudson as chief mate, sir. I believe he does not have a way with the men, and rubs them up the wrong way when things go wrong." I found it very difficult to speak so openly about a superior.

Captain Dethick, good man though he is, does not like to have his judgment questioned. He held out his hand for the paper without another word.

Martha breathed out. She could see conflict looming. Would the *Griffin* be a happy ship on her next voyage? She read on.

September 14th

"So that's it, Edward," says the Captain when I went to the library this afternoon. He tapped a letter on his desk. "We have Thomas Howe as third mate – brother of Commander Howe, y'know. And that's everyone. We're ready to go," he added with the greatest cheerfulness. I have not seen him in such good humour for many months.

September 29th

The Captain has gone to Blackwall to see how the work is
progressing on the fitting out. He says the dock is a marvel
of ingenuity and promises that next time I shall go with
him. He is in despair that everything will be ready in time
and attacks poor Mrs Dethick with his worries. I think
perhaps after all she will be relieved when he sails!

October 10th

I went down with Captain Dethick to see the Griffin safely
back in the water. She made a splendid sight, newly painted
and polished and all her brasswork so fine. It was good to
see her. I shall be very pleased to be aboard again. She is
now at her moorings, and the Captain is aboard, to ensure
that the cargo is properly stowed. We are taking a great
amount of lead and wool. English wool is much prized in
foreign countries.

I am to join her in a week's time, and bring the rest of the
Captain's things. He does not take much, but he likes to
have fine things about him.

It is very instructive to watch the Captain come aboard. He
is here, there and everywhere – you can see the ship is
really his home. He has an eye for the smallest detail, and
the men jump to his every word. In a woman, you would
say it was fussing. In him, it seems the natural mark of a
good captain, ensuring that we shall have a calm and
prosperous voyage, and arrive at our destinations without
trouble.

"Fussing! I like that! Who's the bigger fusspot, master or servant?" thought Martha with amusement.

"Just so with the bags of wool, Mr Kent, if you please,"
the Captain said, showing how he wanted them laid. (Mr

Kent is the second mate. He is new to our ship. Captain
Dethick was no doubt thinking of some little troubles we
had with the stowing of the cargo last time.)
"The accounts so far, Mr Lockhart, for your perusal," he
said to the purser, handing over the heavy volume that he
had brought down from the Company offices. "Perhaps you
will be so good as to find time for us to look through
them together at the end of the watch."
I came home again for the last week with my dear family.
These are trying times at home. Jane is very quiet, I can see
that she does not look forward to my departure. She tells
the children they must be specially good or Papa will not
come back. Little Jamie burst into tears today and would
not be consoled, though I hugged him until he went to
sleep. I could see that Jane was much affected.

"Who would be a sailor's wife?" thought Martha indignantly.
"The husband fathers a brood of children on her and then rushes
off to sea for a year or more. You can see he's dying to get away.
Still, I don't suppose Jane thought like that."

"Closing in five minutes," said a voice behind her. Martha
started guiltily. The pile of papers to be sorted had not gone down
at all in the last half-hour, she'd been so absorbed. She was not
earning her keep. Her mother would be furious.

She decided to take the diary home and read it out of hours.

When she got home, she forgot about it. It was not until she
was back in the library next day that she remembered it. It was
still in her bag.

She started on the pile of newspapers, and worked solidly until
one of the assistants stuck her head round the door and whispered "Tea!"

Martha thought she ought to be offered rum, but then thought
Edward might disapprove. Bit of a starchy fellow, she thought on
reflection. Probably drank water. Don't think I'd like to have
been Jane.

She fished the diary out of her bag. Feeling somewhat dishonest about enjoying herself at her work table, she opened the diary where she'd stopped. She'd used her bus ticket as a bookmark. Just ten minutes reading, and then back to work, she promised her invisible mother. She could hardly wait for the *Griffin* to put to sea.

October 31st

We're away! I know Captain Dethick would laugh at me, but I am sure he feels the attraction of distant places as much as I do. It is one of the difficulties to explain to Jane, who would not leave our dear home for all the world. The pilot, Mr Bromfield, came aboard about 11 am and not long after we weighed anchor and moved out into the channel to catch the tide. We found three other Indiamen already at anchor off Gravesend. We are here to await others, also further cargoes.

November 3rd

We have been joined by four more Indiamen. The captain of one of them, the Clinton, has just left after discussions with Captain Dethick. The season is truly under way. We still await the treasure before we can weigh anchor and leave our native land. Meanwhile the Captain has the crew busy about the ship. We are ever so smart! There is much traffic to and fro between the ships, as the captains dine with each other and take advantage of these quiet times to swap news of foreign shores. Captain Dethick is particularly keen to learn news of new chartings. Charts are much in evidence at these meetings as safe channels are discussed.

"Old gossips, that's what they were," thought Martha. "I bet they were not discussing maps at all."

Then she repented her sarcasm. Safe channels were a matter of life and death for them. Sailing uncharted seas is not like driving along a motorway.

December 1st
Such a fury of holystoning the deck, polishing the brass
and cleaning of paintwork there has been these last two
days! Two days ago the lighters brought the treasure to be
stowed away – forty chests of it there was. You can imagine
the good reasons the men found to be at work on that side
of the ship as it was lifted aboard.
This afternoon, the new husband Captain Hunt came aboard,
and the men were called in one by one and paid their
imprests.

"Bother!" thought Martha. "I'll have to go and look those up."
She found them in the huge Oxford dictionary:
"**husband** An official. A representative of the shipowners in the
East India Company," she read. Hmm. Was that clear? Captain
Hunt must be one of the owners.

"Now, what was the other word? Ah yes:
'**imprest** Advance pay of soldiers or sailors.' "Well, that seems
clear enough." She went back to the diary.

The men receive four pounds ten shillings for signing on
and two pounds five shillings a month for wages. This is a
little more than I receive but I have the honour to speak to
Captain Dethick directly. By this means I am able to make
up my earnings in other ways.
This evening Captain Hunt is dining with Captain Dethick.
No doubt Captain Hunt will have fresh instructions for our
voyage. I have been told to bring out the Captain's best
claret.

December 9th
We slipped down river on the morning tide and are now
anchored off Margate. The weather is turning against us and
I have no doubt we shall be held here for some time.

December 12th
We have four passengers aboard, and two more are still to come. Three of them are supracargoes from the Company, who will have charge of buying the goods in China.
I do admire them. Theirs is such a dangerous business, living among those people and trying to deal like honest Englishmen. Such stories I have heard of what goes on! It seems you cannot trust the Emperor's officials from one day to the next, they will say "Buy, buy!" one day and the next day they will threaten to chop off your head if you do not put twice as much money in their hands as the goods really cost. Really, I should not know how even to begin dealing with such people.

December 13th
I overheard the supracargoes talking at dinner, and I must say they lead fascinating lives. They said more than once how much the Chinese dislike foreigners and look down on them! I heard this on our last voyage but did not believe it. How is this possible, when we come in peace and have guns and wool and gold to offer them, and want to buy their tea and porcelain? I shall never understand them.

"The honest Englishman abroad," thought Martha. A scene in a shop in Majorca last year came to mind, while she was on holiday with her parents. An English family had quarrelled with a German family. They both wanted to buy the last pair of beach mats in the shop. In the end, the owner had asked them all to leave. It was very embarrassing.

Maybe it was like that with the Chinese and the Europeans. Or maybe the Chinese had all they needed and did not need our goods.

December 15th
We are still off Margate because of the weather.

"Shall we return to the shore and go post to Portsmouth?" asked one of the supracargoes as they paced the decks. It is very confining for such active men to be on ship and to have nothing to do. I do believe they would prefer to be on land and about their work. However, the Captain persuaded them to stay. He believes the weather will change and does not want to miss it.

December 29th

The wind veered round to the east and we were able to proceed to the Downs, but were held up there again by adverse weather for some days. I am happy to say we now have a fair breeze behind us and we are out in the Atlantic, on our way to Cape Verde.

We stood well away from Portland Bill as we proceeded down the Channel. Such tales of wrecks and stormy seas some of the crew have to tell of Portland! They say seven currents meet at the tip. I cannot bear to think of sailing in such waters.

And so farewell to my native shores! When shall I see them again?

New Year's Day, 1753

The weather holds steady and we are making a good pace. It does one good to see brighter skies.

The men were celebrating below decks last night, I could hear a lot of singing and laughing. So many fine voices among them, but I fear Jane would blush to hear some of the songs they sing.

The Captain gave a special dinner for the officers and passengers.

"His Majesty, and a prosperous year!" was the toast.

I wonder what Jane is doing. I miss her, although I am glad to be at sea.

"So he's human after all," thought Martha. "I expect she is bustling around with the children and having a hard time, trying not to think of him."

January 5th

I do suspect that all is not well below deck. We hear Mr Hudson shouting a lot, and the singing is much less noticeable now. There may be some discontent among the men.

January 12th

We have reached San Vicente in Cape Verde, and have had our first encounter with a foreign tongue. But it is only Portuguese and sounds almost as familiar as English. Though I myself understand it but little, I heard it a great deal on our last voyage to China. The supracargoes can all speak Portuguese with perfect fluency. They have to deal with the Portuguese authorities in Macao, who can help them negotiate with the Imperial officials.

We have put 2,400 miles behind us since leaving the Downs, in a bare fourteen days. We are glad to restock with fresh food and water, and have filled our decks with animals.

"We must have good food for the men, Mr Davidson," Captain Dethick says to one of the quartermasters. "I want no scurvy aboard my ship."

The men get very quarrelsome if they eat and drink nothing but salt beef and brackish water. However, I fear we shall not avoid the scurvy entirely. Mr Harvie the surgeon is not optimistic we shall escape it altogether.

"Last time we were lucky, very lucky, not to have had a single case," he told Mr Lockhart the purser.

"The Captain knows what he is doing," Lockhart replied. Indeed, I find Captain Dethick is somewhat fanatical about the crew's food, and insists on them having fresh meat and fresh bread whenever possible.

"I'll get a baker aboard in China," he said. "That's the answer."

January 14th

We are heading due south for Cape Horn. The wind is still with us. However, we had an unpleasant event yesterday. The men were called on deck and lined up to watch while one of them was tied to the mast and whipped.

I did not feel able to ask the Captain about this, but Mr Griffiths, the sixth mate, told me what had happened.

"What was his offence that he should be punished so seriously?" I asked.

My question was very quiet. I did not wish to seem to enjoy another man's misfortune.

"Mr Davis found him at cards during the watch," was Mr Griffiths' reply. Mr Davis is the fourth mate.

If that is true, it was indeed a grave offence. Our lives are all dependent on each of us doing his job on the ship.

I could see the Captain does not like it. He does not talk much when he is uneasy. He called Mr Hudson in to his cabin and I believe they discussed the feeling of the men.

January 17th

Another misfortune today. Midshipman Thomas told the Captain that some cheese was missing. Mr Hudson at once ordered all the men's chests to be opened and searched, thinking that one of the men must have stolen it.

After about an hour, I heard someone shout, "Here, sir!" The cheese had been stowed out of sight between decks, no doubt in a position where it could be collected later. But how would the thief be able to eat it comfortably? There is almost nowhere private on the ship, unless a group of men agreed to steal it together and divide it among themselves.

I heard the men talk about it. They do not like to know there is a thief or thieves among them. With all of us at

such close quarters, we have to trust each other.
"I catch 'un meddling with my things, he'll soon feel my
fist in his face!" said one seaman to his fellow, thinking no-
one was in earshot. His tone frightened me, I can tell you.
Captain Dethick has called the officers to his cabin.

January 21st
We are under the Line, the Captain says. We shall pass
along the coast of South America but shall not see it.

January 29th
The lookouts have been told to expect a landfall. I believe
we will soon be passing the small island of Trinidad, if the
Captain's calculations are correct. We shall then be not far
from the Tropic of Capricorn, and head south for colder
climes.

January 31st
Still no landfall. No doubt we have passed the island in the
night, without seeing it.
"Drift, Beardmore," said Robert Dominicus to me as we
looked at the horizon like the lookouts, but saw nothing.
Dominicus is a very earnest young man. He has read many
books on navigation and is very knowledgeable. "We study
the stars and the winds, but we find it difficult to measure
the currents. Currents drift as well as flow."
I am sure he is right, though I do not wholly understand.

"What are you reading?" asked a voice behind her. Martha
instinctively covered up the diary, thinking it was the huffy
librarian, Mrs Trelew, but it turned out to be nice Lisa, the assistant from the children's library.

Martha laughed.

"Caught me at it, I'm afraid," she said. "Just an old diary I
found in these papers. I got carried away. Look at the time! I'd

better get on with sorting, or Mrs Trelew will complain to my mother. Quite right too."

She put aside the diary with great determination, and flew at her work. When she returned to the *Griffin*, things had taken a turn for the worse.

February 18th
A dreadful thing happened a few days ago. We experienced a white squall which made even me, who am generally comfortable in rough seas, feel uncomfortable. During the storm Mr Davidson, one of the quartermasters, tried to make his way along the deck and was washed overboard. So dreadful was the power of the wind that we were quite unable to put about and look for the poor fellow, who is, I fear, lost. The Captain received the news with great perturbation.

February 19th
Money and small valuables have been reported missing. The mood among the seamen is not good. Each suspects his neighbour may be the thief. The Captain is determined to root out the canker before it destroys us all. The ship will be searched from stem to stern.

February 24th
All is not well among the men. One of the crew was found in possession of five bottles of wine and admitted stealing them.
He was given 15 lashes of the whip.
Despite this public warning, the thieving continues. Two days ago, some of the missing articles were found in the possession of the gunner's boy, who has admitted his guilt. He is scarcely older than a child. It is dreadful to see such brazen wickedness in one so young.
"Tie him to the gun!" came the stern order. I could discern

no trace of repentance on the boy's face, either then when
the punishment was pronounced, or as he was given twelve
lashes with the cat-o'-nine-tails. He did not utter a sound
throughout, though his back was bleeding almost entirely by
the end.
I have never seen fortitude like this in a boy, and am
almost able to feel sorry for him.
Yet it was not sufficient punishment in the eyes of the men.
Some of the men whose things the boy had stolen were
muttering that the whipping was too good for him and he
ought to be keel-hauled.

It was harrowing to read, even at a remove of two centuries.
Martha almost felt she could not read on, but her eyes continued to trace the elegant handwriting, whether she wanted to or
not.

March 1st
The devil is among us. A midshipman has reported the loss
of a large sum of money. I do not know how much, but
hear tell that it is more than ten pounds. Captain Dethick is
in a taking, and has ordered the officers to find the money
and the culprit within 24 hours.

March 2nd
The gunner's boy has been brought before the Captain and
has confessed to the theft. He displays the same scorn for
punishment.
"Where is the money?" he was asked.
"I an't telling," was all he would say. "I an't never telling."
"Twelve lashes," was the verdict again, "and twelve again
tomorrow if he don't tell where the money is."
After the first twelve lashes, he was asked again.
"Where is the money?"
A shake of the head was the only answer, at which he was

carried below deck and his wounds swabbed – to no
purpose, I fear, because tomorrow it will happen all over
again.
I believe there is a demon in the boy that puts him beyond
our reach. He cannot help himself.

Martha put the diary aside at this point, feeling it was too
much for her. It was some days before she found the time to look
at the diary again.

"I'll skip a week or two, and see if things got better," she said
optimistically. She leafed forward, hoping to find the *Griffin* in
port somewhere. She found it anchored off Batavia, the capital of
Dutch Java.

May 1st

We are anchored in the Batavia road, I am happy to say. It
is our first sight of other creatures since the hawk landed
on our mast two weeks ago. The men fed it scraps,
thinking it would bring us luck, but two days ago it flew
off again. The men do not know whether to take this as a
good sign or not.

May 2nd

It seems we have to give profound thanks to good fortune
for the skills of our Captain. A Dutch captain came on
board and I was able to talk to him. He was in wonder that
Captain Dethick had safely negotiated the uncharted shores
of these islands without incident. I told him our course had
been as smooth as a trip down the Thames. Myneer
Verhulst said they have lost many vessels in this past year,
though he fears that many good men perish after they are
wrecked and get safely ashore. The peoples of these islands
are not always friendly. They do not see the advantages of
honest trade and kill strangers that land on their shores,
even through no fault of their own. It is mindful for us to

think what risks we run when we voyage to distant shores.

May 3rd

Captain Dethick advises against spending much time ashore as this is a very unhealthy place. However, I have had the good fortune to obtain some curious pieces of timber and am engaged in carving them into animal shapes. It is satisfying work.

The men are not permitted to go ashore. It is feared that they may run. Discontent simmers among the crew, I believe as much because of the way they are handled by the Mate. Captain Dethick is unwilling to give approval for women to be brought on board instead. He says it would lead to an unwholesome and degrading spectacle. The Captain is a very upright man.

"Prude!" thought Martha.

But on reflection, it must have been an awful choice for the captain: either let the men loose on the shore, where they would run riot and cause destruction and half of them might never be seen again. Or use the ship as a giant brothel.

"What an unnatural world a ship is!" thought Martha, "even with the best-intentioned captain."

She shuddered for the sensitive Edward.

May 4th
We have had more trouble with the men. Seaman James Murray has been brought before the Captain for attacking Mr Parslow, the Fifth Mate, and promising to kill him if he got a chance. He also struck Mr Hudson, the Chief Mate. It is as I feared with Mr Hudson in charge.
Murray has been clapped in irons while the Captain decides what to do with him.

May 5th
Overnight Murray escaped, taking the pinnace moored alongside. The Captain does not know how he undid his irons. Can it be that his fellows sympathised with Murray and helped him to escape?

May 7th
Captain Dethick has given up hope that Murray will be found. He has now gone ashore with the supracargoes.

May 22nd
The Delaware arrived yesterday. Captain Dethick rejoiced, thinking to see his good friend Abraham Dominicus again. Mr Dominicus was Chief Mate on our last voyage, and now his son Robert is with us as a midshipman.
Alas, the news is all bad. Mr Dominicus is dead, and the crew of the Delaware have suffered greatly from the scurvy. Captain Dethick is sorely affected by the news, I can tell, and has been very gruff with the men.
Our second carpenter Samuel Gregory is to go across to the Delaware as the ship has lost its own carpenter and cannot sail without one. As I have myself seen on my voyages, a carpenter is one of the chiefest of the crew. There is always work for him to do, especially after rough weather. If the mast breaks and cannot be repaired, we are lost.

Gregory was not too pleased at the promotion and asked to speak to the Captain. The Captain would not change his mind. He feels he has a duty to his dead friend.

The Captain is to go ashore with the supracargoes. They have been invited to stay with the Governor of Batavia, who is a very hospitable man, Myneer Verhulst told me. The Captain has told me I am to accompany him. I am very much determined to enjoy my visit to Batavia.

It will be a very short visit. We are due to sail in two days' time.

Martha turned over the next page. It was blank. There were no more entries. She leafed back, thinking to find some clue as to why the steward had stopped keeping his diary. There were none.

"Can he have run? Most unlikely. Not the sort of man to run. He was quite happy with his lot," she speculated. "Can it be there was some trickery ashore and he never came back on the ship?"

The possibility was too ghastly to consider. She had become very fond of her diarist. She pondered on other possibilities.

"Maybe he got involved in a fight in Batavia, defending the captain. In the fight, he broke his arm, and so couldn't write."

All pure guesswork. It was most upsetting. She had become too involved in the loquacious steward's account.

Dissatisfied, she put the diary in her bag and forgot about it.

"Martha, you're finishing at the library next week. Why don't you and I go to the *Griffin* exhibition next Saturday? You don't have to come, of course, but I'd love to go."

Martha had forgotten about the *Griffin*, but she knew all about her mother's fascination with chinaware. She thought for a moment. She might get a clue as to why Edward the steward's diary had stopped.

"Of course I'll come with you, Ma. Though I'm not promising I'll stay as long as you."

And so they went. Martha was surprised how much of an appetite for the exhibits she did have. The *Griffin* had sunk in the dangerous uncharted seas that Mijnheer Verhulst had shaken his head over. Captain Dethick and the crew had survived, but of course all the valuable cargo had been lost.

The underwater archaeologists had done a brilliant job in rescuing whole crates of things from the ship. A selection of these were beautifully displayed. Seeing them brought the whole story in the diary to life.The exhibition was full of fascinating details, including information about the lives and names of the crew.

It was one of these displays, taken from an earlier voyage, which arrested her attention just as she was ready to go. The display contained a contemporary illustration of some Europeans in a yawl being attacked by dark-skinned people of indeterminate race in another boat. A text from the ship's log accompanied it:

May 24th
1 p.m. Returned from Batavia with the supracargoes after a most agreeable visit to Government House. The Governor afforded us every courtesy. On our return, we were alarmed to find that our servants and the seamen with them were not aboard the ship. They went on ahead last night but did not arrive here. I have sent a boat ashore to make enquiries.

6 p.m. The boat has returned with distressing news. The officer found a servant who was in the boat last night. He reported that near midnight they were attacked by about ten people in a prow. Everyone in the boat was killed except him. He was able to escape only by feigning death. They took everything from our boat and scuttled her, so as to cover up their dastardly crime.
We have lost six good men. I regret to say my own steward Edward Beardmore was among them.
I shall be very pleased to leave this benighted shore.

Martha was stunned. So that was what all the hopes and expectations had come to! Instead of fascinating experiences coupled at the end with a profit that would give him and his family a comfortable existence, the luckless Edward had ended his existence at the bottom of a Malay harbour, murdered for a few pence.

She walked up and down the displays aimlessly, not seeing. Then slowly her eyes focused on another display in front of her.

It was a list of crew names. Her eye travelled down the list: John Read, ship's steward...died at St Helena. John Banton, bos'un's servant... drowned 5th August. Thomas Oldfield, captain's tailor... died 13th November. Edward Hugil, seaman... drowned 26th August...

Another voyage, other deaths. A commonplace, death.

She turned away. She had had enough for one day.

"Coming, Martha? I think I've seen everything I want."

"Yes, of course, Ma. Let's go."

They stepped outside. It was good to be alive.

On the bus, she took out the diary. As she did so, a piece of paper dropped out of it. She had not noticed it before. She unfolded it. It was written in an old, elegant script:

Dear Madam,

I have the honour to return the papers of your husband Edward Beardmore. He was a most valued member of our crew. I regret his death most deeply. Please accept my sincere condolences. Yrs etc. Th. Dethick, Captain.

Nice to know they valued him in his time. There've been many worse lives, she thought. Must return the diary to the library.

CHAPTER 20
VISITORS

"**W**e have visitors, Ted."

Ted lifted his head and screwed up his eyes, looking to the west.

"Hand me my field glasses, Natalie, would you?" he said.

"Here," said the third member of the party, Luis, who was nearer.

They did not say much, the three of them. Speaking was quite an effort in the extreme cold, and they always tried to conserve their energy.

"Strangers," said Ted, fiddling with the focus. "They have sails, I think. Or maybe it's a contraption from outer space."

"Tourists, maybe," said Luis hopefully. He liked the occasional change of company. Arctic explorers and scientists can get a bit intense.

"They may have a bit of walking to do," said Ted. "The ice is broken this side, but it looks solid further out. More ice than sea, I'd say."

"How can they do that in a boat?" asked Luis.

Ted put down his glasses and brushed some ice off his beard.

"Have to see. The sea'll have changed by tomorrow, I expect. It'll be frozen solid, or all water. They'll probably find a way through. We just can't see it from here.

He picked up his glasses again. In his mind, he was already busy imagining what the visitors looked like. He wondered if they had any problems.

"They must have come a long way," he said. "I wonder if they have enough food to get here."

"What time is it?"

"Nearly midnight."

"They'll be here tomorrow evening, I reckon," said Natalie dismissively. People she couldn't see didn't interest her.

Their little observation station consisted of a low wooden hut and a trio of tents, set up on the barren shores of a northern Canadian island within the Arctic Circle.

In front of the station, where they were standing, the icy easterly breezes blew a pattern of sharp ripples on the metallic blue of the sea channel. Beyond the navigable channel lay a solid strip of white. It stretched apparently unbroken to the horizon, a soft greyish streak that might have been sky or sea or land. Here and there, rougher, shadowy patches showed the existence of ice floes and small bergs.

"Time for me to turn in, I guess," said Ted.

"Yup. Busy day tomorrow, what with all these visitors."

He soon retired to his tent, which was hidden behind a rough wall made of blocks of ice, to protect it from the Arctic wind.

"Leave those boxes – I'll put them away," said Natalie. "I'll just take a breath of air, then I'll get down to those figures."

She followed Ted out of the door and stood outside, staring at the landscape. It was awe-inspiring, a symphony in grey and yellow major. Wonderful to look at, as the sun tinged the horizon. Not so wonderful to be in. Her face burned with stiffness.

She changed her mind and returned to the room and sat down. She bent to her figures.

When Ted reappeared at the flap of his tent, the contraption from outer space was near enough to show itself as a boat of sorts. At least, he could see it had bright red and green sails.

"Single mast, two sails, I'd say – genoa and mainsail, most probably."

He made a note in his log. He kept a strict log on everything he saw or that happened at the station. It was like a ship's log.

His attention was distracted by a call from Luis. Luis was a marine biologist, and was there to study the behaviour of white whales. He pointed to the sea channel in front of the station. Ted looked but could see nothing.

"Let's get the dinghy out and see if we can get closer this time," said Luis animatedly. "Look, there it is again."

This time, Ted caught sight of a whale blowing out in the channel, close to the ice edge. Or rather, he heard the distinctive sound of the blow, and then quickly located the source. Its gleaming white bulk broke the surface about a hundred yards away, moving slowly west. Shimmering white flashes beneath the surface indicated the presence of a small pod of perhaps five or six animals.

Every July, thousands of white whales head for the region of Somerset Island, where they stuff themselves with squid and cod and roll around in the shallow gravels of the inlets. The stones pull off the dirty old yellow skin and reveal the new glossy white skin underneath. It is a high point in the white whale social calendar.

"Probably a family. Some of them are calves."

Indeed, the brownish grey of two or three of them indicated quite young animals.

With all due stealth, Luis and Ted hastened to get the inflatable dinghy into the water. Unfortunately, the slight splashing of the first foot in the water sent the animals plunging out of sight. Sound carries for miles under water, and whales have an immensely keen sense of sound.

Luis grunted with annoyance and took his foot out of the water.

"Doesn't normally have that effect here," he said. "This water's quite deep. I must have dislodged something." He added, "I'll leave the boat here. I'll do a session out in the channel later."

"Sure," said Ted, his mind elsewhere. "Listen, I'm going to see if Natalie can locate them on the radio. They must be trying to call us."

"Who?" said Luis, his mind on the whales and his morning's work.

"Those people out there." He nodded in the direction of the red and green sails.

"Yeah. Why not? Invite 'em to supper," said Luis facetiously.

Ted looked at him suspiciously. He did not like being mocked.

"They may be in trouble," said Ted. "Broken a leg or something. That's no joke out on the ice."

He went back to his work, making a mental note to think about the matter later.

It was an hour or two before Ted got round to it. He hurried back to the prominence on which the permanent hut stood. Natalie was not there, so he started fiddling with the equipment himself. He was very keen on modern communications. However, not being very expert at using it, he was still at it when Natalie came in.

"Had enough of us, Ted?" she said good-humouredly. "Trying to get an airlift out? I bet you can't even find Resolute."

Resolute was the nearest settlement, permanently populated by some 170 residents who ignored them as much as possible.

As she spoke, Ted hopefully twiddled another knob he had not touched before. A sudden blare of raucous music filled the hut.

"Out of the way, Ted! You're way off course. What are you try-ing to find?"

"I thought maybe those poor souls out there on the ice would attempt to call us up. I mean, don't worry if you're too busy to rescue fellow creatures in difficulty."

Save us from Ted in his pathetic vein! thought Natalie.

"Why are they poor souls, Ted?" she asked with a kindly air. "I expect they like it out there. That's why they're doing it. Just like the other freaks that pass this way from time to time."

She watched Ted pick up the handbook to their sophisticated new radio equipment, and was struck by another thought.

"Have you checked recently to see if they're still heading this way? They may have a busy social diary and not be intending to visit us at all. Or they may have gone to dinner with a Polar bear."

Ted had not looked, of course. He flung out of the hut in a tem-per. The wide, white horizon was completely bare of human activity.

"Tcha!" said Ted.

The visitors arrived when they were not looking, of course. This was no mean feat, given that it was virtually impossible to hide anywhere in that bare, frozen land and seascape.

Ted was asleep, Natalie was hunched over her computer in the hut and Luis was out of sight behind a bluff. He had a hunch that a family of Polar bears were in residence on an island across the sound, and was awaiting a sighting. He suspected that the passing traffic in white whales heading for Somerset Island would be of more than little interest to the bears, who preyed on whales.

He was rewarded in an unexpected way. A loose ice floe appeared from behind the headland, moving slowly with the wind. On board was what appeared to be an ancient male bear. No doubt the bear did not intend to be aboard – that was just its bad luck. In front of it were the remains of some animal, so it was clearly a well-fed bear. There was so little left, it was impossible at a distance even to identify the species of the victim. It could even have been just seaweed, which bears eat when they cannot find meat.

The sight brought Luis to near frenzy, though to the outward eye he was the icy cool scientist.

He picked up his camera.

Natalie was stirred into action by the sound of strange voices outside. She got up and went to the door.

"Hi!" said a bearded stranger, some twenty paces down the slope. He was dressed from head to toe in green.

Natalie stepped outside and shut the door behind her, to keep the warmth inside.

The stranger attempted to beam, but his face was too frozen to allow more than a twitch at the corner of the mouth.

"I'm Vitus. That's Maarti."

He waved slightly behind him. By Arctic standards, it was an expansive movement. Natalie followed the direction of the gesture. There was no one else to be seen in any direction.

"Well, she's there somewhere. We've come several hundred

miles together, so I can't have lost her, can I?"

He continued twitching, looking expectantly at Natalie. An increasingly embarrassing silence was finally broken by a voice emerging from behind the hut.

"Hello!" said another frozen voice.

"Ah, there you are, Maarti. I thought for a moment the ice had devoured you. Maarti, this is ... uh ... ?"

He gestured at Natalie, who said,

"Natalie."

Maarti was dressed entirely in red. Evidently she and Vitus were a matching pair. As both were entirely wrapped in water-tight survival suits that left only their faces visible, the colours – and Vitus's beard – were the main means of identifying them.

"Sorry," said Maarti, her lips hardly moving. "I was thrilled by the local drama going on behind the hill. We've had wolves, and rabbits, and seals to deal with, but not Polar bears."

She nodded in the direction of Luis.

"Bears?" said Natalie. "We've never had bears round here. Luis! Luis! Where is that man? He won't want to miss this."

"I think you'll find he's there already," said Maarti.

"I must wake Ted," said Natalie. "I'm not sure I can cope with bears. Ted! Visitors!" she yelled.

"I think you'd better go and help your colleague behind the hill," said Maarti. "A full frontal face-off was on the point of developing."

"You're joking!" said Natalie, staring at Maarti. "I'd better get Ted. Ted! Ted!" she yelled again. "Bears!"

"The poor man will be having nightmares," murmured Vitus to Maarti. "Why don't we all go down?" he suggested aloud. "Polar bears do not attack humans unless very hungry or provoked, or are defending their cubs," he murmured to himself, quoting from his survival guide.

"What did you say?" asked Maarti.

When they rounded the bluff, the face-off was still in progress.

The stiff breeze down at the shore, which made the air temperature minus twenty or so, had brought the ice-floe within swimming distance of land. It was snagged on an underwater obstacle.

Despite the intense cold, Luis had put down his camera and was trying to terrify the ice-floe away by some kind of wild dance.

"Is this an Inuit bear ritual?" asked Vitus.

"Luis is Mexican," said Natalie, heading as fast as she could to the shore. "I don't think they have Polar bears in Mexico."

The bear appeared to find the dancing ritual embarrassing. It clearly wanted nothing better than to slither off the far side of the floe and vanish from sight. However, the nearest pack ice had considerably retreated out to sea since the day before and was now more than a mile off. A rather daunting prospect.

To Natalie, the bear's movements visibly indicated that it was injured or very infirm. Luis was obviously of the view that it represented a menace even so.

Just as the others came within hailing distance, he stopped still and waited. The reason for this soon became clear: the floe broke loose of the underwater obstacle and began to drift away from the shore again.

Luis picked up his camera.

"I'm not usually so inhospitable to passing visitors," he said cheerfully, "but I can't have my whales scared off. I see we have company. Hi! I'm Luis. You must be our long-awaited visitors."

He held out a hand in greeting to Vitus and Maarti.

"Wonderful!" said Vitus, putting down his knife and fork and belching with pleasure. "Real food. I can't stand the local offerings myself – sealmeat, squid, that sort of thing."

"What you been eating, then?" asked Ted.

"Frozen dishes which we heated up, dried fruit, and so forth. It's not the same as real cooking."

Natalie, who had been brought up in Montreal, grimaced. The rough food they were eating was hardly 'real cooking'.

Over the meal of beef and peas, Vitus and Maarti had related the tale of their trip across the North-West Passage. They were promoting a new type of catamaran, but the trip had been dogged by ill fortune. The helicopter that was to track them had broken down two days into the trip, and another was not available at short notice. In any case, it was only due to follow them from time to time, to make advertising shots.

Then a bag of food had mysteriously disappeared after they had unloaded the boat in order to repair some holes. Maarti was convinced it was an Arctic wolf that had made off with the bag.

"I hope it choked on the plastic," she said with animosity.

"So why didn't you let us know you were coming?" asked Ted. "I mean, we saw you yesterday. I was very concerned about you – thought maybe you'd had an accident or something. There were hours when you seemed to be getting no nearer."

Vitus laughed.

"Yeah, well, that was probably when we were dragging the boat over the ice. Seemed to us at the time like we were getting nowhere, too. I guess we dragged it a couple of miles or so yesterday. Here, look."

He showed them blisters on his hands from the tow lines.

"How much does it weigh, your boat?"

" 'Bout 400 pounds. 600 or so with everything aboard. It slides fairly easily, but it don't do your hands any good."

"Vitus even rigged up a crow's nest, to see if could see the end of the ice," said Maarti. "I begged him to come down. He could have fallen and broken his leg."

Luis looked incredulously at the frail craft down on the shore. It seemed unlikely anyone could even stand on the twin hulls, let alone hoist himself aloft in the riggings.

"True, though," said Maarti with a laugh, noting his sceptical look. "He rigged up a sling."

"So why didn't you let us know you were coming?" persisted Ted. "We live in the age of communications, for God's sake."

"Yup, we certainly do," said Vitus tersely. "We had a battery problem, then lost our spares. Also, there's something else wrong with the radio, I can't figure out what."

"Scary, that," said Ted, shaking his head profoundly. "I mean, being out there and unable to touch base with the world. Communicate or die, that's how it is out here."

Ted's pessimism is more than a little oppressive at times, thought Natalie.

"Maybe I can do something about the radio," she said. "We've got some spares. I'll have a look at it when you've had a rest, see what we can come up with."

Vitus and Maarti apparently needed only five hours' sleep, and were no sooner up and breakfasted than they were pressing Luis to take them somewhere where they might see a white whale.

Over breakfast, they had been regaled with Luis's recordings of white whale sounds. An extraordinary concerto of whistles, creaks, trills, flaps, clicks and birdsong poured out of the speaker.

"Sea canaries, the whalers used to call them," said Luis.

"I've been nagging Vitus all the way, we must get a picture of a beluga," said Maarti. "My boy's mad on them. He says they're brighter and more fun than humans. In his view, a world full of whales would be a deal more fun than Toronto. I have to take a photo back to prove I've seen one in the wild."

"Shouldn't be too much trouble," said Luis. "We had a pod pass us yesterday, only they didn't stop for coffee. I admit, I took it amiss. You want your friends to drop in when you live in a place

like this. Not that we're short of company – it's kinda like Times Square here, the number of visitors we get."

Vitus was unembarrassed.

"So where do we get to see these belugas?" he said briskly.

"We'll get the dinghy out and go round to the river inlet, see what's new round there," said Luis. "The whales often call in on us there, we've got some mighty fine squid that side."

"Tell you what, Vitus," said Natalie, "I'll try to fix that radio while you're away with Luis."

And so it was agreed.

The whale chase was exceptionally successful. Not only did a solitary beluga suddenly pop its head out of the water to have a look the strange rubber craft – spy-hopping, as it is known – but they also came across a young female stranded by the tide in the shallow waters of the river inlet. The whale was absolutely still when they reached it.

"Hold it, hold it!" breathed Maarti excitedly when she saw it. "Don't move, please, dear almost white whale. I must get my camera out."

"Don't worry, she won't move one inch," said Luis. "It might attract the attention of our ageing friend the Polar bear I sent on his way yesterday."

They circled round the whale and beached the boat on the stony gravel. Luis got out into the sea and scrutinised the young whale.

"I don't know, though. Maybe the three of us could just about move it back into the deeper water."

Maarti sucked her breath in as she put a foot gingerly into the icy water.

"How can you bear it, Luis?"

"A shock, huh? Think noble thoughts. Think of the glorious beast you are going to help to freedom."

Vitus waited until Maarti had both her feet in the water before he even set a toe in it. Maarti turned round and saw him hovering.

"Get your feet in that water or I'll take a picture of you and send it to all your friends," she said in high dudgeon.

Luis approached the animal carefully, but if it was alarmed, it showed no signs of it. He bent over it and tagged its back with identification patches of green and red, in honour of the visitors.

"Great," he said. "This is terrific. I've been able to tag very few specimens this year. Right. C'mon. You two take the tail, I'll take the head."

With a great deal of effort, they were able to get the animal back into deeper water. It swam off in great indignation.

"Could have done it myself, if you'd've let me," proclaimed the magnificent tail as it splashed out of sight finally.

Maarti devoted a whole reel of film to the occasion.

"Bobby will go spare when he sees these," she said. She rewound the film and took it out.

"Hey, Luis, you got a pocket there? Can you carry this till we get back to base? I don't want it to get wet."

They returned exhilarated, to find Natalie had given up on the radio.

"It's missing something vital," she said. "It must be a Friday machine. Look, why don't you borrow our old radio? It works, only it's a special adapted model. I'll write out some notes about how to use it."

Within the hour, the red and green catamaran was on its way again.

"Thanks for the radio!" called Vitus as they pushed off from the shore.

"Bye!" said Natalie. "Bon voyage! Let's hear from you when you arrive. Send the radio back to the Institute in Toronto. It belongs to them."

Ted watched them go with great satisfaction, pleased to have communicated so well.

"Great people," he said to Luis. "That's what makes living today so satisfying. People crisscross your life in a busy place like this and you hit it off. Instantly. I like that."

Two hours later, he went out to monitor their progress again.

The red and green sails were a speck on the horizon. He grunted, and went inside again. Time to go and monitor one of his test stations. He put on Luis's coat, which had pockets for carrying samples. He felt in the pocket for the pencil which was always there. His fumbling hands came out with a roll of film.

He called over to Luis, who was working at his computer.

"Hey, Luis, this yours?"

Luis looked up, paused a minute, then let out a suppressed oath.

"Something wrong?" asked Ted.

"It's Maarti's," said Luis, "the pictures she took for her son. She'll kill me for not giving it to her before she left."

"How's she gonna do that?" said Ted. "She's gone. You'll have to send it to her."

Luis thought for a minute.

"Yeah," he said, "I'll send it to her, only I don't know her name or where she lives."

"Call her on the radio," said Ted.

"Natalie," called Luis, "can you call Maarti and Vitus, tell them they've left a roll of film behind and ask them where we should send it."

Natalie rummaged in her drawer.

"Sure, just let me find the handbook for the old radio."

She pulled open the drawer. There on top was a piece of paper.

"Luis," she croaked. "Come and tell me what you see here."

Luis went over.

It was Natalie's instructions for using the old radio.

At the end of the season, as the long Arctic summer drew to a close, Luis, Ted and Natalie passed through Resolute on their way back to Toronto. They called at the mail office to check out, leave a forwarding address.

"This yours?" asked the man behind the counter.

It was postcard from Montreal, sent about two weeks earlier.

Hi, Natalie, Luis, Ted! Great to meet you. Thanks for the hospitality, I thought we communicated really well. Nice radio – we managed to speak to the Canadian embassy in Moscow on it. See you again sometime. V + M

PS You can have the radio back when you let me have the roll of film. I'll send you a print of any nice belugas. Ciao!

"She's forgotten to write their address," said Ted.

CHAPTER 21
A DATE WITH DESTINY

The Douglas Dauntless rumbled down the long deck of the aircraft carrier *USS Enterprise*, engine roaring. Its progress seemed agonizingly slow.

The plane reached the critical point of no return. The pilot, Captain Jim Lengel, glanced anxiously at the speedo. Barely 60 knots.

Must be something wrong. The engine was not supplying full power.

He glanced down at the controls. Too late to do anything.

He raised his head and stared at the runway fast disappearing under him. Nothing to be done. Just carry on and hope for the best.

"We're not going to make it," he said aloud. "Goodbye, folks. This is the end."

He wondered if he was sweating.

His gunner, Private Marvin Beck, nodded and said nothing. He was sitting behind in a separate cockpit and could not make out Lengel's words above the engine roar.

A hundred yards.

Fifty yards.

Twenty-five yards.

The Dauntless lurched over the end of the carrier at about 75 knots, weighed down by a single 500 lb bomb and full load of fuel. Firm metal gave way to grey, choppy sea, producing a sudden sickening drop in the stomach. It felt like the first time he'd ever done it.

Instinctively he pulled sharply at the joystick. Instead of producing the usual kick of power as it left the deck, the aircraft responded in a sagging arc as it finally picked up a stiffer breeze over the water. All too slowly, the sea gradually receded.

He breathed out. They were airborne.

Lengel hummed tunelessly, as he always did while flying. He was in his element. He felt at home in the air, and fretted while on board the carrier.

He looked across to the right. Two other members of the squadron were visible, peeling off ahead of him. He followed them up into a calm blue sky flecked by just a few white clouds. It was perfect flying weather.

They circled, waiting for the whole squadron to come up. Thousands of feet below, the *Enterprise* looked like a grey slug leaving a trail of white.

———————

It was June 1942 and the United States Navy was at bay.

With single-minded determination, for years now the Japanese had been preparing to extend their empire and gain complete control of eastern Asia and the Pacific Ocean.

It was no sudden idea. The strategy was worked out long before the Second World War began. In fact, the Japanese had been actively developing their Navy for seventy years. The results were formidable. The Imperial Navy was determined that its forces should become better than the best.

By 1941, the Japanese were ready to conquer the world. Germany and Italy had shown that might was right – a well-oiled military machine could really do what it liked with weaker countries.

The Japanese plan was breathtaking in its audacity. The aim was to knock out the US Pacific Fleet before it could interfere in the Japanese takeover of the Pacific.

On Sunday, 7 December they launched a massive surprise attack on Pearl Harbor, in Hawaii, where the main part of the US Pacific Fleet was stationed. The US was not at war with Japan at the time.

Hawaii is almost at the centre of the Pacific. Sunday was chosen because it was a day of rest. No one was on the alert, planes and ammunition were put away for the day, the naval and air crews were enjoying a day off.

At 7.55 in the morning, the first wave of Imperial aircraft reached Pearl Harbor and began an attack of unprecedented ferocity. The Imperial force included 43 fighters, 51 bombers, 49 dive-bombers and 40 torpedo bombers.

Half an hour later, the attack was over. The effects were devastating and visible for all to see. Pearl Harbor was a shambles. Five US capital ships had been sunk, eight cruisers or destroyers had been knocked out, the navy yard and airfield had been disabled, 106 out of 228 aircraft were destroyed and nearly 2,500 US servicemen were lying dead.

The surprise had been total. Complacent in its assumed peace, America was stunned.

The shock became almost paralysis when, two days later, the Japanese launched a second lightning attack on Manila, in the Philippines. They destroyed half the US aircraft fleet, bombed the navy yard to bits and sank more ships.

The US was well and truly dragged into the war. It had no choice, but it was not prepared.

The only surviving obstacles to total Japanese domination of the eastern hemisphere were four US aircraft carriers which had not been blown to bits in Pearl Harbor. One of these, the *Lexington*, was sunk in the Coral Sea as the US tried to hold up the Japanese advance on New Guinea and Australia.

That left just three carriers and their fleet of aircraft, to stop the Imperial Japanese war machine achieving its next target: to occupy Midway Island and knock out the US Pacific Fleet once and for all.

The US island of Midway guarded the other end of the Hawaii chain of islands. It was 1000 miles nearer Japan, and would provide Japan with a land base to occupy Hawaii. Hawaii already had a large population of Japanese ...

It was a day of destiny for the US and the whole world.

It was a good thing that Jim Lengel and Marvin Beck did not know how much depended on them and their colleagues when they took off from the *Enterprise*. They might have thought the task hopeless.

But probably they would have taken off just the same. They were like that.

Gradually Bombing Squadron 6 assembled in attack formation. The crews of the next planes were close enough to identify. Lengel signalled by hand to his neighbour. They could not use radio.

It was hardly a world-beating force, consisting of thirty-seven dive-bombers.

"Numbers aren't everything," thought Lengel. "Sure does help if there's a lot of us, though."

It felt quite a crowd, from his seat. Comforting feeling, that.

The radio crackled into life. "Bogey carriers reported bearing 320 degrees distant 180 miles course 135 degrees speed 25 knots," came the dry tones.

Bombing Squadron 6's task was to dive bomb the carriers. That meant flying steeply into the attack over the enemy, straightening out at the last minute to fly over the ship, dropping the bomb and peeling off smartly heading for the sky and home.

If you could avoid the Zero fighters that buzzed around the carriers and the anti-aircraft guns whose sole aim was to drop you in the sea. No easy task, given that the Zeroes were much nippier than the Dauntless.

"How many carriers are there?" came Beck's voice over the intercom. He was young, and sounded anxious.

"Dunno. Two, three, maybe," said Lengel. He thought about the announcement he'd just heard. "They can only be heading for Midway, on that course."

It was always a guess, trying to figure out what the enemy intended to do. The Japanese were prepared, as usual. They knew what they wanted.

Lengel looked at the sea below. It stretched 50 miles to an almost cloudless horizon. It was cool and fresh, a day for clear thinking. There was not a ship in sight, but the Japanese were out there somewhere. This was a war where enemies did not see each other until the last minute, when black death fell abruptly out of a clear sky.

He looked down. The sea was a patchwork of blue on blue.

"Jenny's got a shirt that colour."

Jenny was his long-standing girl. Her father was something big in the Navy back home, top secret, Jenny never would say what.

He was glad he was not one of the top brass. It was their job to worry that the Japanese had occupied the whole of the Dutch East Indies and Burma, beaten the British and Dutch navies out of the Far East and virtually wiped out the European colonies in eastern Asia. They were ready to advance on Australia and India.

It was their job to worry that they only had three aircraft carriers to stop the Japs, and that their planes and weapons were not up to Japanese standards.

His job was to worry about Midway.

"No way are they going to get there, if I have anything to do with it," he told himself grimly. "Just a little bit of luck and a lot of TNT when we get to the contact point."

―――――

Had Lengel known what had happened to the earlier American Dauntless bombers sent out from the *Enterprise* and its sister carrier *Hornet*, he might have swapped the quantities of luck and TNT.

When they got to the contact point an hour or so earlier, where the enemy fleet was supposed to be, the *Hornet* aircraft had found empty sea. The Japanese fleet had changed course.

Frustrated, the *Hornet* dive-bomber squadrons had headed south to search the seas in the direction of Midway, over 100 miles away. They thought the Japanese fleet must have gone that way. That must be their target.

It was the only guess the *Hornet* squadron could make. They could hardly comb thousands of square miles of sea looking for ships.

Soon fuel started to run short. Fifteen bombers made it to Midway, the rest headed back for the mother ships. The escorting Wildcat fighters were less lucky: they ran out of fuel very quickly, and all of them crashed at sea.

It had apparently been a wasteful, pointless trip.

"What d'ya make the time?" asked Lengel.

"We been running nearly two hours, I'd say," came Beck's voice down the intercom. "Shouldn't we see something by now?"

"Yeah, sure we should. Quarter hour to contact time."

They lapsed into silence, and let the engine do the talking.

"Funny thing. We haven't seen a single Val or Zero. You'd think they'd be up here looking for us. Are we that invisible?" said Beck, still anxious. He wasn't flying the plane, and had more time to worry.

"Maybe," said Lengel, who had been wondering the same thing but did not want to alarm his young gunner. "Dumb thing worrying about what we can't see, though."

Vals were the Japanese equivalent of the Dauntless. Both they and the Zeroes were much faster than the US planes.

"Yeah," said Beck. He sounded none too convinced. "You think Jeff knows where he's going?"

Jeff was what they called the squadron leader. He was a man they greatly admired.

"Nope. I reckon we're lost."

"It's nearly contact time."

"Yeah."

"What the heck...?" muttered Lengel a few minutes later.

"What's up?" came the crackling voice from behind.

"Jeff's just wiggled."

The squadron leader wiggled his wings to indicate to the squadron: follow me.

"Can't see what he's seen. Maybe we're just gonna look somewhere else..."

"What's that down there?"

"Hell!"

Even at 12,000 feet, the outline of a single destroyer was clearly visible. They stared at it, mesmerized.

All at once, the adrenalin started pumping through their systems and they came alive. It was as though they had been asleep for the last hour or two.

"Making some speed. Look at that wake!"

That was what had caught the squadron leader's attention. The Japanese destroyer was travelling full out.

"Must be heading to join the rest of 'em."

"That's my reckoning too."

As if to second their thoughts, the squadron leader had taken them round in a loop to head in the direction indicated by the wake of the destroyer.

The destroyer was the *Arashi*, which had spun off from the rest of the Japanese attack fleet to deal with an American submarine that had accidentally strayed in the fleet's path. The submarine had escaped the *Arashi*'s depth charges, but the *Arashi* was not to know that. The destroyer was now desperately trying to catch up, and was generating an extraordinary amount of foam.

Such are the chances of war. The Japanese ship had shown them where to find their target.

The aircraft ahead of him peeled off abruptly to starboard. Lengel followed suit smartly. It was an automatic reaction. He almost jumped out of his skin when, a moment later, the radio suddenly broke into life.

"Enemy carriers in circular disposition fifteen miles ahead, steaming north-west."

He focused his gaze, raking the rippled sea.

There they were, three carriers. How come he hadn't noticed? His mind had been on another planet, that's how.

Despite the tension that had gripped him, Lengel found his brain coolly analysing what he saw.

It was not the neat, tidy fleet formation he had been led to expect and which would have been the best defensive formation.

Two of the carriers were closer together, the third was several miles away. Were there more?

He scanned the horizon. Another large grey splodge a long way off. A fourth carrier. Some organization! It must be out of sight of the main fleet. What were they up to?

"Zeroes!"

It was Beck behind him who noticed them. From 12,000 feet, they looked like insects zuzzing in irritation just above the water.

"There's more on deck."

It was a perfect set-up for a dive-bomber. An apparently surprised, disordered enemy, most escort fighters not even in the air and a clean run at the target – if they could avoid the AA guns.

Without thinking, Lengel let out a whoopee of delight that even Beck could hear.

Lengel and Beck were not to know that they had benefited from the fruitless attack by the *Hornet* squadron earlier. Although little damage had been done to the Japanese fleet, the ships had scattered in order to avoid being hit by the torpedo bombers. A defensive ship twists and turns to prevent a bomber getting into firing position.

What next?

"Attack two carriers to port," said Jeff on the 'phones. He might have been reading a menu, so dispassionate did he sound.

Lengel took a quick glance at the target. Could they have been seen from the carriers? Zeroes were being scrambled from the deck.

Had they been down there, they'd have heard Admiral Nagumo, in charge of the Japanese fleet, issuing the order for take-off not five minutes earlier. The first of the fleet's 93 aircraft were just taxing to the start. The destruction machine was ready for action, to crush the remains of the American fleet once and for all.

In ten minutes, the Japanese fleet would be on its way, ruthlessly hunting down the *Enterprise*, *Hornet* and *Yorktown*. In two or three hours, the war in the Pacific could be over.

It was the moment of destiny.

The American planes dropped out the sky, in neat order. The sharp change of altitude brought a new surge of adrenalin to Lengel's brain. He felt a tightness at the pit of his stomach.

As they lost height, the target began to swell and take on individual features. Before long, their arrival triggered off a visible

surge of activity on board the ship. Puffs of light smoke indicated that the Japanese AA guns were firing. Soon he could pick out individual people scurrying back and forth on deck.

There was a rat-tat-tat from somewhere close at hand. It was their own gun. Beck was firing at Zeroes that had managed to climb from sea-level and were indulging in elaborate aerobatic manoeuvres somewhere above them. He caught sight of one rolling overhead.

"What the hell are they up to?" Lengel's brain wondered briefly. Maybe the ghost of the Red Baron had come back to teach them. Or was this a cat and mouse game with a scorned enemy?

His attention was diverted. A Dauntless to the right of him was hit from close range, caught fire and went spinning out of control. He stared dispassionately after it. "Tough luck," he thought. "Wonder who it was."

A hail of bullets hit his own plane as they levelled out in a circle round the plane. It was not time for the big dive yet. They had to wait their turn to go in and drop.

Their own gun had fallen silent. Lengel picked up his intercom and shouted to Beck.

"What we doing, then? Where are we?"

"Gun's jammed," was the terse reply.

"Jesus Christ!" thought Lengel. "Just when we need it."

He took a deep breath and held steady.

"Just point it at them!" he screamed to the invisible Beck. "Look busy!"

He had completed a circle round the target. All at once, the

Dauntless two ahead of him went crazy. It jerked sideways and zoomed skyward at an unnatural angle, leaving a trail of grey-black smoke as it vanished from sight somewhere above him.

True to its name, the following Dauntless held its course, then peeled off smartly to port and dropped into the void. Thousands of feet to be covered in seconds.

"We're next."

He mouthed the words silently. His mind seemed to be focusing on both his predecessors.

Without even consciously deciding the moment had come, he dipped his wings and headed for the bright yellow deck of the carrier. In the middle of it was a huge orange circle. It loomed larger and larger as he headed straight for it, picking up speed as he dived. Wisps of thought raced across his brain like tracer bullets.

The rising sun.

Target practice. A bull's eye. Pow!

More bullets buried themselves in his fuselage. He was being followed. Another shower of lead. Down, down!

He was almost buried in orange. Nightmare!

He pulled back the lever. The plane responded. At least the controls had not been hit. The nose lifted and they zoomed over the bright deck and out over the sea.

As he gained height, Lengel turned to look back. Did he hit the target? Had he even dropped the bomb?

He felt for the bomb release. Must have done. Don't know when.

He turned to more pressing matters.

Must keep low, to stop the Zeroes getting under us.

There was dark cloud of smoke over the carrier he had just left. Can't worry about that now, he thought.

Funny, that. Come all this way to do something, and you've no time to think about it when you get there.

There was a burst of fire from an unseen Zero, then a shout of pain from behind him. He grabbed the phone.

"You OK?"

"I been hit," said Beck.

"Bad?"

There was a pause.

"My arm. Can't do anything anyway. All the instruments are gone as well."

"Here too," said Lengel. "Leakier than a sieve up this end."

It was meant as a joke, but neither of them laughed.

"Can you hold on?" he asked presently.

"Sure," said Beck.

A fine kid, thought Lengel. Nothing I can do anyway.

He made to wipe sweat from his eyes. When he brought his arm down again, his wrist was covered with blood. It was blood, not sweat, trickling over his eyes.

"This is it," he thought. "I'm dying. This is really it. This is goodbye."

A feeling of faintness washed over him.

The next few minutes were like a film. He sat and watched events as if they did not involve him.

Another Zero crossed his vision, the sound of bullets whistled close by, then he heard his own engine cut out.

"Lengel's going to ditch," he thought. "Lengel's last landing." Sounded like a good title for a book.

The Dauntless started losing height fast. The pilot turned the nose down in preparation for landing on the sea.

"Must have shot away the fuelpipe," the cool spectator in him thought. "The fool hasn't tried the other tank. That'll be the end of the movie."

He lifted his head and tried to concentrate on what was happening outside, in another cinema. The

Zeroes seemed to be withdrawing.

"Perhaps they think it's the end, too," he said aloud. There could be no other explanation as they headed off looking for other prey. Lengel the spectator watched them go. Marvelous technique they had – shame they were Japs.

He turned back to see what was happening to the pilot in the first film.

Maybe he was not such a fool after all, this Lengel guy. He was manipulating the pressure pump from the other tank. Good thinking, man!

There was a brief cough from the engine and all at once it surged into life with a terrific vibration.

The film was not finished. The stricken Dauntless started to climb. It roared and whistled away from the sea and soon vanished in a patch of cloud.

What's the next scene? wondered Lengel the spectator.

Somewhere in the cloud, Lengel rejoined his body. When the plane emerged on the other side, he was staring at his instruments, pondering what to do. The control instruments were shot away, though the gas gauge seemed to be working.

The next scene was finding the way home.

He fiddled with the radio, addressed it several times. He shook it, tapped it, swore at it.

"Goddam thing!"

Eventually he found himself yelling at the top of his voice, as if to make himself heard in Midway. He thumped the fuselage viciously, and in his carelessness cut his arm on a sharp metal edge where a bullet had passed through.

Stupid thing to do. Blood started welling up on his arm.

He put his hand up to his head. The hair was tangled and caked with dried blood. At least the bleeding had stopped there.

What was he trying to do? Can't remember... ah yes, finding the way home. Where's home? Can't remember.

He scanned the horizon, hoping to see fellow Dauntlesses or even a friendly ship, someone to follow back home. Wherever that is.

Nothing.

He dipped below the cloud layer, which had appeared from nowhere. Possibly someone coming up behind?

Nothing. They were alone. He sat sullenly wondering what to do. He was not even sure they were heading in the right direction.

"You OK?" he called through the intercom. Silence from Beck.

That was dead, too. Maybe Beck was dead as well. He hadn't said anything when he'd been yelling his head off down the radio earlier. Usually they could hear each other if they shouted.

"Head for Midway, that's it," he thought. "No hope of finding the *Enterprise* without instruments or radio."

He hoped Midway was in the direction they were heading.

The plane droned on. Several times he looked down at his hands and wondered whose hands they were. Jenny always said he had such long, elegant fingers. Who's Jenny?

Couldn't be his, these gnarled joints stiff with pain and swelling. When did they get hit?

Hours later, or so it seemed, there was a noise behind him. Beck was alive, and trying to draw his attention.

Painfully, Lengel turned to look in the direction where Beck was pointing.

There was a small patch of green below, with a reef visible beyond it. He'd guessed right! That must be home.

He started to make his descent, then leveled out sharply when he saw that they were approaching just a small island where it would be impossible to land.

"Stupid, stupid!"

He pulled back and started to climb. A glance at the gas gauge told him they had enough fuel for perhaps another half an hour.

Half an hour passed. He could feel the acid burning in his stomach as the tension got to him. He'd have to ditch in the sea – there was nowhere else to land.

He consoled himself. They'd be all right. They'd survive the landing, get out of the plane before it sank, get the life raft out and hope someone would see them.

He began to worry. How long could they survive in the water?

The Dauntless lost height, and sank into the cloud. The feeling of detachment swept over him again and he waited for Lengel to say something. Lengel mouthed but said nothing. Silent actor.

The gas gauge showed zero.

———————

All of a sudden he was jerked back into himself as they drifted below the cloud layer. There directly below him, looking like a moth, was one of his own squadron. He recognized the markings.

He could not believe it. He stared. This must be a scene from a different film. Then he shook his head abruptly.

"I must be losing my wits. Get down."

He started an immediate descent, then pulled up quickly as he realized that he might be taken for an enemy and fired at.

With an anxious eye on the gas gauge, he turned into a slow circle to show the white stars on his wings, then slotted in beside the Dauntless. He made the thumbs-up sign to the other pilot, and dropped behind, content to follow.

The horizon came up before his eyes. A pall of smoke lay ahead.

It was Midway, burning from the fires started by the Japanese attack in the very early morning.

That was a century ago, this morning. The dazed feeling began to return. He was beginning to lose consciousness.

Then, without warning the runway was ahead.

A shot of adrenalin brought him back awake. He opened the doors to let the wheels down. No pressure there. He hoped the wheels stayed firm. Flaps down.

No flaps. No pressure. Nothing to slow me down.

The Dauntless screamed on to the tarmac too fast, lurched as a tire collapsed, started to wobble badly, then recovered as Lengel jerked at the controls savagely. They bumped forward for a few hundred yards, then ground to a halt.

The engine spluttered and died. The fuel tank was empty.

"Quite the hero," said a voice somewhere above him.

The speaker's face was grossly distorted, like a face in a cracked mirror. Lengel shut his eyes and opened them again. It was a medic in a rumpled white coat.

He was in an improvised hospital ward. The regular hospital had been bombed.

"How's Beck?" he croaked.

"He's OK," said Beck, somewhere of sight, painfully. The boy was lying in a bed nearby.

"We did all right, didn't we, kid?" said Lengel, with a frozen grin. "Showed them a thing or two."

He tried to prop himself up and look round. He couldn't. A question buzzed round and round inside his head, but he could not remember what it was.

"It'll come to me," he murmured.

It came to him before he drifted off again.

"We still have a navy?" he asked.

The medic bent over to hear him.

"Sure, captain," he said. "We still have a navy. That's more 'n the Japs can say right now."

Lengel lapsed into slumber, seeing patchworks of vivid blue and orange.

CHAPTER 22

THE PEARL DIVER

Tasman was too shy to say anything to the strange woman. She stood beside him on the beach, in the shadow of a beached prahu, asking him questions in a language he did not understand.

Despite the shyness, the admiration was mutual.

She thought he was exotic because of what he was about to do. A wiry boy, he was clutching a battered diving helmet borrowed from the nearby oyster lugger. He was – she understood – about to make his first deep dive. So much the guide had gathered, with his smattering of the island language.

He thought she was exotic because of her clothes, bright red mouth and thick sunglasses. In fact, she was wearing a smart blouse and jeans, but the lipstick was a bit overdone for the beach.

Most of all, it was the the pearl on her crucifix that fascinated him. As she bent over to talk to him, the crucifix dangled away from her neck. He could have reached out and pulled it. It was not like the pearls he had seen, but it was there right in front of him. He gazed at it.

Pearls were the core of his existence, though he had hardly seen one to handle.

When a pearl was found on the reef by one of the divers, it rarely stayed in the hand long. It represented income, and was sold. Anyone lucky enough to find a pearl might become a rich man.

"He doesn't understand a word you're saying, Myrtle," said the woman's companion. "C'mon, let's wait for him to get diving. You're just holding him up. I wanna get some reel in the can."

He waved his camcorder.

"I just wanna know what his name is, Abel, so I can tell the Junior League when I get back home."

"Aw. Make somp'n up. No one'll know."

Tasman would have been amazed to learn that a group of young women in Philadelphia would have been interested in his name, even if he knew where Philadelphia was.

Myrtle smiled encouragingly at him, making a lot of gestures at him which were equally mystifying. She kept pointing at his helmet and waving her hands beside her head.

"Abel, he won't put his helmet on, so I can take a photo. You tell him – he'll listen to you. You've a louder voice."

"Honey, I just want some diving reel in the camcorder, so we can tell 'em back home we've seen a pearl diver at work."

"Abel, that boy is not going to go diving here on the beach, use your brain! He's gonna get on that boat there and go out of sight to do it, so we gotta get some footage of him in his helmet right here. OK? That's my thinking."

Abel sighed, gently took the helmet from Tasman and placed it on his head. Tasman would not let it down over his head, so Abel took his footage with it perched on top, like a grotesque cap.

The film was in the can, so to speak.

Tasman gathered that the interview was now over. They parted with goodwill and total misunderstanding.

Myrtle and Abel wandered off, pleased with their trophy. They were not the sort of people to hire a boat to go out and watch a dive take place. Moreover, they did not have the time. The tour only allowed one hour for this village.

In any case, there was a more promising group of exotic locals further down the beach, wearing feathers and beads.

Tasman's life was not at all exotic. It was hard and confined. He had never been out of his village. His elder brother and father worked as divers for the oyster luggers, though the father was about to give up because his success rate was too low. Tasman was due to take his place.

Tasman looked at his father standing impatiently by the lugger, waiting for him. He was bent double. His brother was beside him, laughing and still erect. Tasman was not looking forward to his first deep dive.

He scrambled aboard for his first trip as a professional diver.

"How was the little diver?" said Bob. He had come along with the Philadelphia tourist group because there was transport available. "Did you get your shots?"

"No," said Abel. "Myrtle wanted me to film some of the local big noises. Gorgeous outfits they had."

He lowered his voice to a confidential murmur.

"The thing was, the boy didn't tumble to what Myrtle wanted. Seemed a bit slow on the uptake, to be frank," he said.

Bob looked sceptical, and changed the subject. He doubted that Myrtle could make anything clear, even in English. As US tourist groups went, the Philadelphia party ranked fairly low in his sophistication ratings.

———————

The tourists departed. Bob sighed with relief, thinking he could now get on with his work. He was writing a travel guide to the islands, and had come with his co-author Mansur to do on-the-spot research. He really enjoyed this part. The writing he could take or leave, and often did leave. That's why he often had no money in his pocket.

The idea of the little diver had stuck in his mind as unsettled business.

The next morning he challenged Mansur over breakfast.

"You speak the local dialect, Mansur. Can we go and see what we can find out about the oyster divers? I think there may be a story there."

"Sure," said Mansur, American college-trained and prolific in many languages. "I don't think you'll get much. These people are very reticent."

What he meant was, please don't let's ask them questions. I'd rather sit on the beach today.

They encountered Tasman on the edge of the beach, heading for the lugger. Tasman shook his head at Mansur's question and continued on his way. They watched him run down to the boat and clamber aboard. His run seemed lopsided, painful.

"Has he hurt himself?" asked Bob. "What did you say to him?"

"I just said, can we ask some questions," said Mansur. "I don't think he's bubbling with enthusiasm about anything at the moment. Maybe he hasn't hurt himself, maybe he just doesn't like diving."

"Can we find out when they are due back from the dive?" said Bob. "Perhaps he'll be in a better mood then."

They made their way down to the shore.

There, all was a-bustle on the wooden deck. Mansur put his hand on the flat wooden rail surrounding it and beckoned to the nearest villager aboard. The man stooped to listen - Mansur's head hardly reached up to the rail.

A conversation followed that Bob could not hear, then Mansur looked enquiringly at the sailor. The sailor nodded.

"OK?" said Bob.

"Come back later, he says," said Mansur.

"When's that?"

"He didn't say."

They were back later in the day, guessing when the lugger would return. They almost got it right. They met Tasman returning home.

He had not been diving more than a short time, Mansur gathered, but had been helping with the work on the deck most of the day.

Mansur asked him how his day had been. Tasman opened his palm, grinning shyly. A tiny pearl glistened wetly on his hand.

"Is that worth anything?" asked Bob.

"I doubt it," said Mansur, "but it obviously tickles him pink. I think, in his position, it would give me a kick too."

Bob felt something of an outsider in the conversation that followed, and contained his impatience to have everything translated for him. It was only after a series of exchanges that he felt able to break in.

"C'mon, now, Mansur, let's have it! What's he been saying?"

Mansur smiled.

"There you see one happy boy, at least for today. He said yesterday was dreadful, which was why he didn't want to talk to us this morning, but today he found a pearl. This is astounding, unbelievable, he says. His brother has not found one at all yet, in twelve months."

"It's a very little pearl," said Bob. "Almost a fragment."

"Don't be negative," said Mansur. "Apparently only one in every 50,000 shells contains a pearl."

"Uhuh. So what are they looking for?" asked Bob in astonishment, who believed that pearls were what pearl-diving was all about.

Mansur quickly conferred with Tasman.

"How d'you call it?" said Mansur, clicking his fingers with irritation. "Nacre. The shell of pearl."

"Mother-of-pearl?" asked Bob. "That makes sense. Hey, one thing I don't understand: if he's working for them, for the boat owners, how come he's been allowed to keep the pearl?"

"Don't know that one," said Mansur. "I'll ask him."

It turned out that the divers were allowed to keep the pearls. The owners of the luggers were in it for the shells, the mother-of-pearl.

They accompanied Tasman back to his house.

"Any more questions?" said Mansur, thinking he had better earn his keep.

"Yeah," said Bob, his mind blank. "Has he ever dived before?"

He had.

"When? How? How does he do it?"

Mansur held up a hand, laughing.

"Wait! One question at a time. I'll ask."

He held his breath, said Mansur.

Yeah, I've heard that one before, thought Bob. I don't believe it. Someone said they could hold their breath for fifteen minutes – a likely story!

"Tell him to show me how long he can hold his breath," said

Bob. He took a covert glance at Tasman.

Tasman smiled a mischievous smile, but refused to rise to the bait. He did not want to show off. He shook his head.

Mansur questioned him at some length.

"It seems he takes deep breaths and only breathes out slightly each time. He says can only do it when he has to – it would make him dizzy if he did it now," said Mansur.

"Don't believe it," said Bob innocently. "I think he's making it up."

The small boy rose to the provocation, and darted off to the sea. The two men strolled after him.

Carefully, he took off his shirt, making sure the pearl was in a safe place. Then he stood bolt upright, stock still on the shore, with his shoulders rigid, breathing.

Then he plunged into the sea and disappeared from sight.

He emerged many minutes later – how many, they could not tell, as they were not wearing watches – with a challenging look on his face. Bob threw up his hands in mock despair.

"Tell him I believe him now."

They went back in the direction of Tasman's house.

Tasman's father came out to greet them. Bob was shocked to see him, almost bent double. Not only was the father prematurely aged, Bob had not seen a deformity of that severity before. He guessed the cause of it, but not the reason for it.

They waved farewell to Tasman, and went their way.

"Did you see the old man?" said Bob. "Incredible. I've never seen it that bad before. That's the bends, isn't it?"

"I guess so," said Mansur. He was no diver and was not sure what the bends was or what effects it had.

"I wonder why they get it so bad," said Bob reflectively. "Listen, I think we ought to follow this up. I think there's a good story in it."

"Yes," said Mansur, acceding reluctantly. As the local man on the ground, he could see a lot of work ahead for him.

"I think we ought to hire a boat and go out with them for a day," said Bob enthusiastically. "I think we ought to find out why they get the bends – you know, see what the health record is, that kind of thing. Don't you agree?"

"Sure." Mansur's worst fears were being confirmed.

"I'll be away for a week or so. D'you think you can arrange that meantime, Mansur?"

That just about "takes the biscuit", as the English say, thought Mansur gloomily. Still, Bob's publisher was paying for his college fees next term.

Bob returned to the island, full of zest. He and Mansur sat together over a coffee.

"All fixed up, then?" he boomed.

His voice seems to have got louder, thought Mansur.

"Yes, we're fixed up with a boat for tomorrow," he said. "I'm not sure you'll like it."

"Why's that?" said Bob, who usually let nothing disturb him when he was feeling expansive.

"There's a high mortality rate among the divers."

Bob put down his cup, perturbed.

"Why?"

"You saw the helmets they used."

"The ones on the oyster boat? Not close. They looked fine to me. I was quite surprised. A bit battered, maybe."

"They were made before the First World War. All their equipment's like that."

"You're kidding!"

"I'm dead serious, Bob. One of the divers told me that the compressor they use breaks down four or five times a day. Mind you, he seemed very good-humoured about it."

"And when that happens ..."

"They have to yank them up to the surface as quickly as they can or else they die from lack of air. They're not always quick enough."

Bob whistled lightly.

"So they drown. Or get the bends."

"Yeah, they don't stop halfway up to get used to the change of pressure. Fatal," said Mansur. He had learnt a lot about diving in the last few days.

"Yeah, literally, if what you say is correct," said Bob. He gazed at the dense bank of forest foliage not far away, but his eyes were not seeing.

"How far down do they go?" he asked.

"A hundred feet, maybe," said Mansur.

"I think I can manage that. Wait here," he said on impulse. "I'm going back to my room."

He returned a quarter of an hour later carrying what Mansur guessed was pretty up-to-date diving gear. Bob was not a man to stint on equipment.

"I didn't know you were a diver," said Mansur.

"A passion now," said Bob. "Used to be work. I had a job once for an insurance company, inspecting the undersides of ships. What are we hanging around for? Let's go."

Mansur stood up reluctantly. He was enjoying his coffee. Why did Bob have to be so brisk always?

"No sharks, are there?" asked Bob, donning his goggles and breathing tube, as they stood on the side of the hired prahu.

Mansur shrugged. He didn't know. He could just see a trace of a grin before Bob's face disappeared behind his rubber mask.

Bob slipped into the water with a wave of the hand.

He headed downwards, in search of the divers. They had set off just ahead of him. He could not see all that clearly, because of the currents and the distracting variety of fish, which diverted his attention.

Finally he reached the level of the pearl divers. He saw their shadowy figures trailing from the lines to the surface. They were being dragged along with the current as the boat drifted on the surface. With evident haste, they stooped and bent to pick up the shells they could reach as they were pulled along.   As Bob was watching, one of them, a slight figure, lost his balance and slipped. He was yanked along with the line, scraping against the harsh coral.

Bob winced. He could feel the diver's pain through his thin trousers and shirt. He hoped it was not Tasman.

The figure knocked against another reef and stumbled again. This time it looked as if he were in trouble. He started to flail around. Bob's heart was in his mouth. He thought the diver's air tube had become disconnected or severed.

Oh no, what do I do now? he thought. He'll drown without air. Can I get to him in time?

Then he saw that the figure was trying to disentangle his line higher up.

Bob's eyes moved up. The diver's airtube had become caught in a shapeless object floating just beneath the surface. He could not make out what it was.

He panicked.

Up, up, sort it out for him or he'll die, he thought blindly.

Then, just in time, he remembered the folly of rushing straight to the surface. He watched, quivering with anxiety.

The diver managed to shake his line free.

Anyone would think I was the new boy down here, thought Bob, trembling with the memory of the stupidity he had been about to commit. I really deserve to get into trouble.

"Some future for a small boy, huh?" he said to Mansur abstractedly, safely back on the surface. "Being dragged along those reefs day after day until the bends kill you or you drown."

"Sure," said Mansur carelessly. He did not have this habit of thinking himself into other people's shoes.

It was some weeks before Bob returned to the island. He had really only come to collect his belongings, have a last look round and say farewell. He had done all his research, and was going to Australia to write up his work. Mansur would send him his notes in parallel.

On his first evening, Bob went down to the shore to await the return of the oyster luggers. There was no sign of Tasman and his family when they came in. As Mansur was not with him, he could not ask them why they were not aboard. When he went up to Tasman's house, there was no one there either except for some giggling girls. He could not make out what they were trying to tell him. They made gestures, pointing at something along the shore – he could not tell what.

Bob thanked them with the few phrases he had learnt, and left in confusion. He feared that something awful had happened to the family. If it had, the girls seemed remarkably unconcerned about it.

The next day, on the boat back, he stood leaning on the rail, pensively watching the island recede. Next to him stood a rather prosperous islander who knew some English and was obviously inclined to be chatty.

"Nice island, huh?" he said with a cheerful smile. "You come again?"

"Wonderful island," said Bob. "Sure I'll come again."

As was his wont, Bob fell to work, chatting in return. He loved talking to strangers. It gave him lots of material for his book, of course, but he was an outgoing soul and liked people for themselves.

"You fisherman?" he asked.

"No, I'm trader," said the stranger. "Buy this island, sell that island, all sorts of things. Clothes, cameras, watch."

"How about pearls?" said Bob, on an impulse.

The trader made a gesture which combined laughter with cunning.

"You buy pearls?" he asked. "I got marvellous pearl."

He looked round, to see no one was behind him, then took a box from his pocket. He lifted the lid, then unwrapped layers of cloth.

Inside was a glorious golden-yellow pearl, the like of which Bob had never seen before. It was a monster. He was no judge of pearls, but reckoned it was worth a fortune.

"You sell?" said Bob.

"Not to you," said the trader, laughing again and snapping the box shut and putting it away with the swiftness of a magician. "Very excellent pearl, fetch high price. Too much for you." He smiled again, in case Bob took offence.

"Where did you get it?" asked Bob.

"Family on island. Big day for them. Young boy find pearl, just start diving. Very good luck, family very happy."

Bob hoped they were thinking about the same family.

"Father and brother divers too?" he asked, just to check. "Father like this?" He stooped double.

"Yes, yes!" said trader, delighted. "You know family?"

"You pay them for pearl?"

"No, no, I sell pearl for them."

"They'll be rich."

"Lotta rich. Me, I know one person want pearl like this. Pay lots money. Family very happy, very rich. Me too. I happy, I rich."

The trader beamed in the shared happiness.

Bob looked over the rail. The island was just a speck in the distance.

May your luck continue, young Tasman! he said silently.

CHAPTER 23
THE MAN WITH THE GLASSES

It was the glasses they all remembered. They made him look so distinguished and serious.

He was of course very serious, very smooth. He let others do all the trivial work. He did not make an appearance until his associates had taken complete control of the ship.

Pirates of old would traditionally come alongside in a black-sailed boat flying the black skull and crossbones. Unlike them, these pirates were already aboard the ship, as passengers. At the right moment, they simply stepped forward and did their violent work.

They quietly overpowered the armed Indians who guarded the bridge, seized their keys and unlocked the barred entrance to the bridge steps. Before anyone realized what they were doing, they had run up the steps and knocked the officers of the watch senseless before they could raise the alarm. A group of them peeled off to disable the radio and capture the captain in his cabin. It was brilliantly organized and all over in minutes.

The steerage passengers were out of sight two decks down, and saw nothing of all this. When they learnt what had happened, they stayed that way, frightened of getting involved. Most of them were poor, illiterate Chinese peasants travelling to work for British companies in Malaya and Burma. They were in no way able to intervene.

When the dirty work had been done, the pirate leader – Number One – shimmered forth from the First Class section. There could be no mistake about his status: he wore rich silk robes. The few impoverished peasants that actually saw him gasped with amazement.

With his minders following respectfully behind him, Number One stepped over the prostrate Indian guards, set an elegantly shod foot on the steps and mounted them slowly. He was fully aware of the spectacle he was providing. It impressed and frightened. That was good.

The first Captain Pringle saw of him was when he entered the bridge. By then, the guards had brought the captain from his cabin, closely guarded. His chief officer, Beatty, was brought with him.

The *Sunning* was a small British-registered steamer belonging to the China Navigation Company. It plied between Shanghai and Kwangzhou, picking up passengers at various ports along the coast of China. Six officers were British, the rest of the crew were Chinese, including Radio Officer Lok. An official called a comprador or mai-pan acted as manager of the Chinese crew. He was very popular with the men, and highly resourceful.

This was no casual brigand, this Number One. His operation was as smooth as his looks. He had been planning it for months, at great expense. He and his closest henchmen had travelled on the *Sunning* many times in the previous months, watching how the ship was operated, how many crew it had, working out how the attack should go.

Far from wearing patches over one eye like pirates of yore, they normally travelled like successful businessmen having business in many ports.

Number One had bribed a clerk at the office of the navigation company, who told him when anything interesting was going to be carried. A week before this trip, the clerk had sent an urgent message that the *Sunning* would be carrying a huge quantity of gold bullion.

That was what brought him to the bridge on this hot, steamy November afternoon in 1926.

"Set course for Bias Bay, captain," he said calmly.

Pringle was no rash adventurer. Opposition to violent, armed pirates would have been folly. He nodded to Beatty to make the necessary corrections to their course.

Bias Bay was bad news for the *Sunning*, but Pringle decided to let things take their way. At present, he saw no alternative.

Bias Bay was the British name for Taya Wan, a large bay east of Hong Kong. Its wooded, mountainous shores were notorious as the home of pirates. With China in the grip of petty warlords, there was no one except the British authorities in Hong Kong to oppose them. They intervened only when necessary.

"And keys to safe, if you please, captain," continued the smooth voice. It was menacing in its quietness.

Pringle went to a drawer and took out a key.

"And other key?" asked Number One. He was obviously extremely well informed. A hint of threat could be discerned in his tone.

"The comprador has that," said Pringle reluctantly, after a pause.

"And he is ... where?"

"I do not know."

"Find mai-pan," said Number One to his henchman. It was an instruction that tolerated no questioning or delay.

The man went out. Shortly after, barked orders could be heard on the deck.

The mai-pan was not to be found anywhere. Five luckless Chinese crew members were taken at random and lined up on deck.

It was evident from the tone that they were being asked to reveal where the mai-pan was hiding. The first man was asked. He said nothing. A shot rang out and the seaman crumpled.

A shudder ran through the remaining crew members.

The question was repeated. No answer was forthcoming. This time, a further command was rapped out, and the man was thrown over the rail. The crew members did not need to look over to know that within minutes a blood-red stain would discolour the surface. These waters were infested with sharks.

The question was repeated three more times, with the same result.

It was heroism of the highest order, from illiterate men whose yearly pay probably did not equal what the pirates could steal in a minute.

The mai-pan remained undiscovered.

Number One stayed unconcerned. He would have more drastic means of opening the safe, once they reached Taya Wan.

Guards made sure the steerage passengers remained below, on the passenger deck. The officers apart from the captain and chief officer were confined in cabins on the deck above, along with the two elderly European passengers, a widow from Belarus and a retired English resident of China.

Pringle may have been content to wait and see, but the other officers were not. Most were young and spoiling for a fight.

Down in their cabin prison, when they thought the guard was out of earshot, Chief Engineer Cormack and Second Engineer Orr – both of whom were recovering from being knocked out – Second Officer Hurst and Third Officer Duncan started to talk.

"Smashed my best Willow pattern," said Cormack gloomily. He had been hit with his own teapot.

"Wish I had my gun to hand," said Orr, in suppressed fury. "I've got a score to settle with the pig that used a bottle on my head. I have a headache I'd gladly give my worst enemy."

"Where is your gun?" said Cormack, quietly, so that the guard should not hear.

"In the drawer in my cabin," said Orr.

"So is mine," said Hurst.

He hummed a catchy tune of the day.

"We could do with a pack of cards, to pass the time," said Duncan.

"We could annoy them with a few songs," said Orr. "The Chinese think our music was made in hell, have you ever noticed that? We've got some musical instruments. "He added as an afterthought, "They're in your cabin, Hurst."

Hurst looked at him, struck by a thought.

"So they are," he said, dropping his voice. "I have an idea how we can get it."

"Get what?"

"My gun."

The others looked at him expectantly. Hurst looked round, and moved away from the door, so that his voice would not carry.

"I'll ask them if I can fetch the instruments. When I'm there, I'll see what I can do about the gun.'

Amazingly, the pirate guard let him go to his cabin, but Hurst was closely watched all the way. He brought back the instruments, but not the gun. They would have to await a better opportunity.

Meanwhile, they passed the time making weird noises on the accordion and guitar. Like many seamen, they had a passable proficiency, but music it was not. Certainly not to Chinese ears. Most of the pirates moved out of earshot, leaving just one guard on watch.

After an hour or so, Hurst looked out of the porthole and saw a ship.

"That's the *Annui!*" he said, trying to keep the excitement in his voice down. To his colleagues' amazement, he suddenly went to the door and called the guard.

When the guard looked in, Hurst pointed to the ship visible through the porthole.

"Brother ship *Sunning*," he said. "You say Number One." He held up his index finger.

The guard got the drift, and hurried off to tell the pirate leader.

"Keep playing, to cover me," hissed Hurst.

He darted out of the cabin and along to his own cabin, to fetch the gun. Duncan and Orr launched into the most raucous jazz number they could think of.

The minutes that followed were dreadful for the rest of them in the cabin. They waited anxiously to see which footstep would return first, the guard or Hurst.

Up on the bridge, Chief Officer Beatty had also seen the ship.

He suddenly became aware that the muzzle of a gun was being

levelled at the back of his head.

"You signal to ship," said a voice with fine casualness, "I shoot. Him too."

He waved the gun at Pringle, standing opposite.

Pringle was in a state of powerful indecision. Though a good seaman, he was thrown by having to act with a killer at his elbow, whose every action was unpredictable. He would infinitely prefer to deal with the weather and the sea, elements he knew well.

He was in a dilemma. According to standing Company rules, Company ships were supposed to acknowledge each other when they passed. If they did not, it could be assumed that something was wrong.

Pringle shillyshallied. Should he say anything? If he did not, the *Annui* would telegraph Hong Kong and tell them something was up. The Navy would then send an armed gunboat to investigate. But if the pirates found out, they could turn nasty.

He pondered long and deep, this way and that. His whole frame was tense with the imponderables, with his responsibility as captain. Being a captain is a very lonely job, he mused, not for the first time.

At one stage he caught Beatty's eye, and knew he was thinking about the same thing. He would have been surprised to know how different Beatty's thoughts were.

Was it the right thing, then, to say nothing? thought Pringle once again. Would the pirates give up if they knew help was on the way? He thought not.

Beatty looked at him meaningfully. Alas, Pringle was no mind reader: he could not divine what Beatty was trying to tell him. One thing was certain: rescue would be a long time coming, during which time the pirates could do all kinds of unpleasant things.

Still he was tense and undecided. It was such a responsibility.

Throughout the silent drama going on behind him, Number

One peered through the glass, watching the ship passing. His attitude indicated that he too was in a state of alertness.

The *Annui* passed out of signalling range.

The sudden slackening of the tension got to Pringle. Aghast, Beatty watched him beckon to Number One and open his mouth to speak.

"You're making a mistake," said Pringle. "That was a ship from our company. Our ships are obliged to signal to each other...."

Beatty shut his ears in horror. He did not want to hear this.

Number One listened calmly, and then said, "If we die, you will die too."

———————

Duncan and Orr breathed out with relief. The footsteps were from the corridor, from the direction of Hurst"s cabin.

Hurst entered the cabin, triumphantly waving a gun. He shoved it out of sight, promptly sat down and picked up the saxophone.

It was a close-run thing. The footsteps of the returning guard were heard. The saxophone threaded into the melody, as if it had never been away. Everyone in the cabin relaxed.

Almost by telepathy, Beatty picked up the forceful vibrations that Hurst was issuing below. Possibly he was reacting to what he saw as folly on the part of Pringle, who had just thrown away their ace card.

Something had to be done, Beatty decided.

The pirates would now believe that a threat was on its way. They would become excited, and be prepared to use more violence.

"With your permission, Captain Pringle, I have a request," he said. He turned to Number One. "I think we need an extra officer here on the bridge. Could you ask your men to send up Second Officer Hurst?"

Number One considered for a moment.

Really, the glasses are too much, combined with the robes,

thought Beatty. It was odd, given the dire circumstances, but he felt a growing confidence. Or had he misjudged the situation?

"OK," said Number One.

Beatty rendered thanks to heaven. Outwardly, he remained impassive.

Number One signalled to one of the two guards, who went and fetched Hurst.

When Hurst entered, Beatty felt all at once the odds were changing in the officers' favour, though Number One seemed as imperturbable as ever.

Beatty's thoughts focused on the two revolvers he knew were in the chart room.

"Mr Hurst, would you kindly fetch the charts for the Hunghai Wan area," he said. "We are going off our usual route."

A bright young officer, Hurst immediately gathered the implications of the request. Gravely, he left the bridge.

Beatty went over to the guards and called their attention to a minor disturbance going on outside. He did not want them following Hurst.

It was not long before Hurst returned to the bridge, and at the first opportunity he signalled the OK to Beatty – a quick upward flick of the thumb.

He had found the two guns in the drawer, loaded them and left them where they could be collected easily.

More time passed, to all appearances quietly. In Number One's mind, apparently all was well. All was going as planned. Outwardly, Hurst was anxious to please. Inwardly his mind was in turmoil, turning over possibilities. He recalled that Orr had said his gun was in his cabin.

Hurst racked his brain to think of an excuse to go Orr's cabin. He decided he would have to force the issue, but he did not dare ask the captain. Pringle might make the wrong decision.

"Sir, I believe there are some notes on depths in Orr's cabin that will be useful," he said earnestly to Beatty, not looking at Number One.

Beatty appeared to be engaged wholly in his charts.

"Yes, yes, Hurst, go and get them, I'm sure you're right."

Hurst glanced at Number One, seeking approval. Number One's expression was not visible behind the glasses, but he nodded.

Hurst went down, pocketed the revolver in Orr"s drawer and took it to the chart room. He left it with the others. The guards stood aside to let him back into the bridge.

Night fell, with the suddenness of the East, and with it the torpid weather broke. The wind veered round to the south-south-east, and picked up strength. It was blowing straight into the bows, slowing the boat noticeably.

"Faster, captain," said Number One irritably. "We slowing down." He came over to Pringle and stood so close the captain could hear him breathing.

Pringle stood his ground. He hated being crowded, but he thought Number One might take offence and turn violent if he moved away.

"We are at full speed," he said. "We are running into a strong headwind. We cannot go any faster."

Number One moved away restlessly. He did not like things he could not threaten. The wind was outside his control.

Down below, the officers and passengers had been moved to the captain's dining room, where the steward served dinner.

Conversation was subdued at first, because of the proximity of the guards. Eventually the guards lost interest, and moved away far enough for them to talk in subdued tones.

"What are we going to do, then, sir?" Orr asked Cormack. Without Hurst, some of the urgency had gone out of their resolve. Orr was determined to try to recapture their earlier momentum.

"If we could control the boiler room, we would have them in our hands," said Duncan.

"That would be useless as long as they have the bridge," said

Cormack, shaking his head. His mind conjured up the scene.

They would threaten to kill the captain unless I let them into the engine room, he guessed. What would I do then? Would I have the nerve to ignore the threat?

And they have guns to smash the locks ...

The conversation petered out and they finished their meal in silence. It was understood however that Cormack would be on duty down in the engine room, and at a signal from the bridge - a single whistle - would bang the door to the engine room shut. If the others could gain control of the bridge, he would answer for securing the below-deck power.

Waiting, waiting. Each of them had his own private fears and expectations. What were they waiting for, as the night deepened?

The elderly widow, Mrs Proklovyera, expected to be murdered in her bed. Beatty speculated on the likelihood of the Royal Navy rescuing them as the night deepened. Cormack was wondering uneasily when the right moment would come to bang the door to the engine room shut ... the right moment, when was that, for God's sake? Hurst wondered when they could try to seize control. He tried to rein in his natural desire for action.

Not all of them realized that their most likely fate was to be held as hostages in Taya Wan, until the Company paid huge sums to redeem them. The same would apply to any Chinese aboard who looked as if their families had the money to pay.

As they drew nearer and nearer the pirate lair, the hostage possibility became more and more of a probability tending towards a certainty.

Down in the captain's cabin, where Orr, Duncan and the passengers were now imprisoned, this was not at the forefront of their minds. Only radio officer Lok, who was with them, was fully conscious of the fate that awaited them. Kidnapping was a long Chinese tradition. When the hostage's family failed to meet the pirates' demands, bits of the hostage – an ear, a finger – would be sent to the family, to "persuade" them to pay. Lok knew that his family would be unable to meet their demands.

As old China hands, Pringle knew the risk, Beatty knew it, Hurst knew it. Something had to be done before they reached Taya Wan. Once they were there, it would be too late.

By now, Number One had taken himself off to check that all was well with the rest of the operation. He left behind him two armed guards, with strict instructions to summon help at the slightest untoward event. This gave the officers a chance to confer openly without arousing suspicion. The guards knew little English.

With great presence of mind, Beatty created an opportunity to agree a course of action with Hurst. He thought Hurst was the best bet for a partner. He drawled casually,

"Mr Hurst, can I have your opinion on this chart? I believe you know some of these waters better than I do."

Hurst nearly leapt for joy at the chance to do something. He had been chafing at the inactivity. He went over and stood beside Beatty, poring over the chart.

"I believe we are here," said Beatty, continuing the casual naval drawl but gradually letting his voice sink. He pointed at the map. "And there – " he waved his pencil" – is Bias Bay, where we are bound."

By now he was talking in a voice that would be inaudible to the guards. His pencil flicked to the characteristic L-shaped peninsula on the approach to Taya Wan/Bias Bay. It was called Chilang Point. He was careful not to say the name aloud.

"We should sight this L-shaped headland shortly. That is the last possible moment for action. After that we are in Bias Bay."

He paused, without looking at Hurst.

"You get my meaning?"

"Absolutely, sir."

Beatty let the pencil rest under the name Chilang, to make sure. They both stared at the chart.

Beatty continued, apparently still deep in the chart, his pencil resting on the name.

"When I see it, I will say it aloud. I will be outside, pointing it out to our armed friends. I will tell them its name aloud, so that they may rejoice that they are home in their filthy lair. Unfortunately, they will not reach home. You will go and get the weapons and prevent them reaching it. Are you with me? That is an order."

"Yes, sir."

There was no time for discussion. Beatty moved away, ready to engage the guards. However, Hurst's fertile mind was revolving the possibilities.

The guards will notice me going to the chart room, he brooded. And the sound of shots will echo round the ship and bring the wrath of Number One on us too soon. How can I dispose of the guards quietly?

He looked round the bridge. What could he use?

His eye fell on the heavy lead weights that were used to hold the floor matting in place. Could he wield one of those? It had a nice sharp edge.

Shame I can't have the revolver in reserve, he thought. Too risky, though – the bulge in his pocket would be noticeable. Then he reconsidered. He would get it at the earliest opportunity. Better safe than sorry. Once things got under way, there would be precious little time.

First things first, however.

Without calling attention to himself, he worked his way round to the nearest weight. Stealthily, he nudged it with his foot, to check that it would move. It did.

A light flickered uncertainly far ahead to starboard. Land, closer at hand than previous sightings. They had reached the critical point.

Beatty went outside to check, then called the guards over and pointed it out. Hurst could hear his cheerful voice through the open door.

"Chilang Point," he said to the guards. "Chilang Point!" – repeating for good measure - "your home."

The guards nodded agreement, repeating the name as they leaned over the rail to look. Hurst saw his chance.

The first man went down like a ninepin, without the other even noticing. Beatty almost winced when he heard the crack of lead on bone.

As the other turned to speak to his colleague, Hurst whirled his improvised club again, and another body measured its length on the narrow ledge.

Pringle darted out and seized the guard's rifle. Hurst was tempted to pick up the first man's rifle, but decided to use his revolver instead for the time being.

After hours of inactivity, things were happening, he thought with satisfaction.

The rifle lay unused beside the body.

And happen they did. There was no going back now.

Hurst's strenuous attack and the falling bodies had been heard in the captain's cabin, which was directly below. A single guard was on duty, watching the passengers and officers.

Foolishly, he came up to investigate, and was shot dead for his pains. Beatty rushed down the steps and grabbed his rifle before the sound of shots brought up more pirates. He shut the access door to the bridge with a bang. Hurst did the same on the other side.

They were under siege. A buzz of cries from below indicated that they had little time to get everyone together.

"How can we get the others up here?" said Hurst, panting up the steps.

"The skylight," snapped Pringle, stirred out of his indecisiveness now that events were under way. "The skylight of my cabin."

The skylight was set into the floor of the bridge.

Beatty turned his rifle round and with the butt tapped sharply on the skylight, to draw the attention of those below.

"Stand clear!" he yelled. "I'm going to smash it!"

It took three powerful thrusts to break the reinforced glass.

"Bar the cabin door!" shouted Beatty through the jagged gap.

"I've already done that," came the voice of Orr.

"Stand clear!" called Beatty. "More glass coming." He jabbed at the shattered glass until the hole was large enough to climb through.

"Come up here, all of you," said Pringle sharply. One by one, they hastened to obey. The sounds of hammering on the cabin door were too close for comfort.

They were now all together on the bridge, armed with a fair range of weapons but not much ammunition. They would have to fire sparingly and well – and if necessary, use bluff.

In the tumult of the moment, they had overlooked the enemy within.

A slight noise from the direction of the rail drew their attention to the guards Hurst had knocked out. One was still alive. As Hurst turned to see what was happening, he was horrified to see a hand reaching out across the deck to pick up the rifle he had spurned.

"Behind you, sir!" he shouted to Beatty.

Beatty whirled round, but was too late to stop the barrel being raised and levelled into the bridge.

A shot rang out.

It was a tense time below in the engine room. Cormack had waited and waited for a signal from the bridge. None had come, and so he had taken matters into his own hands. He slammed the door to the engine room shut.

The pirates were down on him in no time. They slugged the

locks with their rifle butts until they broke, and hauled Cormack out. His arms were bound, and he was dragged along to where Number One was issuing orders.

Number One rapped out a single sentence. Cormack's knowledge of Cantonese was too sketchy to gather what his intentions were.

He soon found out. A cabin-boy was produced from round the corner, and he and Cormack were pushed to the front, and marched along the deck towards the bridge.

They stopped before they reached the open deck in front of it.

Oh God, they're going to use us as human shields! thought Cormack. His mouth went dry.

Astoundingly, on the bridge the wounded guard's shot had gone wide, as had his second shot. Before Beatty had time to finish him off, the guard had leapt to the safety of his colleagues below.

The besieged officers were in no doubt that they now faced a ruthless enemy. Number One must fear for the success of his plan, and would not hesitate to kill. The officers could prevent the ship from reaching Taya Wan for a while, but they did not control the engine room. But did the pirates? Where was Cormack?

In the darkness, it was difficult to see from the bridge what was happening as the pirates jostled in the shadow on the other side of the open deck.

"What are they up to?" whispered Duncan.

"Wait and see."

The confrontation began.

"Surrender, captain! You have no choice."

The harsh voice of Number One floated up from below. He was hiding somewhere out of sight. The pirate leader was in a fury at being thwarted. Despite his months of preparation, things had suddenly gone awry. He intended to wreak his revenge on the officers slowly and painfully – later. First, he had to terrorize them into submission.

Silence from the bridge.

"You resist, you die," said Number One hoarsely, losing control of himself.

Silence from the bridge.

"We coming for you, captain!" rasped the voice again. It rang eerily in the darkness, echoing off the metal struts. All human sounds were suppressed, as everyone waited to see what would happen.

Eventually a curious shuffling sound reached the bridge over the gusting of the wind. Figures started to move in the darkness, and out into the lighter area. Finally, they could see what they were meant to see. Across the bright open deck came Cormack and a cabin-boy, prodded from behind by rifles. The pirates were going to attack, using humans as shields.

"What you think of that, then? Eh, captain?" sneered the voice.

What indeed? They were aghast. They whispered amongst themselves.

"We can't shoot them!"

"We have no choice. We have to prevent them attacking us, otherwise we are all food for the sharks."

"I can't do it."

"You must. Aim where it will do the least damage."

"How can we? It's dark."

Pringle wondered who was in charge in the engine room, if Cormack was up on deck. No one probably, which was why the ship was losing headway.

There was silence, punctuated only by the occasional scream from a gust of wind. They waited.

Abruptly, on an unseen signal, the attack was launched on the bridge with all the ferocity of professional assassins.

As the pirates rushed the steps, shots rang out from above. The officers had called Number One's bluff. Cormack fell, apparently dead, the cabin-boy was pushed aside.

A second rush followed, with the pirates leaping over Cormack's body. In the ensuing melee, it gradually slipped out of sight, rolling with the *Sunning* over each sea, ignored by all the combatants.

Midnight, one o'clock, two o'clock passed. Still the pirates were being driven at the steps by a maddened Number One, who remained conspicuously out of sight. One after another pirates fell. Their bodies were dragged away and dumped overboard. The men on the bridge did not need to be told what the subsequent invisible splash represented, but they were too preoccupied with the constant attacks to worry about it.

Around half past three came a lull.

"They've stopped," said Duncan wearily. He lay slumped against the wall of the bridge, hardly able to think. It had been a long day.

"How many of them have we accounted for, sir?" asked Hurst.

"I don't know," said Beatty. "A dozen, perhaps? Don't worry, there's plenty more of them down there."

"I'm out of ammunition," said Hurst.

"Quiet!" said Beatty. "They must not hear." He added as an afterthought, "So am I."

Grimly, Pringle looked round the darkened bridge.

"Has anyone got any ammo left?"

One by one they shook their heads.

Bluff was their only remaining weapon.

The thoughts of each of them took a macabre turn as the silence down below persisted. It left them time to speculate what would happen to them in the next half hour. It was not pleasant thinking.

In the unaccustomed silence, they were jolted back to the present by the motion of the ship. It was pitching rather heavily, and, lying inert on the floor of the bridge, the officers and passengers were finding it difficult to stay put.

Left to themselves, the engines had all but stopped. The ship was drifting in a wind that was fairing up to gale force.

Their worries on this score were diverted as they became aware of a new noise from the deck below: a series of muffled sounds that they could not identify.

"What are they doing?" hissed Orr.

"I don't know," replied Hurst with asperity. "I think they're dragging something."

"What can it be?" asked Duncan, listening intently.

They soon found out. Curls of smoke began to drift into the bridge. The crackling sound of flames gathered strength below, fanned by the gale-force headwind.

"They vil fry us!" moaned Mrs Proklovyera.

"Smells like burning hair, sir," said Duncan.

"It sounds like straw burning," said Beatty.

"Mattresses, that's what they're burning," said Orr. "I just caught a glimpse." He coughed as a thick cloud of acrid smoke engulfed him.

"We can't stay here," said Beatty. "I can already feel the walls heating up. We'll burn to death. They've got us just where they want us. For Heaven's sake, let's do something." He began to cough violently.

It's the first time I've seen Beatty lose his composure, thought Hurst.

It was then that Pringle showed them why he was a captain. He had noted earlier that some of the crew, including the bosun, had locked themselves in the foc's'le and were still there. They were of no interest to the pirates.

Pringle now sized up the situation, including the position of the fire, the direction of the wind and the hiding place of the pirates, upwind of the smoke.

Without warning, he stood up and yelled at the bosun, calling him by name until he got acknowledgement.

"Cast the starboard anchor!" He repeated the command until he heard chains rattling, fearlessly exposing himself to the unseen pirates.

"They've heard, sir," said Beatty. He was still puzzled.

The anchor slid out of its housing and slowly bit the seabed.

It was a master stroke. The anchor held the ship far enough back that the bows were free to turn. Exposed to the full force of the wind, the bows were pushed round; for a while, the *Sunning* heeled sharply as it caught the wind along its full length, then righted itself as it continued turning.

The drift of the heat and smoke veered round with the wind. The pirates were caught in their own trap, and started to choke as the smoke carried fumes from the paintwork into their lungs. Soon the timbers of the deck began to burn. There was nowhere for them to stand. Puffed up by the wind, the fire grew white-hot. The pirates retreated until there was nowhere further to retreat. They were well and truly caught.

On the bridge this was all observed with much satisfaction, even if the burning ship threatened their own safety and that of the passengers further below in the long term. At least it would be up to them if they brought it under control.

The final act in the drama was about to open.

"Delegation for you, sir," said Beatty, leaning over the bridge, which was now completely clear of smoke.

Three blackened wretches appeared out of the smoke, clutching damp rags to their mouths to avoid breathing the fumes.

"Yes?" barked Pringle. Neither he nor they were conscious that his face was equally blackened by the smoke.

"You put down guns, we leave ship," said their spokesman in

some agitation. No doubt he could feel the baleful force of Number One driving him on.

Pringle gazed at them. Let Number One wait, he thought – each minute makes it worse for him. Then he recalled the passengers below.

He shook his head, and withdrew from their sight. That was his answer.

The pirates were beaten. The battle was over, and they had lost. Twenty of them put out in two of the lifeboats, the rest tried to "disappear" among the steerage passengers. Captain Pringle had his ship back.

By daybreak, help was on its way, the flames were under control and Captain Pringle had summoned a tow to Hong Kong.

During the day, all the surviving pirates were caught, except for Number One. The man with the glasses managed to spirit himself away. He was clearly a man who knew how to make himself invisible, and let others take the rap with their lives.

And the mai-pan, who had disappeared so inconveniently for the pirates? Where was he?

He emerged from a pile of coal where, with the help of one of the stokers, he had hidden as soon as the pirates took command.

Not far from him, another stoker had placed the body of Cormack, believing him to be dead. He was in fact severely wounded.

Alas, the unlucky ones were the five crew members killed by the pirates for not betraying the mai-pan. Plans had been changed before the *Sunning* sailed. There was no gold aboard – the safe was empty. It was a pointless piracy.